The Handbook of Alternative Assets

Making money from art, rare books, coins and banknotes, forestry, gold and precious metals, stamps, wine and other alternative assets

by Peter Temple

HARRIMAN HOUSE LTD

3A Penns Road
Petersfield
Hampshire
GU32 2EW
GREAT BRITAIN

Tel: +44 (0)1730 233870
Fax: +44 (0)1730 233880
Email: enquiries@harriman-house.com
Website: www.harriman-house.com

First published in Great Britain in 2010
Copyright © Harriman House Ltd

The right of Peter Temple to be identified as author has been asserted in accordance with the Copyright, Design and Patents Acts 1988.

ISBN: 978-1906659-21-9

British Library Cataloguing in Publication Data
A CIP catalogue record for this book can be obtained from the British Library.

All rights reserved; no part of this publication may be reproduced, stored in a retrieval system, or transmitted in any form or by any means, electronic, mechanical, photocopying, recording, or otherwise without the prior written permission of the Publisher. This book may not be lent, resold, hired out or otherwise disposed of by way of trade in any form of binding or cover other than that in which it is published without the prior written consent of the Publisher.

Printed and bound by the MPG Books Group

No responsibility for loss occasioned to any person or corporate body acting or refraining to act as a result of reading material in this book can be accepted by the Publisher or by the Author.

Contents

About the Author	vii
Acknowledgements	ix
Alternative Investments and 'Portable Wealth'	xi
Why Look at Alternatives?	xii
What Alternatives?	xxii
1. Art	1
Basics	3
Collecting Areas	7
Condition	18
Security Measures	19
The Right Alternative Asset for You?	20
Returns	22
How to Invest	25
Where to Go for More Information	27
2. Banknotes	41
Basics	42
Collecting Themes	46
The Right Alternative Asset for You?	48
Returns	51
How to Invest	52
Where to Go for More Information	53
3. Books	59
Basics	60
Collectable Genres	62
Identifying a Rare Book	66
Condition	69
The Right Alternative Asset for You?	71
Returns	75
How to Invest	78
Where to Go for More Information	79

4. Coins	89
Basics	91
Condition	94
The Right Alternative Asset for You?	97
Returns	100
How to Invest	102
Where to Go for More Information	104
5. Diamonds	115
Basics	117
The Right Alternative Asset for You?	126
Returns	128
How to Invest	130
Where to Go for More Information	132
6. Forestry	137
Basics	138
UK Tax Benefits From Forestry	140
The Right Alternative Asset for You?	143
Returns	148
How to Invest	150
Where to Go for More Information	153
7. Gold	163
Basics	165
The Right Alternative Asset for You?	169
Returns	172
How to Invest	174
Other Precious Metals	185
Where to Go for More Information	186
8. Stamps	193
Basics	195
Condition	199
The Right Alternative Asset for You?	203
Stamp Prices	206
Returns	208
How to Invest	212
Where to Go for More Information	215

9. Wine	227
Basics	228
The Right Alternative Asset for You?	234
Prices and Returns	238
How to Invest	245
Where to Go for More Information	247
10. Auctions and Dealers	255
Auctions Versus Dealers	256
The Essence of Auctions	259
How Auctions Work	260
Online Auctions	267
Dealing with the Dealers	269
Other Sources of Investment-grade Material	271
Appendix – Resources	273
Art	274
Banknotes	276
Books	277
Coins	279
Diamonds	281
Forestry	282
Gold	284
Stamps	285
Wine	287
Auctions	289

About the Author

Peter Temple trained as an economist and statistician. He has been working in and writing about financial markets for almost 40 years. After an 18-year career in fund management and investment banking, he became a full-time writer in 1988.

His articles appear in the *Financial Times*, *Investors Chronicle* and a range of other publications and websites. He has written more than a dozen books about investing, mainly aimed at private investors.

He and his wife live in the English Lake District.

Acknowledgements

I started out writing the original version of this book knowing a little about some of the areas that I planned to cover, but with huge areas of ignorance about the detail of many of them. Fortunately I have been able to call on several experts, collectors and experienced alternative investors for guidance. I have picked their brains, gone to them for tips about research angles, and in some cases they have been good enough to check the chapter that covered their particular area of interest and alert me to any nuances I had failed to pick up, or to the more obvious mistakes I had made. I have called on many of them again, and also a number of newer contacts.

In no particular order of precedence, therefore, I would like to thank the following for their help, patience and forbearance: Barry Townsley; Val Porter-Godman; Peter Holland; Philip Athill at Abbott and Holder; Peter Blaskett of Signature Gallery in Kendal; Martin and Pat Masters of Thomond Antiques in Kendal; staff at Sotheby's; Bruce and Kim Stanfield, who auction art for P&O Cruises; Barnaby Faull at Spink; Peter Duppa-Miller at the International Bond and Share Society; Keith Hollender; Colin Steele; Julian Roberts; Christopher Proudlove, Simon Roberts and Tim Schofield at Bonhams; Dave Selby; staff at Spink's coin department; staff at Coincraft; Ian Goldbart, Dimitri Loulakakis, Seth Freeman and Stephen Hill of Noble Investments (UK) plc and Baldwin's; Rick Warren and colleagues at Apex Philatelics; Alan Kelly at Mannin Collections; Cathy Roberts at Petra Diamonds; Tim Kirk, Simon Hart and Ruth Roy at UPM Tilhill; Robert Weinberg and Rhona O'Connell; Laurence Chard; Michael Hall, Richard Purkis and Geoff Anandappa at Stanley Gibbons; Adrian Roose; Colin Harding at Scotia Philately; Richard Watkins at Spink; Jim Budd; James Sherry at Vineyards of Bordeaux; and Anthony Foster at Bonhote Foster.

Various publications I write for regularly have allowed me to use their columns to explore some of the ideas contained in both the original version of this book and this new edition. In this respect I must thank Simon London, Kevin Brown and Matthew Vincent at the *Financial Times*, Rosie Carr at the *Investors Chronicle*, Richard Beddard and Steve McDowell at *Interactive Investor*, Andrew Pitts at *Money Observer*, and Frank Hemsley and Andrew Vaughan at Fleet Street Publications for their help. I first got interested in the tangible assets scene through writing articles about scripophily and gold for *Accountancy* magazine in the late 1980s.

At Harriman House, thanks go to Philip Jenks, Myles Hunt, Nick Read and Stephen Eckett for embracing the original idea of this book so enthusiastically and for the subsequent proposal to convert it into a handbook, and for editing, designing and producing the finished products at a speed that puts most traditional publishers to shame.

Last but not least, my wife Lynn Temple, whose idea this book originally was, has contributed to it in many ways. She conducted or sat in on most of the interviews we had with experts in many fields, attended auctions, researched particular topics in depth for me, and compiled and maintained the database relevant websites and information sources on which a number of the tables in this book and its predecessor are based, wrote some of the text, and proofread the finished version of the manuscripts. Completing the books would have been a much lengthier task without her help and she has, as always, my grateful thanks for her diligence and support.

Peter Temple

March 2010

Alternative Investments and 'Portable Wealth'

There has been increasing focus in the investment world in recent years on finding alternatives to the stock market. For many this has involved looking at real estate, at hedge funds and at private equity. The events of the past few years have highlighted the shortcomings of these different options.

The true alternative investments, in my view, are those that are tangible and perhaps even portable. They can serve as a store of value in troubled times when stock markets are volatile, bond markets subject to inflation and fiat currencies depreciating in value. The aim of this book is to show investors and their advisors how they can use such tangible assets – ranging from gold and diamonds to books, wine, forests and more – as a means of diversifying a portfolio, and avoiding such pitfalls.

Many investors may already own, or have inherited, tangible investments like this: a stamp or coin collection, or a set of first editions. Or they may pursue collecting stamps, coins, books or art as a hobby. They may not hitherto have thought of their collections as potential investments to be examined and developed systematically as a bona fide part of their overall portfolio.

There is, however, no shortage of examples of successful investment in this vein. One good painting, carefully chosen and bought at the right time, can prove a fantastic investment. The author's own modest portfolio of investment-grade British stamps (recently sold) delivered a return of close to 50% over a four-year period at a time when the stock market was in disarray.

Each alternative asset covered in this book will be examined systematically, taking in:

- the background to the market
- whether a particular kind of asset may or may not be appropriate for your investment needs
- the long-term returns that can reasonably be expected based on past history
- whether or not there are tax advantages available

- how best to buy and sell, and through whom
- and where to go for more information on that particular tangible investment area.

But first let's outline some of the issues that have led us to the conclusion that looking seriously at alternative, particularly tangible, investments is a good idea.

Why Look at Alternatives?

Investing in tangible assets can often simply grow out of a previous collecting activity or some other interest taken to a more systematic level. It may make sense for an investor to pursue, in the first instance, investment opportunities in an area that they already know. Arguably, however, this should be done only after reviewing whether there are more suitable areas available that offer better growth opportunities.

What investors also need to recognise is that to make a difference to overall portfolio returns, investing in alternative assets still requires a serious financial commitment; and, like any investment, it will repay the attention devoted to research, and penalise carelessness. I venture to suggest, however, that researching tangible investment choices can be just as interesting and involving as trying to spot undervalued companies.

There are many reasons why it makes sense to look at tangible investments in more detail, which are enumerated below.

Conventional investments are untrustworthy

Running through the whole investment process is the axiom that risk and return are closely linked.

Here are a few ways that this axiom manifests itself:

Government bonds are generally considered to be 'safe' but have low returns; pooled investments like unit trusts are safer than individual ones; blue-chip equities are more risky than bonds but tend to produce higher returns over the long term; loss-making enterprises or very young companies are even riskier than blue-chips, but investors in them have the potential to make still higher returns.

Statements like this, however, don't tell the whole story. Government bonds are only safe in the sense that they have a government guarantee that interest will be paid and capital returned at maturity. But in certain circumstances their prices will go down. If inflation rises or interest rates go up, bond prices will fall.

Many pooled investments have proved treacherous. Investing in a unit trust, mutual fund or other form of collective investment doesn't absolve an investor from thinking about the investment. Investors have to pick the right area in which to invest and, however diverse a fund, it will lose money if the area it specialises in moves out of favour or if the manager is incompetent.

UK investors also don't need to be financially sophisticated to know that insurance company with-profit funds have not yielded the returns that investors in them once expected. Granted, there are generally some guarantees: but recent events have shown that returns, in the form of bonus rates, can change both dramatically and arbitrarily.

Property is also problematic. Recent big movements in residential property prices in countries as far apart as the US, Spain, the UK and Dubai, as well as collapsing prices of real estate investment trusts and commercial property unit trusts, have demonstrated that it is by no means the sure-fire investment it is (or perhaps was) popularly supposed to be.

The 2007-09 bear market in shares should have taught investors that there are no short cuts to investing success. If investors can't discover where the risk in an investment might be, it doesn't mean there is no risk, but simply that investors have not looked in the right place for it.

Predicting where equity and bond markets will go from here is difficult. At the time I wrote the original version of this handbook in 2004 there were those who believed that the strong rally in world stock markets that began in March 2003 was the beginning of a new bull market. And indeed the market did approach its earlier high before the credit crunch, banking crisis, and deep economic downturn intervened.

It is a moot point now whether tentative signs of economic recovery and the recent share price revival are durable. One possibility is that markets will move sideways for an extended period, rather as they did in Japan since the pricking of the property-based bubble there at the beginning of the 1990s. The prolonged period of low interest rates in the US, UK, Europe and elsewhere, together with the massive increases in public spending as a result of the bailouts of banks and other industrial sectors, may usher in an era of much more rapid global inflation.

In any case, the inherent volatility of stock market returns should prompt any rational investor to look elsewhere to invest at least part of their assets. This is why, in my view, tangible investments are worth closer investigation.

Diversifying your assets is good

Conventional wisdom in investing is that diversification reduces risk. Academic studies have measured how and why this works. Theory suggests that holding as few as eight individual shares, for example, will reduce risk significantly, in fact by almost as much as holding 50 or 100 shares would do.

Professional investors and many individuals also reduce risk by investing in other types of securities, notably in fixed-income investments like bonds, but also in less conventional (but still essentially stock market related) investments like hedge funds and venture capital.

The aim of all this activity is to produce a smoother pattern of returns, in other words to reduce volatility. The assumption is that rational and affluent investors do not want the value of their investments to fluctuate alarmingly. They would rather see returns that are predictable, and for the value of their portfolio to show a smooth upward trajectory.

One of the ways volatility is reduced is by having a mixture of different types of assets that are not strongly correlated with each other. Bonds generate income constantly and may show capital growth when shares are weak, for example. And when shares are strong, bonds may be weak. Hedge funds pride themselves on performing well whatever the market conditions, although in many cases this claim has proved to be illusory and any returns have been eaten up by the generous fees paid to managers.

The flaw in this diversification argument is that all of the investments that are widely used by professional and amateur investors alike are based around the securities markets. Securities markets are highly liquid and the securities that are traded there have a real-time price. At any moment of the day investors can tell how much their investment is worth.

There are times when this is not necessarily a good thing. Stock and bond market investments, and those like hedge funds and unit trusts that are related to them, are vulnerable to shocks to the financial system, such as those seen in the 2008-2009 crisis. The fact that they are liquid can tempt investors to sell when they should hang on for a better price, and to buy when they should take their profits or avoid investing in them. Markets like this are feverish places, and however diversified a portfolio of stock market investments may be, it will still reflect the market's mood swings.

Owning a range of tangible investments is a good counterweight to this febrile background. Most categories of tangible asset (with the particular exception of art) have low volatility, minuscule correlation with stock markets, and in many cases a negative correlation with bond markets.

Returns over 20 years (1976-2006) from selected alternative investment categories

	Art	Books	Coins	Stamps	Wine
Annual returns (%)	9.1	7.9	3.0	6.4	11.7
Standard deviation (%)	25.0	3.1	3.8	4.2	4.1

Source: Campbell, Koedijk & De Roon

Academic research demonstrates that over the long term the volatility of returns for tangible asset categories (with the exception of art and diamonds) is extremely low, typically in the 3-5% area.* Compare this with typical stock market volatility in the 'teens.

Tangible investments of the sort I describe later in this book are less liquid than stock market investments, although not as illiquid as is commonly supposed. At first sight this lack of liquidity might seem a disadvantage. But it can mean that investors are less prone to making poor short-term market-driven decisions when they own them.

---

*The statement is based on research commissioned by Emotional Assets Management & Research.

Long-term asset allocation is an underrated technique

It is accepted that serious investors should diversify the type of asset they own, whether it's a bond, share, hedge fund, unit trust, or other form of investment, and diversify within each of those categories. In the same way, it also makes sense to diversify investments according to the length of time they may need to come to fruition.

Rather than micro-managing their portfolios, experienced investors look towards asset allocation as the correct way of viewing investment and maximising returns. It makes more sense to switch assets between stocks and bonds, or between stock market assets and tangible assets, over the course of a few years, depending on the ebbs and flows of the economic cycle and trends in the respective markets. Academic research also shows that asset allocation is a far more potent way of influencing long-term returns than is individual investment selection.

The longer-term nature of many of the most worthwhile investment decisions is the key point, and this chimes in quite well with investing in tangible assets. Many alternative forms of investment – wine and forestry, for example – can take years to reach their full value but, if bought wisely, *are* likely to increase in value. Trees grow each year; high-quality wine improves with age. This means that the patient investor can, other things being equal, make significant percentage returns simply by sitting on the investment and doing nothing.

What is significant too about tangible asset investing is that in almost every category, dealers themselves use their asset of expertise as a home for at least part of their long-term savings. Many avid collectors use their chosen field in the same way. Indeed many a banker's bonus has been invested in tangible assets like art, wine and forestry, and portable forms of wealth. That is one reason for the recent price volatility seen in both the art market and in wine.

Supply restriction means security

There is a simple but fundamental reason why tangible assets work as an investment medium. Supply is restricted.

There is only one Van Gogh 'Portrait of Dr Gachet', only a limited number of bottles of 1990 Château Pétrus, only a limited number of Shakespeare First Folios, only a limited number of high-quality 1840 Penny Blacks, and only a limited amount of gold bullion.

This means that, ordinarily, the greater the amount of purchasing power in the world economy, the more the value of objects like this should rise over time. Scarce objects should at least keep pace with inflation and should rise in value with greater affluence in countries where collecting and investing is common.

The same argument is sometimes made about residential property, although this is more questionable. While residential property prices tend to rise over time, they are subject to the vagaries of the planning regime, location and demographic changes. Investors can try and second-guess the potential shifts in the market, but, even if successful in this, property values are also governed by interest rates and the knock-on effect in rental yields and therefore capital value.

Where the character of a particular property cannot be replicated, the scarcity argument may be valid. A period property that is a couple of hundred years old, or which has unusual architectural features, is in many respects the same as a long-term investment in an 'old master' painting. Because it is old, first-rate and unrepeatable, it has a value all of its own. It is therefore desirable in its own right and its value should in theory be immune to the more extreme trends in the wider property market. This argues for seeking out both quality and inherent and proven scarcity. Buying run-of-the-mill collectables is not likely to result in the best returns over time.

Absence of yield is less important when rates are low

Few tangible investments produce income. Or to put it another way, all of their return comes in the form of capital growth. Of the ones we will look at in this book, possibly the only exception to this is forestry. Forestry investment can be structured in such a way that investors (if they are UK taxpayers) can receive a regular tax-free income from harvesting timber.

Is this lack of income a drawback? It depends on your viewpoint. Some investors need to derive income from their investments. But many long-term investors will go for years without taking dividends. In fact it is often an advantage to let income roll up inside an investment to allow compounding to do its work. And there are many commonly-used investments, like zero coupon bonds, that investors use in order to save for specific long-term goals such as retirement or school fee provision, and which have no income paid in the form of dividends.

So, rather than think of tangible alternative investments as having no income, investors should think instead of the total returns and the hidden income that is rolling up inside them.

The income available from 'normal' investment categories may be less of an issue at times when interest rates are extremely low and bank savings accounts return next to nothing. In the UK, following the economic events of 2008, even long-term savings accounts fell to providing an income of little more than 3%, even for quite substantial sums, and only then with drawbacks in terms of lack of liquidity, and less than this when tax is deducted. Gross yields on conventional long-dated government bonds reduced to less than 4%, while index-linked UK gilts ended up in late 2009 at around 1%.

A low interest rate regime means that there is less of an income penalty for people who choose to put money in investments that yield no income. What investors give up in interest on a bank deposit is much less significant than it would be if rates are much higher.

Critics may say that holding tangible assets for investment yields a negative income. This is because valuable items held for investment need to be stored and insured. This imposes a cost that is supposedly not present in investments made through the securities markets.

This is true up to a point, but the cost is not really that significant. Some items (such as gold) can be held in such a way that storage and insurance costs are eliminated. In other cases insurance costs do not add significantly to normal household contents insurance bills, particularly if investors have good security measures in place at their home anyway. Some items, like stamps, are easy to hide away, and their true value is not apparent to the untutored eye.

It is also worth remembering that holding stocks, bonds or unit trusts is not cost-free either. Most brokers and asset managers impose administration charges, charges for valuations, and for other services. Unit trusts frequently have both initial and annual charges. They can be reduced (if investors buy through a fund supermarket, for example) but rarely avoided. For UK taxpayers, ISAs, PEPs, and other tax-sheltered investments are also almost invariably subject to charges.

Liquidity is better than often assumed

In the stock and bond markets, even investments that do not pay interest or dividends are sufficiently easy to sell, so that investors seeking an income are able to periodically sell small amounts to raise funds.

This is less of an option in the case of tangible investments. A collection of coins, books, stamps or art, for example, may have a value as a collection that exceeds the value of the sum of its parts. This is recognised in UK tax law, which can place an upper limit on the amount of the gain that is chargeable to tax when a collection is sold. This is because collections are best sold as a whole. Selling individual parts of a collection separately may diminish its total value disproportionately.

Even disregarding this point, with tangible investments generally, selling a small lot may be uneconomic. Alternatively an investment may be concentrated in a few items of high value, and therefore it may be 'lumpy' or difficult to sell if the investor only wants to cash in a small amount.

Investors in tangible assets who feel they may need periodically to realise part of their portfolio for income, ought therefore to pick their tangible investment area(s) with this in mind. The more homogeneous the item, or the lower the individual value of the pieces that comprise a collection, the easier it will be to realise a regular 'income' from the portfolio. Gold bullion, stamps, coins, or lower-priced art (like limited edition prints, for example) as opposed to fine art or fine wine might be a better choice if this is an issue.

Dealers and auctions provide liquidity in the tangible investment market. But selling through auction rooms does take time and commissions can be hefty. Sellers do, however, have some control over the minimum value realised. This is done by setting a reserve price: although there may be a charge for this, and the risk that the bids from would-be buyers will not reach the reserve and the item is left unsold.

Price data from auctions is, however, readily available and makes it possible to check the price of many items beforehand and get a good idea of what an item might fetch, or how many pieces might need to be sold to raise a specific amount.

Despite the commissions that have to be paid, in a strong market the saleroom can be a good place to sell because of the potential for a bidding frenzy, with competing buyers eager to own a sought-after piece. On the negative side, as mentioned earlier, there is no guarantee that an item will sell. In addition, if the category in which the investment has been made is an esoteric one, an investor may have to wait several months for an auction in which it can be included to come along.

With tangible investments, however, investors can control from whom they buy and to whom they sell. This might be an auction, but it could equally be a trusted dealer who specialises in a particular tangible investment area and with whom the investor has built a relationship.

There is one big advantage with tangible as opposed to stock market investments. In contrast to the financial markets, works of art and other tangible investments, cannot really crash. Investors do not run the risk of dividend cuts, and the depredations of greedy, incompetent and dishonest management teams.

It follows therefore that in testing economic times and on occasions when the stock market is under severe pressure, investors in tangible assets feel less pressure to hurry a sale simply because they may feel the climate has changed for the worse. There is always the option of retaining the item for the time being and selling it later when conditions have improved, secure in the knowledge that the item has an intrinsic value in its own right and in many cases an aesthetic appeal that the investor can enjoy in the meantime.

The one caveat here is that in times of extreme financial distress, tangible assets may ironically be the only source of liquidity available. Much of the explanation behind the sharp drop in the price of contemporary art and fine wine in late 2008 was because investors were selling tangible assets to raise cash to relieve financial pressures brought on by the credit crunch and financial crisis. Those were, however, exceptional times and pressures of this nature are now unlikely to occur for many years, if not decades.

Aesthetically appealing

Aesthetic appeal can sometimes become the biggest plus point for those attracted to tangible investing. Collecting is often a passion indulged in before any thought is given to an item's value as an investment medium.

Of course, there are several practical and emotional reasons why investors are attracted to collecting. One is because it has a similarity to stock market portfolio investing; the second is because it is comparatively easy to invest regular amounts to build up a portfolio over a long period. Many areas like stamps, autographs and coins also have well-documented price histories. In many markets, there are safe ways of investing, and riskier 'counters' that might produce a bigger return, but which are likely to display greater price volatility.

But the aesthetic dividend from tangible investments is important to many, and a common thread that runs through all facets of this form of investing. Items from a collection can be a conversation piece, and a source of pleasure. Looking at a painting on the sitting room wall or handling a Graham Greene first edition, or a rare coin, gives an investor or collector a reason not to be too worried about the shorter-term ups and downs in the market. If an investor can't achieve the price they might want when they come to sell, then there is always the option of waiting and continuing to enjoy their collection's beauty in the meantime.

They yield an aesthetic dividend, and this is another way in which they provide a chance of making decent returns that are not strongly correlated with the stock market, but rather with the general level of economic prosperity.

There remains the question of which area to choose, why some areas are suitable for tangible asset investing while others are not, and the characteristics that all of the tangible investments we look at later in this handbook have in common.

What Alternatives?

What marks out those areas that make suitable investments from those that are best confined just to collectors? The impulse to collect is strong and often indiscriminate: there are collectors of postcards, used railway tickets, garden tools, antiquities, Victorian rocking horses, model cars, and much more. But few, if any, of these are suitable for the purpose of serious investment. Those areas that are suitable have particular essential characteristics.

Must have a network of dealers and regular auctions

This is essential simply from the standpoint of liquidity. Competing dealers ensure that prices are likely to be fair. Collectables suitable for investment should also have a regular auction calendar, since this also provides a way of checking dealers' prices against auction results to ensure fairness. This is true of virtually all of the categories included in this handbook. There are a number of more modern areas where collectors do exist, often pursuing their interest in relative isolation. While more offbeat collectables may increase in value, there may not be a large number of collectors with whom to buy and sell. They may be interesting in a collecting sense, but not from the tangible investing standpoint.

Must be permanent and lasting assets

Many tangible investments are paper-based (banknotes, stamps, autographs, books) and therefore inherently fragile. Coins likewise can be damaged by inept handling. Forests can burn down or be affected by pests. But, carefully looked after, assets like this are essentially permanent. Serious investors should avoid investments that have a finite life. Racehorses and greyhounds are an example. While investors can make money from owning racehorses, the fact remains that they are high-maintenance items. They will also die sooner or later, at which point the investment ceases to exist.

Similarly, it is worth avoiding those areas that have high maintenance costs in a conventional sense. Classic cars are perhaps the best example. Classic cars also fall down for most would-be investors when it comes to having the space to store them in conditions that can properly preserve them.

Must not be securities-based

For reasons that we explored earlier, we want to avoid looking at investments that reflect the tangible assets we are interested in but which are based around tradable securities. So while it is possible to buy shares in auctioneers, stamp dealers, gold mines, timber companies and various others, the focus in this book is generally on the physical ownership of the items themselves.

This isn't a hard and fast rule. There are good collective investments possible in art, coins and forestry, for example, and there are securities that investors can buy that give direct exposure to the price of gold. But in all of the areas we have looked at, direct physical ownership of the item in question is both possible and for the most part preferable.

Should have measurable returns

One of the characteristics provided by a network of dealers and a regular calendar of auctions is that in many cases they provide the opportunity for establishing a well-documented price history from which it is possible to derive an estimate both of the returns that can be generated and the volatility of prices. Price histories like this provide a degree of comfort to investors and a basis on which to assess the prices of potential investments, the amount of capital required to acquire a range of investment-grade items and a benchmark for determining quality.

There has been considerable academic research on returns from categories such as art, and there are regular standard price catalogues or informal price histories for areas such as coins, stamps, banknotes and autographs. In some areas, such as banknotes, the development of standard catalogues is relatively recent. In some areas (books is a good example) there is little formal data on prices, although research has been done on long-term returns. In gold, wine and forestry, extensive data on prices is available.

Must not be conventional property

Finally, we have avoided conventional property as an alternative investment. Though for many people residential property has been a favoured investment area, as the UK buy-to-let boom of the early 21st century attests, its inadequacies are profound and could be the subject of a book in their own right. And there is another simple reason for avoiding it. If one of the prime reasons for tangible asset investing is to achieve diversification away from existing assets, then many investors already have a sizeable stake in the property market, if only through the home they live in. (If investors don't already own a house, then of course this doesn't apply. But most people need to look at the assets in which they have invested or the cash they have available for investment, and include the equity in any property they might own.)

Investing further in property might, of course, be the correct decision at a particular point in the economic cycle. But it does not achieve the goal of diversification away from existing assets, a diversification both desirable and necessary.

Though forestry is sometimes regarded as an offshoot of the property market, it has particular attributes (permanence, favourable tax treatment, inherent underlying growth and income-generating characteristics) that make it suitable for inclusion as a tangible asset investment.

Should ideally be portable wealth

Again, with the exception of forestry (which has, as noted, other positive attributes), all of the tangible investment categories explored in later chapters have the attribute of being – to a greater or lesser degree – portable.

This characteristic is cited by many dealers in, for example, stamps and coins as being one of the important factors that play a part in decisions by some investors to invest in these areas. Many stamps, rare coins, books, art, diamonds, gold bullion and other items are small, high value items that can be moved from place to place with comparative ease.

This is not to imply or condone their use as a medium for smuggling, tax evasion, or money laundering, but simply a fact of life that gives many investors comfort and is to some degree a counterweight to the supposed lack of liquidity that some of these items are held to possess.

By way of illustration, the table shows how it would be possible to move $1 million using the items, discussed in later chapters of this book, in the appropriate quantities.

Ways to move a million dollars – or portable wealth in action

Banknotes	12 Bank of England £1 notes from 1797 (highest-price banknote sold by Spink)
Books	1 Shakespeare 'First Folio' or 5 first editions of *Oliver Twist*
Coins	2 Edward I 'double leopards' sold for £460,000 (with $250,000 in change)
Diamonds	40 one-carat polished diamonds
Gold	28 one-kilo gold bars at $1100 per troy ounce
Paintings	1 Willem de Kooning 'Women Singing' (sold for £700,000 in February 2009)
Stamps	8 'inverted Jennies' 24-cent airmail stamps of 1918, or 2 Mauritius 2d blue 1847 (unused)
Wine	6 bottles of Château Lafite 1787 (one sold for $160,000 in 1985) or 4 bottles of Château Margaux 1787

With all of this in mind, what areas do we think fall into the tangible asset category as potentially lucrative areas into which diversification can and should be made?

Most of the markets I describe are not completely homogeneous. In some (art, for example) there are many different markets, each with its own dynamic and price structure.

Many investors may not, for example, consider themselves to be in the market for 19th century French Impressionist painting, which even now have eye-watering price tags. But there is affordable art available from around this time period in the form of collectable early photography, watercolours and limited edition prints. Similarly, books, coins, stamps, and various other areas have modestly priced sub-sectors that provide investment opportunities at reasonable prices.

With this proviso, here are the broad categories I have selected to explore further in the chapters that follow.

Tangible investment categories and their characteristics

Market	Volatility	Investor presence	Auction calendar	Standard catalogue	Price indices	Offshoots
Art	High	High	Yes	No	Yes	Photography; limited edition prints
Banknotes	Low	Low	Yes	Yes	No	Old bond and share certificates
Books	Low	Low	Yes	No	No	Atlases; maps
Coins	Low	Medium	Yes	Yes	Yes	Tokens; medals
Diamonds etc	High	Low	n/a	n/a	Yes	Jewellery; watches
Forestry	Medium	Medium	n/a	n/a	Yes	n/a
Gold	High	High	n/a	n/a	Yes	ETFs; sovereigns; other precious metals
Stamps	Low	Medium	Yes	Yes	Yes	Postal history
Wine	Medium	High	Yes	No	Yes	Whisky

Source: Various

There are several obvious omissions, including bloodstock, classic cars, antiques, and film and theatre finance. Antiques fail the test on the grounds of space required for storage and lack of price transparency. Classic cars (as previously mentioned) fail on maintenance costs and space. Film finance fails because the favourable tax-deferral characteristics have largely disappeared for UK investors; and theatrical productions, because they do not represent tangible wealth, and lack durability.

The following chapters each cover:

- the basics of the markets that do make good alternative asset investments
- the returns that can potentially be generated by each of these areas
- how to buy and sell sensibly
- and where to get the data and advice to help make an informed decision.

The last chapter of the book looks specifically at auctions as a medium for buying and selling – their advantages and disadvantages, and the intricacies involved. Then, at the back of the book, a carefully researched directory is supplied, so as to make it easy to find the information and contacts required to begin successfully investing in tangible assets.

My aim has been to look at each particular area as objectively as possible from the standpoint of an investor approaching the subject for the first time, and to analyse each particular category in the same way, particularly with reference to potential returns, costs of ownership and transaction costs.

I have talked extensively to many collectors, investors and dealers in the course of researching and writing this book and some have been good enough to comment on a draft of a relevant chapter. Nonetheless it is inevitable that established and experienced individuals like this may find that this book provides too brief a coverage of their favoured area. However, a handbook cannot be encyclopaedic; I have instead set out to provide a systematic, investment-orientated approach to the chosen assets, and one that might be thought-provoking and challenging, even to expert collectors and investors. It might even encourage them to explore new avenues.

In short, there should be something for everyone interested in or involved in the world of tangible asset investment.

ART HK 10

HONG KONG INTERNATIONAL ART FAIR
香港國際藝術展

HONG KONG CONVENTION AND EXHIBITION CENTRE
27-30 MAY 2010

Lead Sponsor
Deutsche Bank

Education Partner
asiart ARCHIVE

PARTICIPATING GALLERIES

10 Chancery Lane Gallery, Hong Kong / 100 Tonson Gallery, Bangkok / Galerie313, Seoul / acb Contemporary Art Gallery, Budapest / Galeriá Álvaro Alcázar, Madrid / Alisan Fine Arts, Hong Kong / Galerie Anhava, Helsinki / Arario Gallery, Cheonan/Beijing/Seoul/New York / ARATANIURANO, Tokyo / Ark Galerie, Jakarta / ARNDT, Berlin / Art Beatus Gallery, Hong Kong/Vancouver / ART ISSUE PROJECTS, Beijing / aye gallery, Beijing / Aye • Eastation Gallery, Beijing / Ayyam Gallery, Beirut/Damascus/Dubai / Beck & Eggeling International Fine Art, Dusseldorf / Beijing Art Now Gallery, Beijing / Beijing Commune, Beijing / Bernier/Eliades Gallery, Athens / Boers-Li Gallery, Beijing / Marianne Boesky Gallery, New York / BREENSPACE, Sydney / Ben Brown Fine Arts, Hong Kong/London / CAIS Gallery, Hong Kong/Seoul / Leo Castelli Gallery, New York / The Cat Street Gallery, Hong Kong / Charest-Weinberg Gallery, Miami / James Cohan Gallery, New York/Shanghai / The Columns Gallery, Seoul / CONTEMPORARY BY ANGELA LI, Hong Kong / Galleria Continua, Beijing/Le Moulin/San Gimignano / Contrasts Gallery, Shanghai / Conny Dietzschold Gallery, Cologne/Sydney / DNA, Berlin / The Drawing Room, Manila / Eastlink Gallery, Beijing/Shanghai / Thomas Erben Gallery, New York / Eslite Gallery, Taipei / F2 Gallery, Beijing/Los Angeles / Faurschou Beijing/Copenhagen, Beijing/Copenhagen / Galerie Forsblom, Helsinki / Frey Norris Gallery, San Francisco / Gagosian Gallery, Athens/Hong Kong/London/Los Angeles/New York/Rome / GALERIST, Istanbul / Gana Art, Busan/New York/Seoul / Gandhara-Art, Hong Kong/Karachi / gdm, Paris / Robert Goff Gallery, New York / Galerie Grand Siècle, Taipei / GRANTPIRRIE, Sydney / Green Cardamom, London / Greenberg Van Doren Gallery, New York / Grotto Fine Art, Hong Kong / Hakgojae, Seoul / Hanart TZ Gallery, Hong Kong / Hauser & Wirth, London/New York/Zurich / Galerie Kashya Hildebrand, Zurich / Galerie Ernst Hilger, Vienna / Michael Hoppen Gallery, London / Galerie Caprice Horn, Berlin / Hwa's Gallery, Shanghai / GALLERY HYUNDAI, Seoul / Gallery IHN, Seoul / Ingleby Gallery, Edinburgh / Taka Ishii Gallery, Kyoto/Tokyo / Galerie Michael Janssen, Berlin / JGM. Galerie, Paris / Amelia Johnson Contemporary, Hong Kong / Paul Kasmin Gallery, New York / gbk - Gallery Barry Keldoulis, Sydney / Keumsan Gallery, Beijing/Seoul/Tokyo / Tomio Koyama Gallery, Kyoto/Tokyo / Kukje Gallery, Seoul / Kwai Fung Hin Art Gallery, Hong Kong / L.A. Galerie Lothar Albrecht, Frankfurt / Langgeng Gallery, Central Java / Lehmann Maupin Gallery, New York / Galerie Lelong, New York/Paris / LEVY, Berlin/Hamburg / Lisson Gallery, London / Long March Space, Beijing / m97 Gallery, Shanghai / Galerie Urs Meile, Beijing/Lucerne / MEM, Osaka / Mizuma Art Gallery, Tokyo / The Modern Institute/Toby Webster Ltd, Glasgow / Mori Gallery, Sydney / Nadi Gallery, Jakarta / NANZUKA UNDERGROUND, Tokyo / Anna Ning Fine Art, Hong Kong / ONE AND J. Gallery, Seoul / Osage Gallery, Hong Kong/Beijing/Singapore/Shanghai / Ota Fine Arts, Tokyo / Other Criteria, London / Roslyn Oxley9 Gallery, Sydney / Pace Beijing, Beijing / Galerie Paris-Beijing, Beijing/Paris / PARK RYU SOOK GALLERY, Jeju/Seoul/Shanghai / Pékin Fine Arts, Beijing / Galerie Emmanuel Perrotin, Miami/Paris / Platform China, Beijing / Plum Blossoms Gallery, Hong Kong / Primo Marella Gallery, Beijing/Milan / Max Protetch Gallery, New York / PYO Gallery, Beijing/Los Angeles/Seoul / Galerie Quynh, Ho Chi Minh City / ALMINE RECH GALLERY, Brussels/Paris / Red Bridge Gallery, Shanghai / Red Gate Gallery, Beijing / Röntgenwerke AG, Tokyo / Galerie Stefan Röpke, Cologne/Madrid / Rossi + Rossi, London / Sakshi Gallery, Mumbai/Taipei / SCAI THE BATHHOUSE, Tokyo / Schoeni Art Gallery, Hong Kong / SCHUEBBE PROJECTS, Dusseldorf / Michael Schultz Gallery, Beijing/Berlin/Seoul / ShanghART Gallery, Beijing/Shanghai / ShugoArts, Tokyo / Silverlens Gallery, Manila / Singapore Tyler Print Institute, Singapore / Soka Art Center, Beijing/Tainan/Taipei / Sperone Westwater, New York / Star Gallery, Beijing / Starkwhite, Auckland / Sullivan+Strumpf Fine Art, Sydney / Sutton Gallery, Melbourne / Tang Contemporary Art, Bangkok/Beijing/Hong Kong / Tokyo Gallery + BTAP, Beijing/Tokyo / Tolarno Galleries, Melbourne / WAKO WORKS OF ART, Tokyo / White Cube, London / x-ist, Istanbul / YAMAMOTO GENDAI, Tokyo / Galerie Zink, Berlin/Munich

SCMP | ART FUTURES GALLERIES

140sqm Gallery, Shanghai / AANDO FINE ART, Berlin / Galerie Lena Brüning, Berlin / Chatterjee & Lal, Mumbai / Chi-Wen Gallery, Taipei / Pilar Corrias Gallery, London / Gallery EXIT, Hong Kong / Input/Output, Hong Kong / Man&Eve, London / Ooi Botos Gallery, Hong Kong / Paradise Row, London / PLATFORM3, West Java / Project 88, Mumbai / Rokeby, London / Take Ninagawa, Tokyo / Y++/Wada Fine Arts, Beijing/Tokyo

T + 852 2918 8793
www.hongkongartfair.com

1.
Art

There is good precedent for treating art as a worthwhile investment medium. Many investment bankers and other wealthy individuals collect art. They use it as an alternative to the stock market and property. Public companies also hang art in their offices. Some even have full-time curators, although corporate art is often either bland or very abstract, for fear of somehow transgressing the bounds of political correctness. More importantly, perhaps, there is at least one well-known example of a leading pension fund making a substantial long-term investment in art. The facts surrounding this may help to make the case for art as an investment medium.

Railpen (or the British Rail Pension Fund, as it was then called) began investing in art in 1974 because it wanted a hedge against inflation. It put a total of £40 million into more than 2,400 works of art. These included sculptures, impressionist paintings, and work in many other genres. Many of the pieces were lent to museums to reduce insurance and storage costs. Of course, once index-linked government bonds made an appearance in the early 1980s, the need for such a hedge disappeared, and eventually it was decided to sell the collection. The programme of sales was interrupted in the early 1990s because of a slump in the art market, but the last of the items in the collection was finally sold in late 2003. Over the period in question, the Railpen art collection appreciated from an initial £40 million to £172 million, a rate of return four percentage points better than inflation. So, though critics derided the idea for many years, the fund made a worthwhile return from its investment.

There is one distinct difference between art on the one hand, and assets such as forestry, wine or gold on the other. Art has no function other than to be decorative. Gold is a long-established store of value; forestry has inherent growth and is tax efficient; wine can be enjoyed by drinking it. But art is simply to be viewed and admired. It has no practical use other than to please the eye. The same is of course true, to a degree, with stamps and coins. But while there are some minor differences of opinion and personal taste in certain quarters of these other collectable areas, with art there is much more scope for disagreement and uncertainty over the artistic merit and long-term aesthetic durability of, say, a minor Victorian watercolour painter, or the latest 'hot' contemporary artist.

It is a matter of personal taste. Technique can be analysed objectively, but differences of opinion remain. Individuals might prefer Turner to Constable, Mondrian to Pollock, Caravaggio to Canaletto, but all are undeniably great artists. This makes art a more hazardous investment medium, as recent trends in the market amply demonstrate, but perhaps a more varied and interesting one.

Basics

Good art is visually appealing. There is no mystery to it. What you see is what you get. But there are a few general principles to cover before looking at some of the main collecting areas.

1. The first is that the art market has increased substantially in size in the last 25 years. Some estimates suggest that there may be a million people around the world now who consider themselves art collectors, compared to perhaps 10,000 a quarter century ago. The estimated 30 million stamp collectors worldwide (some estimates now put the figure at 80 million) dwarfs this number, of course. But then the average art collector spends rather more on his passion than the average stamp collector.
2. The second point is that the art market is not one market but many. Each big-name artist is a market in his or her own right. Particular schools of artist and artistic movements are separate markets, and prices on works of art by individual members of a particular movement may move in and out of favour together. Unlike some other tangible investment areas, art is hard to standardise.
3. Third, there are also various forms of art: not just painting, but sculpture, prints, photographs, and even video. Each of these constitutes a separate market with its own dynamic and price trends. Within these separate markets there are also different price strata, each with distinct patterns of price behaviour and subject to different market influences. This is true to some degree of the markets for other types of collectable – stamps and coins, for example – but very important to bear in mind in the case of art.
4. Fourth, the art market is undeniably cyclical in character and appears to move in sympathy with trends in the stock market. Historic volatility of expensive art is not dissimilar to that of stock market indices, although art prices tend to follow the stock market with a lagged effect. Since the start of the global credit crunch, prices of expensive art sold at auction have dropped sharply as wealthy collectors and investors have sold, or been forced to sell, to raise cash. Impressionist and modern art sales in 2008 saw prices drop sharply and many works were left unsold. Some estimates claim that contemporary art was at that time selling at prices some 75% or more below the levels seen at the peak, although more sober calculations put the fall – for the better-known artists at least – at more like 30%, albeit with further falls widely expected.

Volatility

This is nothing new. Like the stock market, art prices dropped sharply in the 1930s and did not recover until after World War II. They also fell in 1974-75, when stock markets were reeling from the oil crisis; and again, more mildly, in 1982, and in the early 1990s. Peak to trough changes in prices can be as much as 50%. Substantial price reductions were seen in 2008 and 2009 due to the impact of the banking crisis, credit crunch and global recession.

In some ways, if one can be reasonably sure that the shakeout is complete, the early part of a cyclical recovery in the stock market might be a good time to buy art with a medium to long-term view. If, on the other hand, a stock market rise is simply a bear market rally, that would be a costly trap for art investors.

In normal times, the market is frequently driven by the spending power and taste of wealthy collectors, be they European, American or, more recently, Russian. Of these, US collectors have probably always been historically among the more prominent. Going back to the 19th and early 20th century, for example, wealthy industrialists collected art as a matter of course, often with a philanthropic urge to bequeath it to a museum, or endow their own gallery, on their death. With this in mind, leading auction houses also hold many sales in America. And the vibrancy or otherwise of the American economy and the international value of the dollar is a potent influence on the health of some parts of the art market. For example, the dynamic US economy in the 1990s drove up the price of paintings by American Impressionists, and iconic American contemporary art. American Impressionism in particular was hitherto a respectable, but fairly low-profile area. Similarly, prices of German Abstract Impressionist painting have been buoyant during periods when the euro has been strong, and in the age of the oligarch, Russian collectors set world records by bidding aggressively in the art market (and in stamps and rare coins). An earlier sharp upsurge in interest in oriental art reflected burgeoning wealth in China.

Portfolio strategy

If they can endure this periodic volatility to which art has shown itself to be prone, new investors in art face the simple question of where to begin. Should they simply collect paintings or other forms of pictorial art like prints and photographs? Should they collect sculpture as well as painting? What era should they collect? To some degree the answers will be regulated by the space investors might have available at their office or in their home(s) – hanging paintings normally takes less space than bulky items of sculpture – as well as on the budget available. Recent falls in price notwithstanding, Impressionist paintings tend to be expensive. Victorian watercolours are relatively modestly priced. Photography performed best in the last art bull market.

Contemporary art, another favoured area, can be cheap – although recent price trends show it can be highly volatile. Post-war and contemporary art did well in the long upswing in the market from the mid-1990s onwards. But it is hard to discern which contemporary artists have the staying power to make good long-term investments.

Some critics of the art market also point to the role that leading dealers and gallery owners, who also often own large inventories of favoured artists' work, play in supporting prices of their work at auction. They are sometimes accused of attempting to massage the prices of individual works to such a point that it may not really be supported by their artistic merit.

There is one cast-iron rule that overrides all others: only after an artist has died does one know for certain that the supply of his or her work is restricted, and hence some form of scarcity value can start to be incorporated in its value. Many famous artists' work sold poorly during their lifetimes but flourished after their deaths. Paradoxically, though, it is only through producing consistently good work in some volume throughout their lifetime that artists can come to the attention of dealers and achieve recognition. Picasso was a prolific artist, yet with a style so distinctive that he remains one of the most collected artists and one of the best performers in the auction market, as this table shows. The same is true of Andy Warhol.

High turnover artists by auction results – 2008

Artist	Turnover	Lots sold
Francis Bacon	256	100
Edgar Degas	111	81
Lucio Fontana	95	227
Alberto Giacometti	132	111
Damien Hirst	230	445
Yves Klein	91	59
Claude Monet	174	25
Pablo Picasso	262	1,764
Gerhard Richter	122	166
Andy Warhol	236	1,164

Source and © Artprice.com

One astute private collector describes his approach as being to buy 'icons'. They are pictures and artists that are instantly recognisable. They attract buyers like a magnet and ultimately command a premium price. Think of Andy Warhol's screen prints of Marilyn Monroe, for example. In another example, a Sotheby's sale had a set of limited edition, abstract photographs of a graffiti-covered Berlin Wall, by Fritz von der Schulenburg. An example of a modern icon, perhaps?

Most knowledgeable and experienced art investors say that the wisest policy is to invest only in the best pieces one can afford, to buy a few good pieces rather than many mediocre ones, and for an investor to buy what they like personally from an aesthetic standpoint, and hope that their taste coincides with the affluent art buyer of the future.

It is also important to recognise that some art is derivative; that is to say, it apes another style. The result can be equally appealing in terms of its visual impact, but from an investment standpoint the prudent course of action is to seek the original rather than the derivation. This means investors need to study the history of art, even contemporary art, before they begin their investment quest; or else take along an expert to evaluate a piece they want to buy. It is probably also wise, before making a major purchase, to canvass the opinion of more than one expert. Paying the extra cost this might entail is better than making an expensive mistake in choice of artist, or paying an inflated price for a mediocre work.

Collecting Areas

The price range

The collecting areas chosen ultimately depend on the depth of an investor's pocket, but it is not necessary to spend lavishly to get a good investment. The most up-to-date record price paid (as of mid-2009) for a painting was for the 1948 work 'No. 5, 1948' by Jackson Pollock, sold by Hollywood mogul David Geffen for $140 million in 2006 to a private buyer, closely followed by Geffen's $138 million sale of Willem de Kooning's 'Woman III', also in 2006, to hedge fund manager Steve Cohen through the New York dealer Larry Gagosian.

On an inflation-adjusted basis, the highest sale through an auction house (rather than a private sale) remains at $82.5 million ($136 million adjusted for inflation) Van Gogh's 'Portrait of Dr Gachet', bought in 1990 by the Japanese businessman Ryoei Saito via a Christie's New York sale at the peak of the Japanese property boom. In an auction two days later, he paid $78 million ($129 million on an inflation-adjusted basis) for Renoir's 'Bal au Moulin de la Galette'.

Those prices arguably still represent something close to the high water mark for Impressionist paintings. Taking Artprice (www.artprice.com) data on 19th century painting as a proxy for the Impressionists, the 'peak to peak' (1990 to 2008) price movement was in the order of 15% overall, but prices have since fallen back around 20%.

A list of the top fourteen highest-priced paintings of all time, in absolute and inflation-adjusted terms is shown in the following table.

Top fourteen highest-priced paintings of all time

Work	Artist	Year created	Year last sold	Sale price ($m)	Adjusted sale price	Seller	Buyer	How sold?
No. 5, 1948	Jackson Pollock	1948	2006	140	150	David Geffen	Undisclosed	Privately
Woman III	Willem de Kooning	1953	2006	138	147	David Geffen	Steve Cohen	Privately
Portrait of Dr Gachet	Vincent van Gogh	1890	1990	83	136	Kramarsky family	Ryoei Saito	Christie's NY
Bal au Moulin de la Galette	Pierre-Auguste Renoir	1876	1990	78	129	Betsey Whitney	Ryoei Saito	Sotheby's NY
Garcon á la Pipe	Pablo Picasso	1905	2004	104	119	Whitney family	Undisclosed	Sotheby's NY
Irises	Vincent van Gogh	1889	1987	54	102	Whitney family	Alan Bond	Sotheby's NY
Dora Maar au Chat	Pablo Picasso	1941	2006	95	102	Gidwitz family	Undisclosed	Sotheby's NY
Portrait of Joseph Roulin	Vincent van Gogh	1889	1989	58	101	Private collector	MOMA	Privately
Portrait de l'artiste sans barbe	Vincent van Gogh	1889	1998	72	95	Koerfer family	Undisclosed	Christie's NY
Portrait of Adele Bloch-Bauer II	Gustav Klimt	1912	2006	88	94	Maria Altman	Undisclosed	Christie's NY
Massacre of the Innocents	Peter Paul Rubens	1611	2002	77	92	Undisclosed	Ken Thomson	Sotheby's London
Triptych 1976	Francis Bacon	1976	2008	86	86	Undisclosed	Roman Abramovich	Sotheby's NY
Les Noces de Pierette	Pablo Picasso	1905	1989	49	86	Fredrik Roos	Tomonori Tsurumaki	Binoche & Godeau
False Start	Jasper Johns	1959	2006	80	86	David Geffen	Kenneth Griffin	Privately

Source and © Artprice.com

At the bottom end of the price scale are limited-edition prints, the work of new artists, photographs, some watercolours, and other highly enjoyable artistic works that can sell with a price tag of less than £1000 or €1000. Picasso ceramics can be had, for example, for prices under £5000, etchings for £5000-£10,000, and Roy Lichtenstein limited-edition lithographs for under £10,000. In fact, these lower-priced alternatives are sometimes viewed as one of the better areas of the market in which to invest because, as the art market has become more democratic and opened up to a wider section of the public at large, interest in affordable art has increased. Research has suggested that affordable art of this type has on occasion outperformed the much higher priced sections of the market. In other words, investors should let their taste determine what is collected, and not be put off by issues of price. It is not necessary to pay a high price to get a valuable investment. Some might even say that prices of museum-quality art are driven more by the egos of individual collectors than by the 'fundamentals'.

The outperformance of lower-priced art happens because the art market is to a significant extent governed by fashion. Particular movements and artistic media come into and out of fashion and collectors are always seeking undervalued items. It makes no sense therefore to chase the latest fad. Better to find areas that seem to have gone to sleep, buy quietly, and wait for a revival of interest.

Collecting areas are of course too numerous to select more than a handful for individual mention, but here are a few where there is a ready market.

Old Masters

The saying in the art world is that new money buys new art. It follows perhaps that many Old Masters are owned by old money, reluctant to sell paintings that may have stayed in the same family for generations. Old Master paintings therefore come up less frequently at auction than contemporary works, but that's not to say there is any shortage of material. The best works fetch high prices, although investors and serious collectors tend not to pay up for lesser quality work (which many of the Old Masters produced, notwithstanding their reputations) or works in poor or indifferent condition. But Old Master prices rarely reach the stratospheric levels reserved for Impressionists and more modern works.

In contrast to contemporary art, for example, prices are said to be much less volatile, and the market therefore much less risky. Nonetheless prices fell sharply after a peak reached in 1990, dropping by around 50% over the following few years before stabilising. Estimates are that Old Master prices doubled during the last upswing, but that they have since fallen back by around 30%. However, one trend noted recently in the Old Master market is that, rather like other areas of the art world, the top-quality works remain in strong demand but lesser works often fail to sell at auction if priced too ambitiously. Even in crisis periods, major works by Old Masters attract fierce bidding at auction. In late 2008, for example, a major work by Tiepolo sold for £2.5 million, triple its catalogue estimate.

Nevertheless, high prices like this need not rule out the average investor from the Old Master market. For example, Old Master drawings can also be had for relatively low prices and are often works of great beauty. Collecting Old Master drawings has been a tradition among British art lovers since the 18th century. Depending on the reputation of the artist in question, drawings can be bought for prices of £1000 up. In 2003, a drawing by no less an artist than Rembrandt was auctioned off, with a catalogue estimate of £15,000-£20,000, while Sotheby's offered a Tiepolo caricature with an estimate of £8000-£12,000, which sold for £16,800 including the buyer's premium. A drawing by Rubens was offered at £55,000.

The scale of work on offer varies considerably. Michelangelo destroyed many drawings made as preparation for his most famous works, and instances of his drawings in private hands are rare and fetch commensurate prices, usually in the hundreds of thousands. In many Old Master sales, however, beautiful drawings from lesser names sell for a few thousand rather than tens of thousands.

One reason for this is that there is sometimes an issue involved with identifying the work of Old Masters. Prominent artists employed pupils who in some instances did as much work on a picture as their master, and who in later life faithfully imitated their master's style. I once contemplated paying a low four-figure sum (perhaps suspiciously cheap, even so) to buy a small watercolour reputedly by Turner's contemporary Thomas Girtin, but in the end rejected it because I was not sure that it was wholly his work. Differentiating between the work of master and pupil can be a tricky business. But if attribution is in doubt, the price paid should reflect this uncertainty.

Impressionists

Works by French Impressionist painters are sometimes mistakenly regarded as the 'bankers' of the art world, perhaps because Impressionism is thought more accessible than either Old Masters or contemporary art.

It is true in that many, if not most, of the highest priced paintings sold at auction fall into the Impressionist category. This reflected a vogue for French Impressionist art on the part of well-heeled Japanese buyers in the late 1980s;

with its passing, paintings of this genre fell back in price by an estimated 55%, before beginning to recover. In 2003 prices stood at about 65% of their peak 1990 level, but the period between 2005 and 2008 saw a near doubling in prices, taking values back close to their previous peak. Prices are expected to be substantially lower in 2010, however, as the economic crisis put an end to speculative buying of the sort seen a few years previously. Artprice estimates for 19th century paintings as a whole, for example, showed prices in Q4 2009 at 30% down from the peak.

French Impressionism is not the only genre to be popular. As the number of collectors reached by the art market has broadened, so tastes have become more cosmopolitan. Other art movements, such as the Modernists like Modigliani, Klimt, Leger and others, have come into vogue.

And Impressionism was not just confined to France. As mentioned earlier, there was a parallel boom developed in American Impressionist art during the 1990s. This came about as a result of keen interest from new American collectors, particularly those enriched during the internet bubble. Whether these price levels will prove any more durable than those seen a decade previously for French Impressionists remains to be seen. Prices of US Impressionist paintings more than tripled between 1993 and 2002, but it is likely that prices have fallen back sharply here as well in the aftermath of the 2007-2009 economic crisis, given the link between economic activity and price levels.

Similar, though less extreme, trends have been seen in Impressionist drawings and watercolours. While the market for the best American Impressionist paintings has since largely dried up, drawings and watercolours in this category are considered by some experts eventually to have potential for further appreciation. They are often much more modestly priced. British Impressionist watercolours have followed a similar trend.

Unless one's pockets are exceptionally deep, however, this is generally an area for investors to avoid. It has been thoroughly mined over many years and the chances of finding an undervalued gem are strictly limited (although the setback in the market circa 2009 may provide *some* opportunities).

Watercolours

On the whole available for modest prices, out of favour for a while but becoming more fashionable, watercolours represent a good medium for the would-be investor. The market for English and Scottish watercolours and drawings is well documented. A lot of watercolours are in private hands, coming onto the market as a result of deceased estates and as new generations swap traditional art like this for contemporary pieces.

Britain is reckoned to be the spiritual home of watercolours and there are many themes available, not just landscapes. Artprice has information on ten different movements within the British watercolour and drawings market, and prices vary considerably.

- The Post-Impressionists have the best long-term track record. They rose almost sixfold in value over a decade from 1993, with Pre-Raphaelites doing next best, notably Dante Gabriel Rossetti and Edward Burne-Jones. Works by minor members of the Pre-Raphaelite Brotherhood also sell well.

- 18th and 19th century landscape and portrait painters are perennially popular. Impressionists and Modernist artists in this medium more than doubled in value over ten years from 1993. Classic British watercolours from the 1760 to 1830 period increased in price by almost as much. Inevitably prices slipped back with the economic events of 2008, although this part of the art market has probably attracted much less 'hot' money than areas like contemporary art.

- Some Pop art is also included in the watercolour category but prices of such work appear more volatile. Prices here have doubled over ten years from 1999-2009; but in 1999 were selling at less than their 1993 level.

This market is one where knowledge can pay off. Watercolours still occasionally find their way into provincial antique shops and charity shops. The knowledgeable buyer can pick up a bargain. On the other hand, condition is very important for watercolours, in particular avoiding any fading or foxing in the picture.

Photographs

Photographs have often been promoted as affordable art, and photography shares some artistic movements in common with painting. In the last ten years the acceptance of photography as an art form has increased dramatically, a factor reflected in prices. Indeed it is now common to see major galleries rightly including photography in their collections and exhibitions.

From an investment standpoint there are a few rules to bear in mind. For investment purposes it is best to buy those examples where the print was made close to the time that the original negative was taken. Some dealers will also, in some instances, sell negative and positive together.

One intriguing area is macrophotography. This is close-up photography, particularly of plants, printed to significantly larger than their real-life size. Would-be investors need to be aware that a specialised genre of this sort means that the avenues for liquidating their investment through auctions may be less frequent. They may prove a good investment, but they are a less liquid one than some other categories.

Contemporary photography is also an interesting area. Here, prints are issued in limited editions and the negative subsequently destroyed. Some dealers reckon that buying the work of new photographic talent early is the best policy. The reason is that prices at early showings of new work are generally under-priced, and photography is an artistic medium where differences in quality and talent are perhaps more readily apparent than in other forms of contemporary art. Another technique (a leading exponent is Gary Fabian Miller) is making photographic images in a darkroom using a light source and other materials to create a peculiar effect. This can produce striking and highly attractive images.

It used to be the case that some seasoned observers of the art scene regarded the photography market as rather fickle, and subject to the whims of relatively young collectors, although this perception is probably changing as time goes by, not least because prices have done very well.

Artprice calculates that overall prices of fine art photography doubled between January 1998 and January 2008, though subsequently it estimated that prices came back to 2004 levels as a result of the credit crunch. From a longer-term perspective (see table) photographs showed a trough to peak percentage gain of 284%, a 1990 peak to 2008 peak gain of over 100% (a measure of its increasing acceptance as a collectors' medium) and a relatively modest 23% drop in prices since the 2008 peak.

Art market genres – long-term trends

	Early to mid-1990s Q1 1990 to trough % change	Mid-1990s trough to recent peak % change	Recent peak to current % change	Cumulative % change from Q1 1990	Cumulative % change Q1 1990 to peak
Paintings	-54	143	-32	-23	12
Prints	-55	107	-40	-45	-8
Sculpture	-36	125	-30	1	44
Photographs	-46	284	-23	60	108
Drawings	-55	134	-30	-26	5
Old Masters	-49	112	-31	-23	11
19th century	-44	104	-31	-21	15
Modern	-59	134	-28	-31	-4
Post-war	-61	282	-33	-1	49
Contemporary	-60	242	-29	-2	37

Source and © Artprice.com

The big names in photographic art begin at Gustave Le Gray and continue to Man Ray, Ansel Adams, Henri Cartier-Bresson, and more modern names like Richard Avedon, Robert Mapplethorpe, Cindy Sherman and many others. Photography from the 19th century naturally fetches premium prices. Interest in American photographers like Adams exploded during the 1990s, with many newly rich internet entrepreneurs opting to collect American art, of which this was simply one manifestation. Prices of Man Ray's work have often also seemed to defy economic gravity, despite occasional instances coming to light of his work being forged. In general terms, in times of crisis and art market setbacks older photographs tend to hold their value better than the more contemporary, offbeat names and styles.

While recent auction results for photography have been less than spectacular and buy-in rates have been high, there is little doubt that photography remains of considerable interest and will be a durable part of the art market from the standpoint of collectors and would-be investors. According to Artprice, buyer confidence is relatively undiminished provided that works are available at prices that reflect the current climate. Overall then, and despite recent falls, photography stacks up well in terms of long-term returns. Research suggests that price rises in the region of 8-10% a year have been seen on average over a 25-year period. This is also consistent with the price trend seen in the decade to January 2008.

Limited-edition prints

Prints, typically produced by a serigraphic (silk screen printing) or lithographic process, are an interesting way for those with modest budgets to gain exposure to the art market. Prints are produced in limited editions, after which the silk screen or printing plate is destroyed. Like photography, there has been an increasing recognition of printmaking as a venerable, legitimate and highly skilled art form in itself.

The obvious rule applies that the more limited the edition, the more collectable it is. A print from an edition of 25 is likely to be more collectable than one from an edition of 250, unless the artist in question is particularly well known.

This table provides examples of prices of limited edition prints from some well-known artists.

Current prices of limited edition prints

Artist	Price (£)	Edition size
Beryl Cook	750	495
Sir Terry Frost RA	295	150
Stephen Bartlett	350	75
Donald Hamilton Fraser RA	325	175
Derek Piliotis	75	500
Vassilena Nikiforov	200	225
Ellie Barnes	125	395
Alexander Ivanov	100	385

Note: Based on gallery catalogues and author's own purchases.

Other items that add value to prints are an individual signature by the artist on the mount, and any embellishment to the print done by the artist after printing. Some artists make limited-edition prints available to be sold in non-gallery marketplaces such as the art auctions held on some cruise ships. Those buying at auctions like this can rest secure in the knowledge that the artist is making great efforts to promote their work and this can only have a positive affect on subsequent prices of the items.

Prices of prints are said generally to be slower to increase in value, but on the other hand are much less volatile than the prices of original works of art, and form a distinct market with a cadre of specialist collectors. According to Artprice, print prices just about recouped the early 1990s setback in the subsequent bull market, but are currently around 40% below the peak levels reached in 2008.

Nonetheless there is some surprising value on offer. Recent sales at the 2009 London Original Print Fair saw, for example, a David Hockney work, 'Small Dogs (Vertical)', in an edition of 80 on offer for £7,500. An engraving of 1621 based on one of Ruben's paintings, by Lucas Vorsterman the Elder and dedicated to Philip IV of Spain, sold to an American museum for £1,500. At the other end of the scale, a Damien Hirst print, 'Opium', sold for £5,500.

Contemporary art

This is a huge area, and the best-known names are well publicised: Tracey Emin, Damien Hirst, Andy Warhol, Beryl Cook, John Piper, John Bratby and many others. Prices range from the affordable to the expensive and the trick here is to spot a coming artist before his or her work attains wide recognition. Those who spotted the potential of early work by John Piper and John Bratby, for example, were rewarded for their perception by a fivefold increase in prices over less than a decade. The following shows a league table of the richest artists, based on their cumulative auction sales since 1970.

Top ten richest living artists

Artists	Value of auction sales since 1970 ($m)
1. Jasper Johns	151
2. Gerhard Richter	124
3. Cy Twombly	88
4. Robert Rauschenberg	61
5. Fernando Botero	57
6. Frank Stella	57
7. Karel Appel	56
8. Antoni Tapies	43
9. David Hockney	38
10. Georg Baselitz	34

Source: Art Sales Index; Art Review

Would-be investors need to take care in areas like this, however, because – more than most alternative assets – art is subject to the whims of fashion, and the scale and long-term durability of an artist's body of work, especially that of a living artist, is hard to judge accurately.

Prices of contemporary art, in addition to post-war art, were among the strongest performers in the art market over the period since the price trough in the mid-1990s, showing a more than tripling in prices over that period, with post-war art doing marginally better. Prices of both categories in Q4 2009 were down in the region of 30% since the peak, but, on the evidence of past downturns, may have further to fall before some semblance of stability is reached.

Condition

With art, condition is important, but in some cases less of an issue than it is for other items like books and stamps. But there are still problems with a work of art that need to be checked for and, if humanly possible, avoided.

Tears and rips in canvas, loose or badly fitting frames, poor or unsuitable quality frames, art that has slipped in its mounting, or discolouration due to acidity in the mounting are all important issues and should definitely be addressed before buying. If the piece is being bought 'as is', then a price adjustment should be made to reflect the cost of any remedial measures that might be necessary. A specialist craftsman should always undertake these repairs. If in doubt on these points, walk away.

Condition is a particular issue when buying watercolours. Here it is vital to avoid buying pieces that are faded as a result of having been hung in direct sunlight. Investors and collectors should also avoid any discoloration in the main body of the picture such as foxing, or brown spots like those that commonly occur in old books.

Security Measures

Like antiques, art is regularly stolen, especially since it is normally small enough to be easily portable. There are a number of precautions investors and collectors must take to protect their investment.

First, keep receipts for any items acquired and any other documentation such as certificates of authenticity. Keep track of auction results for the artists in whose work the investor or collector has an interest, and, if necessary, have a collection periodically revalued by a professional.

Investors and collectors should keep photographs of their art. All items should be photographed individually with colour film, preferably in natural light and against a plain background, and a note made of any identifying marks. An inventory of all items should also be kept, with details of any identifying marks and the dimensions of the work, much as would be done for antiques.

All pieces should be marked on the reverse side with a postal code and perhaps even with an abbreviated address.

All items should be insured for their full market value, and investors and collectors should ensure that this can be verified to an insurance company's satisfaction and that the stipulated security measures are in place. Depending on the value of the pieces, it may be necessary to take out specialist insurance, but if the scale is more modest (£50,000 or less) a home contents policy may be able to cover it, and this will not necessarily add an outlandish amount to the premium on the policy.

The Right Alternative Asset for You?

As with other categories in this book, there are a number of questions that investors and/or their advisors need to satisfy themselves on before deciding whether art is an appropriate investment medium in which to participate alongside a wider portfolio of more conventional investments.

A medium to long-term investment?

Most individuals buy art to keep it for the long term, but prices can move rapidly in the art market. As the examples earlier in this chapter show, it is perfectly possible, provided one buys well at the right time, to achieve significant price appreciation in as little as two years. But buying at the wrong time can lead to heavy losses, much as is the case with stock-market investments. What also complicates the rosy scenario of price appreciation in favourable circumstances is dealing costs, particularly if the investor wishes to buy and sell at auction. The buyer's premium and seller's commission paid to auction houses need to be taken into account when calculating potential profits. It is the scale of these charges that tends to make art investors hold on for the long term. In effect, there is a 40% spread to overcome before an investor starts making money.

Capital required?

This is a vexed question. At the top end of the market, museum-quality art sells for millions. From an investment standpoint, however, it is not necessary to invest at this level to make useful gains: rather the reverse. Serious pieces can be had at auction for upwards of £1500-£2000, and a reasonable portfolio put together for £25,000. If the capital the investor wants to devote to this part of the tangible asset scene is less than this amount, there are certain sections of the market where art is eminently affordable. These include limited-edition prints, watercolours and photography. Lower-priced art is by no means the poor relation. It performed very well over the late 2000s, whereas middling pieces produced more pedestrian returns.

Insurance and maintenance costs?

An investment in art will yield no income, although the Japanese owner of one masterpiece did attempt, unsuccessfully, to persuade people to pay to see it. Owning art entails extra costs for insurance, framing and perhaps some gentle restoration. These costs should be quantified before the investor commits to a purchase.

Portfolio diversification potential?

As we have seen, art reflects the whims and affluence of different sections of the collector base, as well as wider trends in global prosperity. International art market trends tend to reflect the fact that most collectors buy the art produced in their own country. Upsurges in wealth in one country, for whatever reason, may produce a boom in that country's painters and artists.

The demise of the internet bubble in 2000-2003 and the weakness of the dollar in its aftermath, the more recent credit crunch and global recession, as well as the reining-in of executive compensation in the US and elsewhere, seems to suggest that the art market will be soft for some time to come in the early 21st century and that the influence of US and European collectors and investors on price may wane for the time being, with the tastes of Middle Eastern, Far Eastern and emerging-market buyers becoming more prevalent over time.

So from the standpoint of diversification you could argue that – timing differences apart – the art market is not that different from the stock market. Artists and artistic movements come into and move out of favour like stocks and sectors. From this it might be assumed that art is not sufficiently different to the stock market to offer meaningful diversification. But American academics who have measured price trends in the art market suggest that, though art is cyclical, most art categories have a very low, and in some cases negative, correlation with the stock market. This would make them an ideal investment medium provided their cyclicality is borne in mind, and purchases and sales are timed carefully.

Tax considerations?

The short answer is 'no', although there have been instances where restricting tax concessions on securities-based investment has fostered a boom in art ownership in particular countries that have imposed them.

Returns

The art market is one where it is easy to work out the returns that have been made by investors in particular categories. This is true despite the diverse nature of the market, the reason being that auction houses and statistical services will have kept comprehensive records of prices achieved on the same or similar items as they came up for sale.

The best-known work in this area has been by two American academics: Michael Moses and Jianping Mei at NYU's Stern School of Business. They have tracked art prices at Sotheby's auctions using data from as far back as 1925 and other data going back to 1875. Some 5300 works had been sold more than once, enabling the price comparisons to be made. Their data suggests that works in the bottom quartile by price showed the highest return, around 11.5% a year. Works in the top quartile rose by only 6.6% a year.

In the post-war era, Moses and Mei calculate that annual returns for the art market in total (for the period 1952-2002) were in the region of 13%, marginally better than the stock market over the same period. On their calculations, art has outperformed the stock market, as measured by the S&P 500 index, by 18% over three years and by 8% over five years to 2002. For the most part, the 2002 data was the latest available comprehensive study at the time of writing. Supplementing data like this with more recent indications from the various commercially-provided art-price indices gives one a reasonable perspective of the pattern of returns.

The returns seen for different price categories over shorter time periods, however, tend to be more closely packed together. In the 1999-2002 period, mid-priced art did better than either top-priced pieces or the low end of the market.

The earlier table of data from Artprice showing trends in prices of different categories over various time periods since the acknowledged major peak in the art market in 1990 (see page 14) shows a divergent pattern of price movements for the different segments of the art market, reinforcing the view that art is not one market but many and that generalising about returns can be difficult. In terms of peak-to-peak performance and trough-to-peak performance, photography, post-war art and contemporary art have been far and away the best performers.

Returns generated by other sections of the art market depend crucially on the timing of entry and exit points. The evidence of past downswings and troughs in the art market suggests that prices may fall further over the next couple of years and that only then will it make sense to buy art from the standpoint of trying to generate long-term positive returns. It is a moot point whether or not the better performing areas of the art market in the recent upswing will be the ones to back in the next 'up' phase in the cycle.

Many academic researchers have conducted projects to examine longer-term price trends. The following table shows some of those based on repeat sales and the conclusions they came to.

Art: Returns calculated by academic studies of repeat sales

Author	Date	Genre	Average real return (%pa)	Period covered by data
Anderson	1974	Paintings in general	3.0	1780-1970
Baumol	1986	Paintings in general	0.6	1652-1961
Frey et al.	1989	Paintings in general	1.4	1635-1949
Frey et al.	1989	Paintings in general	1.7	1950-1987
Pesando	1993	Modern prints	1.5	1977-1991
Goetzmann	1993	Paintings in general	2.0	1716-1986
Chanel et al.	1996	Paintings in general	5.0	1855-1969
Goetzmann	1996	Paintings in general	5.0	1907-1977
Pesando/Shum	1996	Picasso prints	1.4	1977-1993
Mei/Moses	2001	Various	4.9	1875-2000

Note: In some instances real returns were estimated from nominal ones.

This shows consistent positive real returns from art, the scale of the returns depending on the period taken and the category in question. In general, data from the more recent era appears to show higher real returns, although these tend only to stop during the period when the art market in general was booming, and hence returns may be skewed upwards as a result. As yet few if any serious studies have been undertaken on prices and returns and included the effects of the aftermath of the credit crunch and subsequent recession.

Some time ago, an article in the *Wall Street Journal* examined auction records for a number of artists over periods of five and 15 years and tabulated a number of them giving recommendations based on the views of experts, as to what artists might be regarded as 'buys', 'sells', or 'holds' at that time. The following table shows some data extracted from this article. The artists in question are generally the pricier ones, and these should not necessarily be construed as my 'buy' recommendations, but they do give an illustration of the types of returns that can be achieved over the medium and long term, and of the variations in returns.

Past returns from artists viewed as 'buys'

Artist	Average in 2003 ($000s)	Percentage price change 5 years	Auction price over 15 years
Albert Bierstadt	773	126	1871
Gustave Caillebot	2,700	469	461
Paul Cézanne	5,500	59	20
Dan Flavin	135	19	217
Paul Gauguin	2,100	259	110
Keith Haring	58	42	300
Damien Hirst	267	131	n/a
Jeff Koons	519	287	1786
Roy Lichtenstein	1,100	185	181
Rene Magritte	1,100	15	261
Roberto Matta	226	251	493
Claude Monet	4,500	55	-17
Sir Alfred Munnings	247	141	427
Mark Rothko	5,400	1889	451
Ed Ruscha	448	865	356
John Singer Sargent	51	-85	-55
Cindy Sherman	67	121	3292
Wayne Thiebaud	430	129	136

Source: WSJ, 29 January 2004

How to Invest

Art is synonymous with buying at auction, not least because auction houses make a point of having frequent large sales of particular genres of art, and produce lavish catalogues containing price estimates.

Not all items at auction are outrageously expensive. Some auction houses like Bonhams, for example, make a point of having a number of modestly-priced lots, and the same is true of provincial auction houses where, away from the spotlight, there may be bargains to be had. A recent Sotheby's sale of contemporary art contained many pieces with estimated prices of under £2000 and several at under £1000.

Elsewhere many cruise lines operate art auctions and this can be a useful source of material, particularly since serious bidders – especially for more offbeat contemporary work – tend to be few and far between. While most material is fairly mundane and arguably priced with reserves that are too high, there are opportunities to acquire investment-grade art for prices in the low thousands, and also attractive originals from up and coming artists who supply material to cruise lines at attractive prices because of the exposure their work receives. For investment-grade art, some cruise lines operate a buyback policy that effectively limits the buyer's downside risk.

Remember, however, when buying at auction to factor in the buyer's premium (usually 10-20% of the hammer price) and storage costs, shipping costs and the like. This can add up. It goes without saying that those attending auctions also need to guard against overbidding for a particular piece. Research the desired piece beforehand and work out a reasonable estimate of what it is worth. Make sure the lot is viewed before the sale. When it comes to the auction, dealers will not pay over the odds because they need to make a margin, but investors and collectors should avoid getting into a bidding war with another private individual. Buying at auction is not, or should not be, an ego trip.

While this is a seemingly costly and uncertain buying process, it can be made to work on the investor's behalf. There are several ways to get the market to work in this way.

- One is to buy against the trend. Buyers should avoid fashionable areas but look in detail at those that have fallen out of favour and where prices have been left behind.
- Buying during a recessionary period – if an investor or collector has the capital to do so – is another way of improving the returns made.

There are sometimes sales following an auction where a number of lots failed to meet the reserve. These may be a way of acquiring interesting pieces without going into the competitive arena of the auction. Sales from deceased estates and forced sellers are another way that art can be acquired at good prices.

A final point to bear in mind is that, like other tangible asset categories, well-informed investors can sometimes get real value for money by buying as far down the chain of buyers and sellers as possible.

Each time a piece changes hands, a dealer will be making a margin on it. As noted in the previous chapter, city centre dealers and auction houses have expensive overheads. Bargains may be had by visiting country fairs, provincial galleries, and small auction rooms. If individual investors and collectors know what they are looking for and are disciplined enough not to pay too much, they might be surprised at what they can find.

Where to Go for More Information

There is plenty of information about the art market on the web, and the following is a brief review of some of the key sites and publications. The data on auction houses given immediately below also includes some information relating to auctions of other tangible investment categories, and general sites facilitating auctions. Remaining comments in subsequent sections relate solely to art.

Auction houses and dealers

The auction house websites all feature online catalogues and auction prices.

The International Auctioneers Group is an alliance of eight prestigious independent auction houses. It has a head office in Geneva. The group shares marketing, catalogues, etc, and produces its own magazine. The members are:

- Dorotheum (www.dorotheum.com) was established in Vienna in 1707 and is the largest auction house in Central Europe. There are branches in other European cities together with a representative in London and other cities. It holds approximately 600 auctions a year.

- Lempertz (www.lempertz.eu) was founded in Cologne in 1845 and is one of the leading art auction houses in Europe. It has representatives in Tokyo, Shanghai, Zurich and Paris.

- Venator & Hanstein (www.venator-hanstein.de), partly owned by Lempertz, specialises in valuable books, manuscripts, prints, Old Master and modern prints and drawings.

- Koller (www.kollerauktionen.ch) was established in Zurich in 1958. It holds four auctions annually in Zurich as well as two in Geneva. It specialises in the art of the 20th century, books, autographs and fine wines. Koller also has offices in Munich, Shanghai and London, plus representatives in Paris, Belgium, Dusseldorf, Moscow and Australia.

- A relative newcomer to the scene is Porro (www.porroartconsulting.it). It was founded in Milan in 2002 with the aim of operating in the highest-priced segment of the art market in Italy.

- Bukowskis (www.bukowskis.se) was founded in Stockholm in 1870 by an exiled Polish nobleman. It holds four main auctions a year with two devoted to modern and contemporary art.

- The Parisian Artcurial (www.artcurial.com) stages 100 sales each year in every auction field.

- Bruun Rasmussen (www.bruun-rasmussen.dk), the leading auction house in Denmark, was established in Bredgade, Copenhagen in 1948. It holds 100 auctions a year, covering most fields. The company has representatives in France, Sweden, Italy, England and the USA.

Auction houses

Entity	Web address	Main location	Email address	Telephone	Category
Artcurial	www.artcurial.com	Paris	On site	33 (01) 42 99 20 20	Auction house
Artfact Live!	www.artfact.com	USA	On site	(617) 219 1090	Online auction database
Bonhams	www.bonhams.com	London	info@bonhams.com	020 7447 7447	Auction house
Bruun Rasmussen	www.bruun-rasmussen.dk	Denmark	info@bruun-rasmussen.dk	445 8818 1111	Auction house
Bukowskis	www.bukowskis.se	Stockholm	On site	46 (0) 8 614 08 00	Auction house
Christie's	www.christies.com	Worldwide	info@christies.com	020 7839 9060	Auction house
Doyle	www.doylenewyork.com	New York	info@doylenewyork.com	212 427 2730	Auction house
Freemans	www.freemansauction.com	Philadelphia	Info@freemansauction.com	215 563 9275	Auction house
International Auctioneers Group	www.internationalauctioneers.com	Geneva	info@internationalauctioneers.com	41 (22) 310 21 80	Auction house alliance
Koller	www.kollerauktionen.ch	Zurich	office@kollerauctions.com	41 44 445 63 63	Auction house
Lempertz	www.lempertz.eu	Cologne	On site	49 221 925 7290	Auction house
Lyon & Turnbull	www.lyonandturnbull.com	Scotland	info@lyonandturnbull.com	0131 557 8844	Auction house
Phillips de Pury	www.phillipsdepury.com	London	On site	020 7318 4010	Auction house
Pierre Berge	www.pba-auctions.com	Paris	On site	33 (01) 49 49 90 00	Auction house
Porro	www.porroartconsulting.it	Milan	On site	02 72 094 708	Auction house
Society of Fine Art Auctioneers and Valuers	www.sofaa.org	Surrey	On site	0207 0968 417	Association
Swann Galleries	www.swanngalleries.com	New York	On site	212 254 4710	Auction house
Tajan	www.tajan.com	Paris	On site	Dept. specific	Auction house
Tennants	www.tennants.co.uk	Leyburn	enquiry@tennants-ltd.co.uk	01969 623 780	Auction house
the-saleroom.com	www.the-saleroom.com	Online	On site	n/a	Online link to auctions
Venator and Hanstein	www.venator-hanstein.de	Cologne	On site	49 221 257 54 19	Auction house
Weschler's	www.weschlers.com	Washington	info@weschlers.com	202 628 1281	Auction house
Whytes	www.whytes.ie	Dublin	info@whytes.ie	353 (0) 1676 2888	Auction house

Pierre Bergé & Associés (www.pba-auctions.com) is based in Paris with a branch in Brussels focussing on contemporary design.

Bonhams (www.bonhams.com) is the world's oldest and largest auctioneer still in British ownership. It offers sales and valuations not only in London, but also in the provinces, with nine salesrooms and 22 offices throughout the UK. All sectors of the fine art, antiques and collectables market are covered. Several of its departments are established world leaders in their field.

Regular sales are also held throughout Europe. In the USA, Bonhams & Butterfields is the principal auction house on the West Coast, with more than 50 auctions a year. In Australia, Bonhams and Goodman conduct 50 sales a year in Sydney. The company also has representatives in Brisbane and Perth.

Bonhams Hong Kong specialises in jewellery, watches, Chinese Art, Modern Asian Art and wine.

Christie's (www.christies.com) has over 80 departments in all areas of fine and decorative art, wine, books, etc. The company has 57 offices in 32 countries and 14 salerooms around the world, including London, Paris, New York and Los Angeles, plus emerging markets such as India and China.

Christie's also operates a real-time online bidding service, offering clients worldwide access to its sales. Buyers can view condition reports, track lots, place bids and watch auctions in real time. In addition, auction reminders and results can be emailed on request.

Phillips (www.phillipsdepury.com) is based in New York and London with further offices in Berlin, Geneva, Munich, Paris and Cologne. The focus is on contemporary art, design, jewellery and photography.

Sotheby's (www.sothebys.com) is one of the oldest fine art auctioneers in the world and the largest. The main offices are in London and New York, with 100 worldwide. All areas of fine and decorative arts are covered. Select sales are open for bids via the internet. Full access to the site, with features such as real-time auction results and fully customised email notices, can be obtained on registration.

Sotheby's Institute of Art offers courses in London, New York and Singapore, varying from evening classes and day courses to degree programmes.

Doyle (www.doylenewyork.com) was founded in New York in 1962 and has auctioned the estates of such Hollywood legends as Bette Davis, Rock Hudson and James Cagney.

Lyon & Turnbull (www.lyonandturnbull.com) was established in Edinburgh in 1826 and is Scotland's oldest firm of auctioneers, with offices and representatives throughout the country. The firm also has a marketing alliance with Freeman's, America's oldest auction house (www.freemansauction.com). A London gallery opened on Pall Mall in 2006.

Tajan (www.tajan.com) is a leading French auction house with a base in Paris and other offices throughout France.

Weschler's (www.weschlers.com) is one of the USA's leading auctioneers, based in Washington DC.

Associations and galleries

The Society of Fine Art Auctioneers and Valuers (www.sofaa.org) is a professional body formed in 1973 for specialist firms throughout the UK. The site has a list of members.

www.the-saleroom.com is a service provided by *Antiques Trade Gazette*. Free registration allows anyone to follow and listen in to auctions in progress in real-time. The service can also be used for live internet bidding.

The International Fine Print Dealers Association (www.ifpda.org) is an organisation of leading art dealers, galleries and publishers in the field of fine prints. Some 168 members from around the world are listed on the site with web links. There is also information about the annual print fair held in New York.

The Association of International Photography Art Dealers (www.aipad.com) has members in the USA, Canada, Australia, Europe and Japan – all of whom are listed on the site, together with contact details.

Trade associations and other organisations

Entity	Web address	Main location	Email address	Telephone	Category
Art Dealers Association of America (The)	www.artdealers.org	New York	On site	212 488 5550	Organisation
Art Loss Registry (The)	www.artloss.com	London, Bath	info@artloss.com	020 7841 5780	Organisation
Association of International Photography Art Dealers (The)	www.aipad.com	Washington	info@aipad.com	202 367 1158	Association
Confédération Internationale des Négociants en Oeuvres d'Art	www.cinoa.org	Worldwide	On site	1 (310) 229 2626	Association
Contemporary Art Society	www.contempart.org.uk	London	info@contemporaryartsociety.org	0207 7831 1243	Association
International Fine Print Dealers Association	www.ifpda.org	New York, London	On site	212 674 6095	Association
Society of London Art Dealers (The)	www.slad.org.uk	London	office@slad.org	020 7930 6137	Organisation

Gordon's Art (www.gordonsart.com) has databases of art, print and photography prices online, many of which are free to access. Others are available on subscription.

Art in Scotland (www.artinscotland.com) provides a guide to over 300 art galleries in Scotland.

The Contemporary Art Society (www.contempart.org.uk) hosts the annual selling exhibition 'Artfutures', with selections made from the best works from student shows and artists themselves. It is a national non-profit making membership organisation for contemporary collectors, professionals and enthusiasts.

Art fairs

The Armory Show (www.thearmoryshow.com) is an international fair of new art by living artists as well as new modern and historically significant contemporary art. It is held annually in March in New York.

Art Basel (www.artbasel.com) is held each June in Basel, Switzerland and features nearly 300 leading galleries from around the world and more than 2500 modern and contemporary artists. The site has a useful link to international art magazines and publications. Each December Art Basel also organises Art Basel Miami (www.artbaselmiamibeach.com).

Art Fair Tokyo (www.artfairtokyo.com) held annually in April features modern paintings, *nihonga* (Japanese-style painting), antiques and contemporary art from selected domestic and international galleries.

Frieze (www.frieze.com) is a leading magazine of contemporary art and culture. It sponsors the Frieze Art Fair held every October in Regents Park, London, which features more than 150 contemporary art galleries from around the world.

Fairs

Entity	Web address	Main location	Email address	Telephone	Category
Armory Show, The	www.thearmoryshow.com	New York	info@thearmoryshow.com	212 645 6440	Fair
Art Basel	www.artbasel.com	Switzerland	info@artbasel.com	41 58 200 20 20	Fair
Art Fair Tokyo	www.artfairtokyo.com	Tokyo	On site	81 570 02 9999	Fair
Frieze	www.frieze.com	London	info@frieze.com	0 20 3372 6111	Fair
European Art Fair, The (Maastricht Fair)	www.tefaf.com	Maastricht	info@tefaf.com	31 411 64 50 90	Fair
Art Dubai	www.artdubai.ae	Dubai	info@artdubai.ae	971 4 323 3434	Fair
Hong Kong Art Fair	www.hongkongartfair.com	Hong Kong	info@hongkongartfair.com	852 2918 8793	Fair
Venice Biennale, The	www.labiennale.org	Venice	info@labiennale.org	39 041 5218711	Exhibition
London Art Fair, The	www.londonartfair.co.uk	London	Various	Various	Fair

The European Art Fair, also known as the Maastricht Fair (www.tefaf.com), is held each year in March with exhibits from 239 art and antique dealers. Every item is checked by one of 25 vetting committees made up of 155 internationally respected experts. TEFAF (The European Fine Art Foundation) also organises Pan Amsterdam (www.pan.nl) with 120 Dutch and Flemish participants.

Art Dubai (www.artdubai.ae) came onto the scene in 2007 with over 60 contemporary art galleries exhibiting, predominantly from the Middle East, North Africa and South Asia. The growth of the region's finance sector has created a new generation of collectors on which the fair hopes to capitalise in the future.

Hong Kong, the third largest art auction market in the world, held its inaugural art fair (www.hongkongartfair.com) in 2008. It brings together 110 international galleries dealing in contemporary and modern 20th century art. The fair hopes to establish Hong Kong as the cultural hub for visual arts in the region and to attract new money from China, Taiwan and Korea.

The Venice Biennale (www.labiennale.org) is a major international contemporary art exhibition. As its name suggests, it takes place once every two years in Venice and lasts from June to November. It was last held in 2009.

The London Art Fair (www.londonartfair.co.uk) is held annually in January. Painting is the main focus but the fair also features sculpture, photographs, prints, video and installation art. The site has links to all the exhibitors.

Kara Art (www.karaart.com) has a list of art fairs worldwide with a list of artists by country/media. A free newsletter is also available.

Information sites

Artnet (www.artnet.com) has an online gallery network linking to 2200 galleries worldwide in over 250 cities. The site includes many useful features such as a list of auction houses throughout the world, a price database, upcoming auction dates, and information on market trends.

The Art Newspaper (www.theartnewspaper.com) has news, comments on the art market and exhibition and fair listings. The free weekly email newsletter has updates, offers and exhibition information. The full print or digital version can be subscribed to online and can also include access to the Art Newspaper TV channel. The magazine also produces a special free daily news update during the main international art fairs.

Art Review (www.artreview.com) is a leading art magazine for 20th and 21st century art and style. It has a wealth of information including interviews, analysis and critics' views. ArtCalendr links to exhibitions around the world, whilst ArtLive has videos, news and blogs. ArtFinder provides a search facility for artists and galleries. The site also incorporates a virtual art fair experience, where it is possible to buy, find and exhibit artworks from around the world.

Artprice (www.artprice.com) collects, processes and analyses sales from 2900 auction houses worldwide. Their reference databanks list 405,000 artists with images from the 4th century to the present day. The extensive free content covers comment and analysis on the art market by way of the Art Market Confidence Index and a searchable database that can be accessed by title, sales date, hammer price or year of creation. The My Art Collection will track the value of all the works in a collection, together with a quarterly update of the portfolio's value. Paying subscribers have access to more detailed information including artists' price levels and indices, biographies and future sales. An occasional user subscription is also available. For further detailed investment information, the firm's econometrics department offers subscribers quantitative information and analysis plus customised tools.

Art

Information and publications

Entity	Web address	Main location	Email address	Telephone	Category
Art Basel	www.artbasel.com	Basel	info@artbasel.com	41 58 200 20 20	Fair
Art Basel Miami Beach	www.artbaselmiamibeach.com	Miami	info@artbasel.com	41 58 200 20 20	Fair
Art Dubai	www.artdubai.ae	Dubai	On site	971 (0)4 323 3434	Fair
Art Fair Tokyo	www.artfairtokyo.com	Tokyo	info@artfairtokyo.com	83 3 5771 4520	Fair
Art London	www.artlordon.net	London	info@artlondon.net	020 7259 9399	Fair
Armory (The)	www.thearmoryshow.com	New York	On site	212 645 6440	Fair
BADA Antiques and Fine Art Fair	www.bada-antiques-fair.co.uk	London	On site	020 7589 6108	Fair
European Fine Art Fair	www.tefaf.com	Netherlands	info@tefaf.com	31 411 64 50 90	Fair
Frieze	www.frieze.com	London	On site	020 3372 6111	Fair
Glasgow Art Fair	www.glasgowartfair.com	Glasgow	artfair@uzevents.com	0141 552 6027	Fair
Hong Kong Art Fair	www.hongkongartfair.com	Hong Kong	info@hongkongartfair.com	852 2918 8793	Fair
International Fine Art and Antique Dealers Show	www.haughton.com	London	info@haughton.com	020 7389 6555	Fair
Lapada Art and Antiques Fair	www.lapadalondon.com	London	lapada@lapada.org	020 7823 3511	Fair
London Art Fair	www.londonartfair.co.uk	London	On site	020 7288 6482	Fair
London International Fine Art Fair	www.olympiaartsinternational.com	London	On site	020 7370 8211	Fair
Venice Biennale	www.labiennale.org	Venice	On site	39 041 521 8711	Fair

The Mei Moses Fine Art Index (www.artasanasset.com) offers indices, graphs, numerical values and research and press reports. The website is organised in five sections. The home page of each has free content with more detailed information available on subscription. The most recent section to be added provides information by way of graphs and statistics on the returns achieved at auction for the works of each of 150 artists, with the largest number of repeat auction sales represented in the repeat sales database.

Galleries (www.galleries.co.uk) is a monthly UK arts listings magazine and is available from galleries, hotels and the like, and also by online subscription. The magazine lists over 500 art galleries and related businesses, together with information on current exhibitions, and reviews of the auction market and new books.

Culture 24 (www.culture24.org.uk) is a not-for-profit online publisher working across the arts, heritage, tourism and education sectors with links, information and news on thousands of UK museums, galleries, archives and libraries.

Artinfo (www.artinfo.com) is the online arm of Louise Blouin Media, a leading cultural media group. It provides a wealth of up-to-date information concerning the art market, with news, auction reports, detailed coverage of art fairs and events, collecting advice, market trends and analysis. A weekly email newsletter is also available. The site incorporates the Art Sales Index, with a search tool to find auction prices. There are other useful links on the site, including a bookshop offering publications such as the comprehensive *Davenport's Art Reference and Price Guide*.

The Art Loss Register (www.artloss.com) is a permanent computerised database of stolen and missing works of art, antiques and valuables, operating on an international basis. Also available is a pre-loss database where possessions can be registered. Before purchasing a work of art it may be worth checking on the site to see whether a prospective purchase is listed as lost or stolen. Other services include investigative and recovery work, and expert provenance advice for works of art and other valuable possessions.

The Society of London Art Dealers (www.slad.org.uk) has around 100 members, all of whom must have been in business for at least three years and have a high reputation for honesty, integrity and expert knowledge. The site has links to all its members as well as artists.

The Confédération Internationale des Négociants en Oeuvres d'Art (www.cinoa.org) has links to its 5000 members worldwide, plus a database containing 30,000 woks of art. The site also has useful information for the collector concerning art law, assessing value, etc, together with a study of international art market sales.

BALDWIN'S
The Name for Numismatics

A Growth Investment for the Discerning Collector

In relative terms, banknote collecting is still a new area and as such it remains an affordable investment with significant scope for growth. Paper money has a solid place in any diversified portfolio and offers an attractive compliment to a broader numismatic collection.

Established in 1872, Baldwin's has a long tradition of advising collectors and investors.

Baldwin's expanding banknote department holds regular auctions of world banknotes in London and Hong Kong and Dubai which have achieved world record prices in this specialised area.

We have a network of specialists internationally who keep up-to-date with current market trends and can source good quality items. We are well placed to assist you with banknote acquisitions both at auction and from retail stock.

Baldwin's is a *Noble Investments (UK) PLC* company
and is the only numismatic house
listed on a London Stock Exchange

For more information
on buying or selling:
contact our principle specialist Seth Freeman
seth@baldwin.co.uk
or contact our London showroom on
+44 (0)207 930 6879

For a free banknote auction catalogue email AIGB@baldwin.co.uk and quote this advertisement

11 Adelphi Terrace, London, WC2N 6BJ
tel: +44 (0)20 7930 6879 fax: +44 (0)20 7930 9450
www.baldwin.co.uk
A Noble Investments (UK) PLC Company

2.
Banknotes

While investors might think that banknotes should be considered alongside coins, they are a distinct alternative investment area in their own right.

British banks began issuing notes in the 1600s. Few of the early notes survive. Most collections begin later, typically in the late 19th century. As with other collectables, condition is very important indeed when determining value. And as paper items, like stamps they have a fragility that can be something of a problem. Alternative investors in both areas need to guard against degradation of their collections; many of the same means of storing collections are used in both areas.

Basics

History

The Chinese developed paper money in the 8th century as a temporary solution to a copper shortage, which limited the ability to mint coins.

Marco Polo brought the idea of paper money from China to a sceptical Europe in the late 13th century. The scepticism meant that paper money did not start out in Europe until the late 15th century. Then, as in China earlier, it was only used as an emergency measure. Banknotes were only issued on a regular basis from the 1660s onwards. Sweden was the first to try out the idea. The Bank of England and Bank of Scotland followed in the late 17th century. Several other countries quickly followed suit.

Fundamental to the appreciation of banknotes for collectors and investors is knowledge of the different printing processes used.

The earliest banknotes were printed from woodcuts. Most notes now are produced using intaglio engraving. This is a process where the design is etched on a metal plate, and printing undertaken at high pressure. A new banknote produced by this process has a slightly raised surface on the face of the note. This detail is discernable to the touch, and matching it is a slightly indented surface on the back of the note. As the note is used, wear erodes this detail.

Banknotes inevitably attract forgers. This has led to a range of security devices being adopted by banknote printers. Countermeasures include an intricate amount of detail in the engraving, use of high-quality paper, watermarking, and numbering, micro lettering on the note that is visible only under a magnifying glass, anti-scanning and photocopying designs, security strips and holograms.

Condition

Condition is important. Poor condition detracts considerably from the value of an item. There are several issues to consider.

Banknotes need careful handling. Notes are normally kept in protective holders made from a neutral plastic material. This will preserve the note and avoid introducing any extraneous chemical change.

Some early banknotes had large dimensions. Once in circulation they were inevitably subject to folding and creasing. More recent issues will fit flat in a wallet and therefore many may be available with only slight evidence of folding.

Counting of new notes used to be done by hand. Even an uncirculated note would have some slight folding. Notes are now counted mechanically or electronically prior to circulation. This leaves little or no evidence of handling. Older items, even if they were uncirculated, may have some evidence of handling that is unavoidable and to be expected. The investor has to be satisfied in having a note in the best possible condition for a specimen of its age and type.

Terms used for the condition of banknotes are fairly standard across countries and are summarised in this table.

Grading terms

Term	Abbreviation	Characteristics of note
Uncirculated	UNC	Perfectly preserved and never mishandled. Paper clean and firm; corners sharp and square
About Uncirculated	AU	Virtually perfect with only minor evidence of handling. Uncreased. No rounding on corners.
Extremely Fine	EF	Very attractive with only light handling. May have some light folds or one strong crease.
Very Fine	VF	Attractive but with more evidence of handling. Limited rounding. No tears. Minimal dirt.
Fine	F	Many folds and creases, minor tears, clear colours, not excessively dirty.
Very Good	VG	Well used, abused but still intact. Small nicks and tears, rounded corners. No pieces missing.
Good	G	Well worn and heavily used, with no large pieces missing. Some graffiti possible.
Fair	F	Totally limp, dirty and very well used, with large tears and large pieces missing.
Poor	P	A 'rag' with severe damage because of wear, staining, holes, missing pieces, perhaps taped together.

In addition, banknote graders use the term 'about' to distinguish items that fall between two categories. So 'about very good' would be somewhere between good and very good, but nearer the latter. Notes graded 'poor' are really only acceptable as collectors' items if they are the only known example of a particular issue.

Price differences between grades have tended to increase as the number of collectors grows. Most collectors, and especially those collecting with an eye to investing, collect only those notes in 'very fine' condition or better. Even here, the difference in price between a note classed as 'very fine' and one classed as 'uncirculated' could be a ratio of 4:1. A 'very fine' example could exceed a 'very good' one in a ratio of 2:1 or even 3:1.

As with stamps, scrip and other similar items, banknotes showing any evidence of cleaning or tampering should be avoided.

Currency terminology

Banknote collectors often have an interest in the names of currencies and how they originated. Many names represent weight. Dirham probably equals dram, or gram. Peseta means 'little weight', Lira is a derivation of the French livre (pound), from which comes the stylised letter 'L' that represents the Pound Sterling. The Livre was yet another high-profile casualty of the French Revolution, replaced by the more proletarian Franc.

Using weights to signify currency names dates from those long-gone days when money was backed by a specific weight of precious metal. Their names lived on even when fiat currencies – backed by nothing more than faith in the note issuer – took over. Other conventions for naming currencies were used too. In Portugal, the word Escudo signifies the coat of arms of a city, from a similar root to the English heraldic term escutcheon. The best guess is that the former Portuguese currency dated from the time when currencies were issued by cities rather than nation states. Some other names are even more obscure. Drachma means 'handful', Forint and Zloty and Guilder mean 'golden' or 'gilded', Rouble means 'cut-off', Rupee means 'beauty' or 'shape' and Kuna means 'marten', which dates from when Croatians used pine marten skins as money. The 'cut-off' signified by Rouble dates from when money was comprised of pieces cut off from a bar of silver, often in multiples of eight. Hence also 'pieces of eight'.

The Romans bequeathed currency names on the countries that fell under their imperial influence. In pre-decimalisation Britain, the letters l. s. d. denoted pounds, shillings and pennies. Pennies took the letter 'd' from denarii, small units of currency in Roman times, from which also derives Dinar, a currency name still used in many Middle Eastern countries to this day.

South American currencies often have more exotic derivations. Simón Bolívar may be one of the few political leaders to have seen his name live on in his country's currency (the Venezuelan Bolivar). In Brazil, the Cruzado was the unit of currency for 1988-1990 until hyperinflation forced the change to the Cruzeiro and then the Real. The Cruzeiro is said, rather romantically, to have echoed the stars of the Cruzeiro do Sul, or Southern Cross, the great Southern hemisphere constellation. In Ecuador, the Sucre might be thought to reflect the importance of sugar in the economy. In fact, as in Bolivia, it carries the name of a popular 19th century leader, Antonio José de Sucre.

Perhaps the prize for the most unusual derivation goes to the Cedi, the currency of Ghana. This appears to derive from the local word for cowrie. Cowrie shells were used in parts of Africa as currency and, to prove the point, cowrie shells feature on Ghana's coins even now.

And the ubiquitous dollar? The explanation is mundane. It comes from the word 'taler' (sometimes written as 'thaler'), itself a contraction of Joachimsthaler. A thaler was a piece of specie from the silver mine of the same name located in Joachim's valley, now Jáchymov, in the present day Czech Republic. How the name got from Central Europe to the United States is unclear.

Collecting Themes

Countries

Once the would-be banknote investor has assimilated all of this, it's time to select a theme for collecting. Most collectors see the older Bank of England notes as the banknote 'blue-chips', together with those of the Scottish and Irish banks. Some collectors also collect US and Canadian official currency issues, and these fall into the same blue-chip category. Notes like this tend to be stores of value and there is a ready market for them. Recent issues, though, are not of investment interest because so many have been issued (as is also the case with stamps and coins). In contemporary times, notes issued in India and China have been popular thanks to the newly emerging wealth in these regions. The same is true of their coins and stamps.

More established markets for banknotes in Continental Europe are not currently very exciting, nor are those of the group of emerging economies in Eastern Europe. This is also true of trends in the stamp market of late. Some collectors believe that, to make money, collectors (or investors) have to try to find countries which will do well politically and financially. Currency trends matter because they influence buying power.

Other favourite areas among collectors are South Africa and the old Colonial notes – especially those of banks in East and West Africa, and notes issued by English provincial banks. Notes from, say, South African private banks issued prior to the Boer Wars, can be bought for prices anywhere between £500 and £10,000. Notes issued by English provincial banks fetch prices between £200 and £2000, with some rarities being appreciably more expensive. Unusual ones are clearly rising in price at present. Proofs also sell at a significant premium because many of the issued notes are in poor condition.

While not regarded as having the same blue-chip status as Bank of England notes, notes issued by leading colonial-era banks like Barclays (Dominion, Colonial & Overseas), Standard Chartered and HSBC are much more predictable than, for example, lesser-known banks like the Wellington Bank of South Africa.

Often historical events may dictate collecting themes. In the US, for example, as well as areas such as the above, collectors sometimes look for currency from the old Confederate states, banknotes from the colonial era, or those from the early 1800s with denominations of less than a dollar.

Proofs, signatures, numbers, denominations & errors

Most banknote collectors and would-be investors should look to build up a collection of issued notes and, of course, proofs and trials. The issued notes, according to one veteran collector, "have romance, but if you want to see them at their best you need a proof." The best investment of all is an issued note in mint condition.

Signatures on notes are also important. When a bank failed, as many of them did, the receiver would usually cancel the note, often by cutting off the signature. Banks might also cut off signatures of used notes anyway, when notes were removed from circulation. So investment-grade notes are almost always signed and numbered with the signature intact. Collectors and investors like to get a run of numbers, maybe a run of dates, whilst some specifically invest in notes with a sequence of signatures.

As with stamps and coins, rarity and condition matter most. High denominations are usually best because fewer were issued, although there are exceptions to this rule. Banknotes in poor condition may be all that is available in some areas, unless one can find a proof. Often, however, no proofs and trials remain. Proof banknotes and colour trials will normally not be signed. So a signed issued note in the best condition is generally the most desirable.

Another interesting theme to consider at the same time is errors – the small quantity of banknotes printed with some form of mistake in the printing process, such as non-matching serial numbers, missing signatures on intact notes, mistakes in cutting, or other flaws (though, of course, not 'flaws' caused by mere misuse, vandalism and damage over the years!). Other themes include collecting older, large-size banknotes.

The Right Alternative Asset for You?

In general terms, as with other collectable areas, the crucial variable in banknotes is the general well-being and affluence of the collector base. Other things being equal, prices should tend to rise as the general level of prosperity increases. However, though there are some similarities in the dynamics of these markets, the banknote market is by no means identical to other collectable areas like coins and stamps. One big difference is that it is smaller, and more specialised. There are an estimated 10,000 active banknote collectors worldwide. That compares to an estimated 75,000 active coin collectors in the UK alone, and many millions of stamp collectors worldwide.

Banknotes form part of the wider field of numismatics, and some collectors of coins will collect banknotes too. Nonetheless, banknotes are a less active collectors' market, and prices reflect that.

With all this in mind, let's look at the questions that need to be considered when deciding whether this area merits a place in a wider portfolio of investments.

A medium to long-term investment?

A long-term perspective is essential. As with most tangible assets, the certainty of good returns increases the longer investments like this are held. And it is essential to make sure that any initial investments are not made when prices are artificially high. In stamps, for example, there was a bubble in prices in the late 1970s. This was less true of banknotes, and this latter market has had an underlying firm tone over many years, which remains true today, although different collecting and investment areas do come in and out of fashion.

Capital required?

Prices of banknotes are generally affordable. The scarcer the item the more expensive it will be, particularly if in pristine condition. But, in the case of banknotes, a glance at recent dealers' catalogues shows few items priced at more than £500 and many priced at well under £100. Scarcer items such as Victorian Bank of England notes can, however, cost well into the thousands in top-quality condition. The following table shows prices of a selection of sought after collectable notes. *The Banknote Yearbook*, from which these examples are taken, has a comprehensive list of current prices for British Isles banknotes in grades suitable for collectors and investors. This reference work also contains details of similar numismatic publications pertaining to the banknotes of a wide range of other countries.

Examples of typical collectable banknote prices

Item	Signatory	Year	Price	Condition
Early Bank of England £1	A Newland	1803	8500	VF
Early Bank of England £2	A Newland	1805	12500	VF
Early Bank of England £5	A Newland	1793	22000	VF
Early Bank of England £10	JG Nairne	1902	1200	EF
Early Bank of England £20	EM Harvey	1918	2500	EF
Treasury Note 10/- (prefix A)	J Bradbury	1914	1150	UNC
Bank of England 10/-(prefix A01)	CP Mahon	1928	1350	UNC
Bank of England £1 (prefix A01)	CP Mahon	1928	1350	UNC
Bank of England 10/-(prefix 01A)	KO Peppiatt	1948	2200	UNC
Bank of England 10/- and £1 in envelope	CP Mahon	1928	7000	UNC

Storage and insurance costs?

Investors can hold the banknotes physically on their own property. As with many other alternative investments, this entails having good security measures and proper insurance. However, rather like stamps, collectable banknotes might not have a readily apparent value to the untutored eye.

It may be possible to store a collection off-site at a bank or safe deposit facility, but, because of the fragile nature of paper items like this, it is very important to make sure that the conditions under which the items will be stored are conducive to preserving them in their original state. As with stamps, temperature- and humidity-controlled conditions are best.

Portfolio diversification potential?

Like stamps and coins, prices of banknotes should rise in line with economic growth and inflation. As is the case with stamps, banknotes may have a slight edge over coins in the sense that they are less durable, and hence there are fewer examples of top-quality 'extra fine' items.

Other than from the standpoint of reduced purchasing power in the hands of collectors, there is no reason to expect that prices of banknotes will be particularly affected by movements in world stock markets. As such, they represent solid diversification.

Collecting banknotes is essentially about history, although enthusiasts would add that it takes in economics, geography, politics and art. Many of the more collectable notes have attractive pictures usually depicting a classical scene or something relevant to the issuer. Banknotes, rather like stamps, are mementos of the economic history of a particular country, telling one of the rise and fall of dictators, monarchs and politicians.

Returns

Returns on banknotes vary considerably from category to category and hard data is difficult to come by. Specialists confirm, however, that returns in some of the better areas have been very respectable indeed. English private banks – the forerunners and original constituents of today's clearing banks – used to issue their own notes, and prices of the better collectors' items have risen perhaps 40-fold in 20 years, a compound annual return in the region of 20%. The best older Bank of England material shows a return over the same period in the region of 12%.

Other good performers until the late 2000s (prices retreated somewhat before the turn of the decade) have been old Hong Kong and other Far East banknotes, where prices in Q4 2009 had appreciated to show a compound return over 20 years in the region of 17.5%.

Returns like this are examples of the best performing items in exceptional condition. Other items may not have performed as well as this, and some items have even gone down in value over this period. There is no guarantee that returns like this can be repeated.

How to Invest

The procedure for buying banknotes for investment purposes is much the same as for coins and stamps. While some lower-value items can be purchased over the web or by normal mail-order methods, for higher-value items would-be investors will need to visit the dealer to satisfy themselves that the item and its condition is as described. Some mail-order banknote dealers offer a money-back guarantee. If a dealer is a member of a reputable trade association, there is no harm in buying on this basis. Many collectors also buy and sell items at shows, which gather a lot of dealers together in the same place.

Auctions remain a popular way of buying, too – either face to face or by mail. Once again, being able to inspect the items beforehand is a sensible precaution, particularly if they are likely to be of high value.

With smaller collectables markets of this type, when an investor comes to sell a collection it is worth considering whether the auction route really is the best, or whether it is safer to simply place the collection in the hands of a trusted dealer who can release items over a staggered period to allow the market to absorb the issues without unduly affecting the prices. There is no single best answer to this, and it is wise to take advice from several sources. There is an active auction market in banknotes, but auctions are probably fewer in number, and the market therefore less liquid, than is the case for stamps and coins.

Those starting out assembling a collection of banknotes for investment purposes need to bear in mind that active collectors may be competing for the same material and that beginners, as it were, need to 'join the queue' to be offered the scarcer and more desirable investment-grade material by the large dealers.

Collectors who are pursuing their interest for pleasure may be prepared to pay more than a particular note is worth in objective terms, simply to have it in their collection. This also makes navigating the market difficult for those whose objective is to earn a worthwhile return.

The usual rules apply: get to know the market first; find a dealer who can be trusted; buy something attractive; and the best that can be afforded, in the best possible condition.

Where to Go for More Information

The following are some brief details, by category, of the information resources available on banknotes. Many coin dealers also deal in banknotes and I have omitted details of these at this point as a comprehensive list of numismatic dealers is given in the chapter on coins.

Dealers

Baldwin's (www.baldwin.co.uk), now part of Noble Investments (UK) plc, hold paper-money auctions in London and Hong Kong, details of which can be found on the site together with prices realised. They also have a limited amount of stock available at their retail premises in London.

Barry Boswell World Banknotes (www.collectpapermoney.co.uk) has been dealing in banknotes since 1986, and has a large and varied stock, all available online.

Bonhams (www.bonhams.com) holds periodic sales of banknotes.

Bowers & Merena Auctions (www.bowersandmerena.com) is a leading American auctioneer of coins and banknotes, based in California.

Colin Narbeth & Son (www.colin-narbeth.com) is a very well-known dealer and sells both online and from premises in London, near Leicester Square.

Dealers and auctioneers

Entity	Web address	Main location	Email address	Telephone	Category
Baldwin's	www.baldwin.co.uk	London	On site	020 7930 6879	Dealer/Auction house
Barry Boswell Banknotes	www.collectpapermoney.co.uk	UK	barry.boswell@btinternet.com	01327 261 877	Dealer
Bonhams	www.bonhams.com	London	On site	020 7447 7447	Auction house
Bowers and Merena	www.bowersandmerena.com	California	info@bowersandmerena.com	949 253 0916	Auction house
Coincraft	www.coincraft.com	London	info@coincraft.com	020 7636 1188	Dealer
Colin Narbeth	www.colin-narbeth.com	London	colin.narbeth@btinternet.com	0207 379 6975	Dealer
Dix Noonan Webb	www.dnw.co.uk	London	auction@dnw.co.uk	020 7016 1700	Auction house
Ian Gradon World Paper Money	www.worldnotes.co.uk	Durham	igradon960@aol.com	0191 371 9700	Dealer
Morton and Eden	www.mortonandeden.com	London	info@mortonandeden.com	020 7493 5344	Auction house
Spink	www.spink.com	London	info@spink.com	020 7563 4000	Auction house
Stack's	www.stacks.com	New York	Via site	212 582 2580	Auction house
Warwick & Warwick	www.warwickandwarwick.com	Warwick	info@warwickandwarwick.com	01926 499 031	Auction house

Coincraft (www.coincraft.com) of Bloomsbury buy and sell banknotes both online and to personal buyers, in addition to their other activities of selling coins and antiquities.

Dix Noonan Webb (www.dnw.co.uk), a London-based specialised auctioneer and valuer, holds four traditional sales a year plus internet-only sales. Online valuations can be requested. For those who prefer more traditional sales methods, DNW also handles high-value private treaty sales.

Ian Gradon (www.worldnotes.co.uk) based in County Durham sells British and world paper money.

Morton & Eden (www.mortonandeden.com) hold regular auctions in London.

Spink (www.spink.com) generally holds five paper money auctions a year in addition to retail sales. They have auctioned many famous collections and realised a number of auction records. Spink has also recently begun active dealing and auctions in old bond and share certificates, sometimes considered a close cousin of banknotes.

Stack's (www.stacks.com) is a leading specialist auctioneer based in New York.

Warwick & Warwick (www.warwickandwarwick.com), one of the UK's leading auctioneers of banknotes and coins, holds six auctions per year of both individual items and collections.

Fairs

The world's largest paper money show is held each year in Maastricht in the Netherlands (www.papermoney-maastricht.org).

Veronafil (www.veronafil.it) is held annually in May and is one of the largest fairs in Europe.

Information

Banknotes.com (www.banknotes.com) has a lot of useful information on banknote collecting for the beginner, as well as on buying and selling online.

Banknote News (www.banknotenews.com) has the latest news about notes, including new issues.

Collectpapermoney.com (www.collectpapermoney.com) is an informative site aimed at beginner and intermediate collectors.

MJP (webhome.idirect.com/~mjp) has numerous links to dealers, collectors and currency-related sites worldwide.

Collector Network (www.collectornetwork.com) has links to dealers and information resources.

The Professional Currency Dealers Association website (www.pcdaonline.com) has links to dealers. It sponsors the National and World Paper Money Convention held each year in October in St Charles, Missouri.

The Society of Paper Money Collectors (www.spmc.org) may be of use for those interested in US notes. The site has brief general comments on the worth of US notes, plus links to US clubs, societies and periodicals. A members newsletter is published quarterly.

Information, trade associations and fairs

Entity	Web address	Main location	Email address	Telephone	Category
Baldwin's	www.baldwin.co.uk	London	On site	020 7930 6879	Dealer/Auction house
Barry Boswell Banknotes	www.collectpapermoney.co.uk	UK	barry.boswell@btinternet.com	01327 261 877	Dealer
Bonhams	www.bonhams.com	London	On site	020 7447 7447	Auction house
Bowers and Merena	www.bowersandmerena.com	California	info@bowersandmerena.com	949 253 0916	Auction house
Coincraft	www.coincraft.com	London	info@coincraft.com	020 7636 1188	Dealer
Colin Narbeth	www.colin-narbeth.com	London	colin.narbeth@btinternet.com	0207 379 6975	Dealer
Dix Noonan Webb	www.dnw.co.uk	London	auction@dnw.co.uk	020 7016 1700	Auction house
Ian Gradon World Paper Money	www.worldnotes.co.uk	Durham	igradon960@aol.com	0191 371 9700	Dealer
Morton and Eden	www.mortonandeden.com	London	info@mortonandeden.com	020 7493 5344	Auction house
Spink	www.spink.com	London	info@spink.com	020 7563 4000	Auction house
Stack's	www.stacks.com	New York	Via site	212 582 2580	Auction house
Warwick & Warwick	www.warwickandwarwick.com	Warwick	info@warwickandwarwick.com	01926 499 031	Auction house

Books

There are several books about banknotes that are well worth perusing. These are reviewed briefly below.

Banknote Yearbook, various authors (Token Publishing, published annually)

This is a UK price guide and collector's handbook. As well as valuations, the book includes a wealth of other information advice for beginner collectors, as well as technical information and a directory of dealers and fairs.

English Paper Money: Treasury and Bank of England Notes 1694-2006, Vincent Duggleby (Gardners Books, 2006)

This is a standard work on the subject of English banknotes, which collectors should find useful for identification and valuation purposes.

Standard Catalog of World Paper Money, eds. Shafer and Cuhaj, (Krause Publications, multiple vols)

This is a three volume series covering specialised issues, and the years 1650-1960 and 1961-Present. It contains hundreds of illustrations, with current values as well. Reference information includes international grading terms, foreign exchange rates and numerous historical facts.

3.
Books

A collection of rare and collectable books can acquire a substantial value. A book collector friend of the author, who lives in Australia, sold a small part of his collection for tens of thousands of pounds a few years ago. The rest of his collection, built up over a lifetime and including many signed copies and letters from authors, is worth a small fortune.

Many book collectors may start forming collections by accident. A liking for books leads them to acquire many, and it is only after looking in detail through a heterogeneous collection that first editions or rarities are discovered, and they are drawn into more serious activity.

First editions are what such serious book collecting is all about. But transforming a random collection into a portfolio of investment-grade quality is a different matter. Indeed some prominent book dealers in the past have scorned the idea of using books as an investment medium.

While there are used and rare book dealers nationwide in the UK, and indeed worldwide, finding a dealer that specialises in the area in which a would-be book investor chooses to collect may take a little more effort. The advent of the internet has, however, made the process of locating dealers and books easier and less time-consuming than it once was. There are details of a number of book dealers' websites and other services at the end of this chapter. Good quality material may be harder to find, however, and the trend in prices of collectable books is much less documented than in some other areas included in this book, such as coins or stamps. In the case of these, a definitive price history is relatively easy to obtain from values in standard catalogues published by leading players in the market.

Basics

History

Collecting books is as old as the libraries of great universities. In Britain, country house libraries also flourished in the 16th and 17th centuries; and in the Victorian era, book collecting spread to the educated middle classes.

Yet while many avid readers have large collections of books, few make the jump into the serious collecting of sought-after items. Fewer still have devoted time to investigating book collecting as an investment proposition. This is not to say that an individual can't pursue book collecting/investment in this way. But what it does mean is that, with a smaller serious collector base and with book collections diffused over hundreds of different themes, it is a much less liquid market than, say, stamps and coins.

The internet has helped to improve the situation. It has allowed collectors to scour the world for the books they require, using specialist websites, whilst sites like eBay have allowed books to be auctioned to a customer base of millions of potential purchasers. Buying high-quality investment-grade books through this medium is still fraught with risk, though.

The subject of buying and selling through online media like eBay is covered in a later chapter ('Auctions and Dealers') but the cardinal point to remember is that with eBay you are buying 'sight unseen'. Condition is important for books, as with other collectables, and some would argue that the would-be investor needs to see and handle a book *in the flesh* to verify that what is being offered is a true first edition, that it is in the advertised condition, and that a signature, if there is one, is genuine.

This reservation aside, the web has made it easier for specialist booksellers to advertise their stock and new acquisitions, in turn making it easier for collectors and investors to locate the book they require from a source within an acceptable travelling time from their home. On the downside, the chances of finding bargains in out of the way flea markets and antique shops have probably diminished.

According to some purists in the book trade, the internet has ushered in the era of speculative buying of books. They appear to deplore the spread of book collecting to a wider market. One view might be that this attitude is simply the self-interest of long-standing booksellers and collectors, who want to keep the rare book market a well-kept and profitable secret. The idea that it could be rewarding to buy books for investment purposes is viewed as rather vulgar. That said, since the first edition of this book was published, even the stuffiest of book dealers appear to have embraced the possibilities offered by the internet in terms of marketing their stock.

Investors and collectors alike are always likely to buy with an eye to the future potential value of a book. While some may claim to collect a particular genre for its own sake and to keep in perpetuity, the salerooms are full of the books of those who are happy to realise the value of a collection and move on to a new area, or else those being sold by the estates of deceased collectors in order to realise their value.

Collectable Genres

Just as some investors favour particular sectors of the stock market, so those wishing to invest in tangible assets often have their favourite areas, and, within each category (books, wine, stamps, coins, etc.), some favoured subsection. What to favour is an open question, but as is the case with stock-market investing, favouring areas where the investor has specialist knowledge or an 'edge' conferred by a particular qualification or interest is also advisable with tangible assets such as books.

There are, however, several obvious genres that are naturally popular.

Modern first editions

Modern first editions are a well-established category for book collectors and investors. The author's book collector friend mentioned at the beginning of this chapter has a collection of modern books, including science fiction and books by the likes of Terry Pratchett. Modern first editions can be worth a lot, and are a legitimate investment area.

How you describe 'modern' depends on your taste, of course, and perhaps your age. But in the book trade, most would date modern as being from the early part of the 20th century. Maggs Bros, the rather grand bookseller in London's Berkeley Square, starts its modern category at 1800.

Literary merit and popular appeal is another important variable. Modern (i.e. 20th century onwards) writers who become prolific sellers may not prove to be the best investments, although first editions of their first novel, before their popularity became evident, would probably have had small print runs and therefore be scarce.

Even established writers of acknowledged quality go out of fashion. While Hemingway, Faulkner and others are always collected, John Galsworthy has gone out of fashion and Steinbeck is currently fading in popularity. Ultimately, would-be investors have to be reasonably sure that an author they wish to collect – take Graham Greene as an example – will either stay in favour or become more popular.

But it is important to stress that it is a popular author's early work that is always the most valuable, and the most likely to be of investment grade. In the case of Graham Greene, for example, a first edition of *Brighton Rock* might sell for tens of thousands of pounds, whereas first editions of Greene's later work, even in the best condition, would probably fetch under a hundred. Size of print run governs scarcity, which in turn governs value.

Another valid approach is to adopt a 'buy low' scattergun approach of buying a first edition of a first novel (or a second or later novel from a relatively unknown author) which has been shortlisted for a literary prize. The key is that the author's work has a low initial print run. By doing this, as a reader the collector or investor will have the chance to enjoy new work; as an investor, they have the chance that the author will become popular and repay the investment many times over. An example from my own collection is a first edition of Monica Ali's book *Brick Lane*, which was shortlisted for the Booker Prize in 2003 and has subsequently sold very well. But this is something of a rarity. I have spent a lot on signed first editions of Booker Prize-shortlisted authors and never managed to pick the eventual winner.

Collecting books of this nature does, however, increase the chance of getting hold of a signed copy, which can in some circumstances add substantially to the value of the item. Collecting at the shortlist stage is the only practical way to do this. Once the winner is announced, the print run increases and the scarcity value evaporates.

Children's books

Classic children's authors like J. M. Barrie, Charles Kingsley, Beatrix Potter, Arthur Ransome, Roald Dahl, Captain W. E. Johns (of *Biggles* fame) and, of course Terry Pratchett (also in the fantasy market) and J. K. Rowling, are a popular and extremely active market. Books in good condition from authors like this can fetch a considerable amount. Christmas annuals issued by popular children's comics are also an acknowledged collecting area.

Crime

Crime is a popular genre for many collectors. Books from authors such as Dashiell Hammett and other American stalwarts of detective fiction are an obvious starting point, as is Agatha Christie and then more modern authors like Ruth Rendell, P. D. James, Ian Rankin and Colin Dexter. Gollancz crime novels with their distinctive yellow dust jackets are a genre in their own right, as are *The Saint* novels of Leslie Charteris. Though not strictly crime, first editions of Ian Fleming's James Bond books are also considered eminently collectable, particularly with the distinctive dust jackets designed by Richard Chopping.

Science Fiction, Fantasy and Horror

This group of genres is also popular and spans writers from the 19th and early 20th century through to the present day. Collectable authors range from Jules Verne, Edgar Allan Poe, Edgar Rice Burroughs, Kurt Vonnegut, Arthur C. Clarke and Isaac Asimov to writers like Frank Herbert, Peter Hamilton, Stephen Baxter, Ray Bradbury, H. P. Lovecraft and Stephen King. The latter is said to be the most collected living author.

The early works of Dean Koontz, who does not fit precisely into this genre, are also widely collected. First editions of his newer work, however, have large print runs and are only worth having to keep a larger collection up-to-date.

Military

Books about military campaigns are popular, with some British collectors focusing on books about key events in history ranging from World War II back to 1066, and from the English Civil War to the American Civil War. In the US, the Civil War is the most popular area and books pertaining to the Confederacy are highly sought-after.

Sport

This is another specialist area, with collections based around early works relating to classic sports such as hunting, shooting, fishing, motor sport and golf. Signed sporting memorabilia is also a major area of interest for many collectors, too large to be included within the scope of this book.

Travel

Many book collectors believe that voyages, exploration and travel represent a classic area that will never lose its popularity, particularly since many books of this nature are lavishly illustrated with maps, photographs and drawings that enhance their appearance.

Identifying a Rare Book

As previously argued, determining rarity really comes down to identifying a first edition, although for some scarce books this is not the be-all and end-all. A reprint of a particularly scarce book could have considerable value in its own right.

The term 'first edition' is also in itself somewhat confusing. What all collectors and investors alike are seeking is books that are 'first edition, first state'. This means, to put it another way, the very first print run of a published book. Often this print run of a book will be small, especially if it is an author's first novel or the early work of an author who has only subsequently become popular.

Only when the popularity of the book has been gauged will a second larger print run be made, sometimes with some errors in the original removed. This book will still be a first edition, but much less collectable because it is less unusual, has fewer errors and will have been produced in greater quantity. This, together with the condition of a book (see next section), is normally the reason for wildly disparate prices for what are seemingly more or less identical books.

There is also a particular nuance related to foreign language authors. The really rare first editions will be those published in the author's own language rather than a translation. So a pristine first edition of Gabriel García Márquez book *Love in the Time of Cholera* in the original Spanish would be worth far more than the equivalent edition of the English translation of the book. Translations only happen when authors have become popular, and hence print runs for translations will be larger. There may of course be exceptions, especially where a particular translation has itself become a classic. For example, a first edition set of the classic Scott Moncrieff and Terence Kilmartin translation of Marcel Proust's *À la Recherche du Temps Perdu* dating from the 1920s would be a valuable property.

Collectors also need to take care that they buy the first edition issued in the country in which the author was first published, even if published in the same language. This is because the books of, say, a popular UK author published, say, in an American edition (or vice versa) would come later, have a larger print run, and therefore be less collectable. In my own collection, for example, is an

American first edition of a fairly scarce book by Ian Rankin, acquired for a much lower price than the UK first edition would demand.

On modern books there is a numbering system that will normally help identify whether a book is a true 'first edition, first state' copy or not. On the page of the book containing the copyright information (or sometimes on the page at the very back of the book) will normally be a series of numbers either in ascending or descending order thus:

10 9 8 7 6 5 4 3 2 1

or: 3 4 5 6 7 8 9 10

or else: 1 3 5 7 9 10 8 4 6 2

The presence of a 1 in the series indicates a first edition first state copy. So the sequence in the top and bottom examples would be such a book. The second example would actually be the third printing of the book (the lowest number is a 3). One big exception to this (although not the only one) among well-known publishers is Random House. It will state 'First Edition' in a first edition and yet have the list of numbers beginning with 2.

This is not, however, a foolproof way of identifying a book. Many publishers have more idiosyncratic ways of identifying first editions, sometimes by printing the words 'first edition' on the copyright page, others in more arcane ways. If it is not obvious, then you need to consult an expert or a reference book to establish the situation beyond doubt. The book *A Pocket Guide to the Identification of First Editions* by Bill McBride takes a comprehensive look at the subject of identifying first editions from publishers' marks.

Another point worth remembering is that, in the case of some modern books, a small number of proof copies may have been issued to reviewers. Because these tend to be even fewer in number than first editions, they can also be collectable and may even fetch more than a conventional first edition.

There are other points to watch for. Some publishers like Cassell, Collier, Tower and others are known only for publishing reprints, and their books, with a few exceptions, are not collectable. The same goes for book club copies, which are generally worthless to both collectors and investors. The only exception to this is books published in numbered and signed limited editions or those authors whose first editions were only published under a book club imprint.

The signature of an author, with or without an inscription, can add considerably to the value of a book, particularly if the author has since died. By the same token, the inscriptions of previous owners in books, unless well known in their own right, detract from the value of a book. Books of one famous author owned by another and inscribed as such, or books dedicated and signed by one author to another are particularly valuable. So a first edition of F. Scott Fitzgerald's *The Great Gatsby* owned and signed by former US president Herbert Hoover would be a valuable collector's item. One signed by the author and inscribed with a dedication to his friend Ernest Hemingway is the sort of book most collectors would love to own, since it would most likely be unique.

Some living authors will sign copies of their books, either on the book itself, or on a bookplate. Investors seeking to add value to an unsigned first edition might wish to contact the author via their publisher to see if getting a signature is an option. Some well-known authors charge for signatures, on the grounds (presumably) that this increases the book's value to the collector. A flat-signed (i.e. directly onto the title page) copy is better than a signature on a bookplate, but either is better than no signature at all. Opinions differ about whether or not a bookplate should be pasted into a book. But keeping a signature separate in a protective sleeve is probably the best policy. Signatures and autographs are a collectors' market in their own right, so keeping a signature separate makes sense. It may be possible to acquire the signature of a dead author to place with a book. Autograph dealers and fairs are the place to seek these out.

Condition

The most important single additional aspect governing a book's value is its condition, and particularly whether or not a dust jacket is present.

What determines whether a book is in good condition or not is obvious. For investment purposes, you need to avoid buying books that have cracked or torn spines, cracked or loose hinges, mildewed or worm-eaten pages, ink or pencil marks on the pages other than an author's signature or inscription, loose or missing pages, and so on.

Condition and grading terms, and the affect they have on prices, are shown in this table.

Price variation of books, according to condition (£)

Mint	Fine	Very good	Good	Poor
200	180	150	80	10
150	135	125	70	8
100	90	75	40	5
75	65	55	30	4
50	45	40	20	3
40	35	30	18	2.50
30	27	22	13	2
25	22	18	10	1.50
20	17	15	8	1
15	13	11	7	1

The table shows prices relative to those paid for a mint copy.

Mint = Indistinguishable from a new unread book. DJ (dust jacket) as new.

Fine = Some evidence of ownership. DJ slight rubbing.

Very good (or VG) = As fine, other than slight foxing or fading. DJ rubbed but colour good.

Good = Complete but obviously secondhand. DJ fairly clean; some marks and small tears.

Poor = Warped, missing pages, damaged spine. DJ tatty, dirty, marked, creased, or torn.

Source: Adapted from a similar table in *Book & Magazine Collector*

The presence of a dust jacket is, however, the biggest single item that enhances the value of a book. The better the condition of the dust jacket the better, but any dust jacket is preferable to none. The difference in price between first editions with dust jackets in good condition and those without is considerable. The next table shows some indicative examples of the difference in price for some well-known collectable first editions with and without the dust jacket present.

Difference in prices of first editions with and without dust jacket

Author	Book	With DJ (£)	Without DJ (£)
Arthur Conan Doyle	The Hound of the Baskervilles	80,000	5,000
Kenneth Grahame	The Wind in the Willows	50,000	6,000
Graham Greene	Brighton Rock	30,000	700
J. R. R. Tolkien	The Lord of the Rings	25,000	3,000
Virginia Woolf	Jacob's Room	25,000	1,000
Ian Fleming	Casino Royale	15,000	1,000
Arthur Ransome	Swallows and Amazons	15,000	2,000

This table shows that the difference in value is anything from eight to fifteen times, and sometimes more. The reason is that the dust jacket is easily destroyed, damaged or removed. Therefore copies with a dust jacket, especially one in good condition, are scarcer and fetch more from collectors.

At some stages of the 20th century, in particular, it was a fashion to remove dust jackets. Books from that era – those by Virginia Woolf are an example – are rarely found with them at all. If one is available with a dust jacket, it will attract considerable interest.

The Right Alternative Asset for You?

Investing in rare and collectable books, generally taken to mean first editions or other scarce material, as with many of the investment categories in this book, should be able to provide investors with a hedge against inflation if the right grade of material is bought at the outset.

Prices of books like this as a whole tend to rise over time. Like stamps, books are perishable if not cared for properly. This means that the supply of good quality material can contract. In many instances the first editions of some books were not produced in large quantities and can be quite scarce. The depredations of time and the actions of those who are not collectors can result in a valuable book being lost forever as a collectors' item.

Rare books, particularly modern first editions (meaning in this instance authors from the beginning of the 20th century onwards), are subject to fads and fashions that affect their value. To build a collection of investment-quality that will stand the test of time necessitates collecting the classic authors that are perennial favourites, and avoiding temporary fads. Even then, some authors go out of fashion. John Galsworthy first editions took a hit in the wake of the Wall Street Crash in 1929 and have never really recovered.

There are a number of questions that need to be posed when working out whether rare books could or should form a place in a wider portfolio of investments, tangible or otherwise.

A medium to long-term investment?

Few people get involved in book collecting simply to make money. It is possible to assemble a solid collection of books and sell it for appreciably more than you paid for it, but probably only after some time has elapsed. Like most of the tangible investment categories in this book, a period of at least ten years probably needs to go by before significant increases in value can be achieved.

There are exceptions of course. Some authors achieve phenomenal popularity in a much shorter timescale and the value of their first editions increases dramatically. The best example of this is perhaps the Harry Potter author J. K. Rowling. A first edition of the original book *Harry Potter and the Philosopher's Stone* cost a few pounds when first published in 1997 and now sells for £25,000.

Examples like this are, however, a rarity. If a would-be investor is fortunate enough by chance to possess a book like this, it makes sense to take advantage of an author's temporary popularity to realise profits from it and reinvest them in more classic items. Another recent example occurred at the time when the *Lord of the Rings* films were on general release, when even second-rate examples of Tolkien's trilogy fetched unduly high prices. Dealers were cashing in – generally by selling to the less well-informed buyer.

Capital requirements?

Throughout this book I explain that using tangible assets as part of an investment strategy means that the proportion of a total portfolio devoted to this broad area should represent perhaps 10-15% of the total amount available for investment. If the investor has, say, £500,000 invested in the stock market, then an alternative asset portfolio totalling £75,000 is probably appropriate.

If books are selected as one of the investor's tangible investing categories, what is spent can be tailored to the depth of the investor's pocket. Books, even from eminently collectable authors, can be found at all price ranges. Worthwhile collections can be built up spending less than £100 per item, rounding off the collection with a scarce work that might cost £1,000 or more. High-quality items can fetch £10,000 or more. Investors can start off a book portfolio with a modest amount, and then build up as their knowledge increases and as they develop an idea for a collecting theme. Buying first editions of newly published authors costs less, but investors should (as mentioned earlier) try and get a signed copy if possible, as this will hold its value better.

What about insurance?

Books are relatively bulky items and it is impracticable to store them in a safe. This means they need insuring to protect them from fire and theft. You need to make sure that your home contents insurance is sufficiently comprehensive to cover your collection, and to keep receipts for your purchases in a safe place (perhaps a fireproof lockable cabinet) in case you need to make a claim. A periodic valuation for insurance purposes is a good idea.

Keeping books in good condition?

Books need careful location and display, in particular to avoid the obvious risks of damp and fire. What is needed is a dry room, with no dampness or overhead water or central heating pipes, a minimum of curtains and upholstered furniture and, for preference, a fire retardant carpet. Books should be kept in such a way that they are not damaged and that features such as dust jackets are preserved from damage and from direct or strong sunlight.

Excessive humidity and excessive dryness and heat should be avoided. Books need to be checked periodically for damage from insects, and if damage is found an appropriate treatment applied. Proper storage, in rigid bookshelves, is essential. Books need to be handled carefully, especially old and leather bound volumes, whose value may be adversely affected by scratching and scuffing.

Repairing very old books is best left to a professional bookbinder. Modern books with defects such as cracked hinges and torn spines may be able to be repaired carefully at home. Leather books need treating with leather dressing every six months. This treatment replaces the animal oils in the leather, which can dry out as time passes.

Care of dust jackets is vital. If an investor buys from a good bookseller or trusted dealer, then dust-jacketed copies will most likely already have the dust jacket protected by a clear plastic sleeve. New first editions purchased from a normal bookshop will not be protected in this way. Plastic sleeving can be bought by the roll, and it is a matter of a few minutes' work for collectors to do the job themselves.

All of this takes time but is time well spent if it preserves and even enhances the value of an investment. If in doubt on points of repair, it is best to seek the advice of a professional before attempting anything radical.

Portfolio diversification potential?

There is probably less documentary evidence about the performance of rare books as an investment category than there is for similar types of collectables like stamps and coins.

Apart from certain classic authors, writers can come into and go out of favour quickly and often for no apparent reason. For example *The Herries Chronicles* by the British author Hugh Walpole, a five-volume set covering the history of a fictional Lake District family, does not merit a mention in most booksellers' catalogues. But Virginia Woolf, James Joyce and other authors writing around the same period are all the rage. John Steinbeck, once a collectors' standby, is now decreasing in popularity.

Some books seem to share a similar level of medium-term price volatility as the stock market, but classics, the blue-chips of the book world, climb inexorably in price. A serious investor needs to decide whether their primary reason for buying collectable books is for the pleasure they bring, or for long-term gain. The two are not mutually exclusive. Some of my own personal favourites – Charles Dickens, George Orwell, Graham Greene, Ernest Hemingway, Gabriel García Márquez and Peter Carey – are all collectable blue-chip authors. One expert calculates that a pristine first edition of Dickens' *Bleak House*, regarded by some as his best book, would have returned 4% a year over the last 30 years.

Even among alternative asset categories, some form of diversification is worthwhile. It probably doesn't make much sense to have too many of the same style of alternative investments in a portfolio. Stamps, banknotes and coins are essentially similar – well documented and dependent on the spending power of the collector, and increasingly the investor base.

Books are, too, but what ranks as classic literature, and is therefore collectable, is constantly shifting. Rather as with art, it is a more subjective judgement than it might be to, say, identify what makes a classic investment-grade coin or stamp. In these latter cases, scarcity is measurable and unvarying. So books can make a good counterweight to other tangible investing areas.

The final indispensable necessity is to have an interest in literature, and the subject or genre being collected. If this sounds obvious, remember that it is possible to regard some other alternative investments, like stamps and coins, as an 'off-site' financial investment that you can leave securely in a bank or a dealer's vault. But books are going to sit in your home, and the pleasure of handling them is part of the collecting and investment process. A love of, and knowledge of books and literature is a vital part of the process, as also perhaps is a love of browsing round bookshops and a tolerance of the sometimes odd characters that frequent the book trade.

Returns

According to Emotional Asset Management & Research, the long-term annual return from books is in the region of 9% (over 20 years) with relatively low volatility (standard deviation of less than 5%). This compares well with other tangible assets.

Unlike stamps and coins, in the case of books there is little systematic organisation of the price information from dealers and auction results. If there were, it might allow investors to calculate returns with reasonable accuracy. However, we can make some estimates from current prices of the sorts of returns that would have been made had a particular book been purchased new in the past.

The method I adopted in the first edition of this book was to use the obvious idea that a hardback book purchased new will have cost a different amount depending on when it was first published. I assume, as a rough guide, original prices as follows: 1900-10: £1; 1911-1920: £2; 1921-30: £3; and so on up to the present day when a new book might be had for around £11. Using this method, and factoring in recent auction results to get the present day price for a particular item, the returns from some modern first editions work out approximately as follows.

Returns from jacketed first editions bought from new

		Year	Price then (£)	Price now (£)	Compound rtn % pa
Arthur Conan Doyle	The Hound of the Baskervilles	1902	1.00	80,000.00	11.8
Kenneth Grahame	The Wind in the Willows	1908	1.00	50,000.00	12.1
James Joyce	Ulysses	1922	3.00	40,000.00	12.4
Virginia Woolf	Jacob's Room	1922	3.00	25,000.00	11.8
J. R. R. Tolkien	The Lord of the Rings	1954	6.00	25,000.00	18.5
Graham Greene	Brighton Rock	1938	4.00	20,000.00	14.0
Ian Fleming	Casino Royale	1953	6.00	15,000.00	16.9
Arthur Ransome	Swallows and Amazons	1930	3.00	15,000.00	12.4
Beatrix Potter	The Tale of Peter Rabbit	1902	1.00	10,000.00	9.6
John Fowles	The Magus	1966	7.00	250.00	10.2
Zadie Smith	White Teeth	2000	10.00	125.00	132.1

Source: Trade estimates for current prices

This is clearly only a guide, but it does seem obvious that annual percentage returns in the low to mid teens can be expected for a book that is or becomes a classic, if bought from new. This argues for a very long-term view of collecting for investment purposes. At the same time, there are the whims of fashion to watch out for. Zadie Smith's *White Teeth*, in first edition first state, would currently fetch around £125 compared to a purchase price in 2000 of around £10, whereas a set of John Galsworthy's *The Forsyte Saga* currently fetches only £350, a very low return for a book published in the 1920s.

First editions of the first Harry Potter book have gone for as much as £25,000, a phenomenal return over the 12 years since publication because only 350 copies were printed in this first state. Subsequent first edition print runs have been massive, so sets will not fetch commensurately more, and later books in the series will probably be virtually worthless to collectors or investors.

What about practical examples of the returns from individual book collections? Examples of collectors calculating the returns they have made from their interest are rare. Well-known US collector Kenneth Hill (a former investment banker) documented the returns from his extensive collection of books mainly related to travel and ornithology, as well as some perennial classics. His data showed returns averaging around 10% a year over as a long a period as three decades, as shown in this table.

Average returns from book collections – the example of Kenneth Hill

Topic	Number of books in collection	Average annual return (%)
Voyages of discovery in the Pacific	14	11
Ornithology	12	7
Classic books	8	10
Explorations of the West & California	15	10

Source: Rare Books as Investments (K Hill), 'Book Collector' Volume 47, no. 3

When it comes to modern or ultra-modern authors, the golden rule remains, therefore, for an investor to collect what they genuinely like and also to go for books that have been well reviewed. For books published in the 20th century, the best returns will be from those authors no longer alive that have stood the test of time – Graham Greene, George Orwell, William Faulkner, F. Scott Fitzgerald, Ernest Hemingway and others. The jury is still out on some living literary lions like V. S. Naipaul, André Brink, Martin Amis and so on. Further back, classic authors like Charles Dickens, Jonathan Swift, Arthur Conan Doyle, the Brontë sisters and Jane Austen are likely to make good investments. Look for the perennially popular giants of literature and avoid paying top price for today's current favourite.

How to Invest

It is perhaps just stating the obvious to say that investors and collectors buy books at bookshops, but that is the truth of it. Antique shops, flea markets, book fairs and the like are other good sources of books, but the astute tangible asset investor has to have a theme in mind, be opportunistic, and able to spot a good value book when he sees it.

With many 20th century authors who do not fall into the 'classic' category, the investor has to take a view, much as you would with any sort of investment. Are Galsworthy or Walpole on the up? Are Zadie Smith and J. K. Rowling overpriced? The rules for investors buying are relatively self-evident: having studied and reflected carefully, investors should buy what they enjoy, in the best condition available, and without paying over the odds.

Selling is another matter. If an investor has built up a collection, even the most hard-nosed may find it hard to part with. A long-standing relationship with a trusted book dealer may provide the best outlet for selling a collection, as opposed to the riskier route of the auction house. On the other hand, many dealers will try to buy a book as cheaply as possible, and it is only when there is a complete and desirable collection that a dealer is likely to offer a competitive market price.

Though auctions may seem expensive, sellers (and buyers) are at least guaranteed a more perfect market than with a single dealer, even though you may have to pay a seller's commission of 15% of the hammer price. Placing a realistic reserve price is vital. See the later chapter 'Auctions and Dealers' for more about dealing at auction, offline and online. The tables have details of booksellers, auction houses, relevant publications and how to find them.

The next section has more information on the various forums for buying and selling. By far the best initial option is to build up relationships with a network of local booksellers and for the investor to contact them regularly and let them know the type of material which they might wish to be shown.

Locating signed copies of newly published first editions, investors can avoid paying a premium by making frequent visits to large bookstores in major cities. It can be a frustrating process. Some authors are prolific signers, but the more desirable signatures are extra-elusive. Firsts in Print (www.firsts-in-print.co.uk), a UK online bookseller based in Taunton, Somerset, specialises in signed and unsigned first editions of newly published titles, and has many signed copies and limited editions available. It is a good first port of call.

Where to Go for More Information

The book trade, which some regard as stuffy, has increasingly accepted the role the internet can play in attracting customers. There are exceptions, of course, but like many other areas of collecting, the ability the web offers a bookseller to reach a much wider base of customers, the ease with which customers can search for a particular title, and the capacity it offers to buy and sell online, have all made the medium a natural one to use.

The following is a selection of sites that I have found to be useful, together with some brief notes on books and publications relevant to book collecting and investing.

Dealers

Henry Sotheran's (www.sotherans.co.uk) is the longest established antiquarian bookseller in the world. Sotheran's will act as agents for clients at sales, providing full condition reports and attending the sale in person. They also sell a wide selection of original antique engravings, lithographs and etchings. All can be ordered by email.

Maggs Bros (www.maggs.com), based in Berkeley Square, London, was established in 1853 and is one of the world's largest antiquarian booksellers. All the stock is available for online purchase.

AbeBooks (www.abebooks.co.uk and .com), a subsidiary of Amazon, is home to thousands of professional booksellers around the world. The headquarters are in Canada, with a European office in Düsseldorf. Over 110 million primarily used, rare and out-of-print books are listed for sale.

Alibris (www.alibris.co.uk and.com) is an online, independent retailer based in California, which performs much the same service as AbeBooks. The site features a glossary of book terms, information on collecting and a newsletter.

Any Amount of Books (www.anyamountofbooks.com) is a shop on London's Charing Cross Road which also has an online catalogue of 20,000 items.

Dealers

Entity	Web address	Main location	Email address	Telephone	Category
AbeBooks	www.abebooks.com	Canada	Through site	n/a	Online dealer
Alibris	www.alibris.com	USA	Through site	n/a	Online dealer
Any Amount of Books	www.anyamountofbooks.com	London	charing@anyamountofbooks.com	0207 836 3697	Dealer
Blackwells Rare Books	www.rarebooks.blackwell.co.uk	UK	rarebooks@blackwell.co.uk	01865 333 555	Dealer
Francis Edwards	www.francisedwards.co.uk	Hay-on Wye	sales@francisedwards.co.uk	01497 820 071	Dealer
Firsts in Print	www.firsts-in-print.co.uk	Taunton, Somerset	peter@first-in-print.co.uk	01823 256 656	Online dealer
Maggs Bros	www.maggs.com	London	enquiries@maggs.com	020 7493 7160	Dealer
Peter Harrington	www.peterharringtonbooks.com	London	mail@peterharringtonbooks.com	020 7591 0220	Dealer
Quaritch	www.quaritch.com	London	rarebooks@quaritch.com	020 7297 4888	Dealer
Robert Frew Books	www.robertfrew.com	London	shop@robertfrew.com	0207 590 6650	Dealer
Sotherans	www.sotherans.co.uk	London	books@sotherans.co.uk	020 7439 6151	Dealer
Spink	www.spink.com	London	info@spink.com	020 7563 4000	Dealer

Biblio.com (www.biblio.com), based in North Carolina, is an online marketplace for rare and out-of-print books. It brings together 5500 professional, independent booksellers worldwide.

Biblion (www.biblion.co.uk) is an online marketplace with over three million items from hundreds of dealers in rare, antiquarian and secondhand books. For personal callers Biblion has premises in London, with a wide range of stock from over 100 dealers. The website has many useful links.

Blackwell Rare Books (www.rarebooks.blackwells.co.uk) sell online as well as from their premises in Oxford. They will also bid at auctions on behalf of clients.

BookFinder.com (www.bookfinder.com), a subsidiary of AbeBooks, will search every major catalogue online and let customers know which booksellers are offering the best price and selection. The purchase is then made directly from the original seller. The site also features a useful glossary of book terms.

Firsts in Print (www.firsts-in-print.co.uk) sell modern first editions and first printings online. They provide a regular email newsletter of new offerings to those interested.

Francis Edwards (www.francisedwards.co.uk) has its main shop in Hay-on-Wye with a smaller establishment in London. All stock can be purchased online.

Peter Harrington (www.peterharringtonbooks.com) is one of London's largest and best-known rare book dealers. Apart from selling books, other services include commission bidding at auctions.

Quaritch (www.quaritch.com) has been dealing in rare books in London since 1847. Other services include commission bidding at auctions and restoration and conservation. Quaritch also runs Bibliopoly (www.bibliopoly.com). This is a search facility which lists the stock of participating antiquarian book dealers.

Robert Frew (www.robertfrew.com) deals in most areas of antiquarian books from premises in London as well as online.

*via*Libri (www.vialibri.net) links to 200 independent booksellers worldwide. The site also has useful links to reference and research sites.

Auctioneers

Bloomsbury Auctions (www.bloomsburyauctions.com) holds sales every two weeks and is the only specialist auction house in England devoted to the sale of books, prints and manuscript material. Bloomsbury also has two other auction houses; one in New York (ny.bloomsburyauctions.com) and the other in Rome (roma.bloomsburyauctions.com).

Bubb Kuyper (www.bubbkuyper.com), based in Haarlem in the Netherlands, has two book sales a year in the spring and autumn.

Burgersdijk and Niermans (www.b-n.nl), based in Leiden in the Netherlands specialise in rare books, manuscripts and prints.

The Munich auction house Zisska & Schauer (www.zisska.de) is an international specialist in rare antiquarian books and prints.

Other auction houses specialising in books include:

Dominic Winter Book Auctions (www.dominicwinter.co.uk) – the UK's leading provincial book auctioneer.

Ketterer Kunst (www.kettererkunst.com), based in Hamburg with an additional salesroom in New York.

Lawsons (www.lawsons.com.au), based in Sydney.

Pacific Book Auctions (www.pbagalleries.com), based in San Francisco.

Reiss & Sohn (www.reiss-sohn.de), based in Frankfurt.

Horta (www.horta.be), based in Brussels.

Gorringes (www.gorringes.co.uk), based in Lewes, Sussex.

Kestenbaum & Company (www.kestenbaum.net), based in New York and specialising in Judaica.

Auctioneers and online marketplaces

Entity	Web address	Main location	Email address	Telephone	Category
Biblio	www.biblio.com	North Carolina	Through site	n/a	Online marketplace
Biblion	www.biblion.com	London	Through site	n/a	Online marketplace
Bloomsbury Auctions	www.bloomsburyauctions.com	London	info@bloomsburyauctions.com	020 7495 9494	Auction house
Bubb Kuyper	www.bubbkuyper.com	Haarlem, Netherlands	info@bubbkuyper.com	31 23 532 3986	Auction house
Burgersdijk and Niemans	www.b-n.nl	Leiden, Netherlands	On site	31 71 512 1067	Auction house
Dominic Winter	www.dominicwinter.co.uk	Gloucestershire	info@dominicwinter.co.uk	01285 860 006	Auction house
Gorringes	www.gorringes.co.uk	Lewes, Sussex	clientservices@gorringes.co.uk	01273 472 503	Auction house
Horta	www.horta.be	Brussels	info@horta.be	32 (2) 741 6060	Auction house
Kestenbaum	www.kestenbaum.net	New York	Kestenbook@aol.com	212 366 1197	Auction house
Ketterer Kunst	www.kettererkunst.com	Germany	info@kettererkunst.com	49 40 3749 610	Auction house
Lawsons	www.lawsons.com.au	Sydney	info@lawsons.com.au	02 9566 2377	Auction house
Pacific Book Auctions	www.pbagalleries.com	San Francisco	On site	(415) 989 26 556	Auction house
Reiss & Sohn	www.reiss-sohn.de	Frankfurt	reiss@reiss-sohn.de	61 74 92 720	Auction house
Spink	www.spink.com	London	info@spink.com	020 7563 4000	Auction house
ViaLibri	www.vialibri.net	n/a	Through site	n/a	Online marketplace
Zisska & Schauer	www.zisska.de	Munich	auctions@zisska.de	49 (0)89 263 855	Auction house

Information

The International League of Antiquarian Booksellers (www.ilab.org) is the home to 20 national associations, comprising 2000 leading booksellers, all of whom have links on the site. There is also information regarding book fairs and exhibitions worldwide, plus a glossary of book terms and a dictionary in four languages.

The association organises the Antiquarian Book Fair, held each year in London with over 150 of the world's leading dealers.

The Book Guide (www.inprint.co.uk) has information on shops, fairs, auctions, binders, etc.

The US Library of Congress Online Catalog (catalog.loc.gov) contains approximately 14 million records representing the materials held by the library in Washington DC.

The British Library (portico.bl.uk) receives a copy of every publication produced in the UK and Ireland. It houses over 150 million items, with three million new items added each year. Personal callers can view such treasures as the Magna Carta, Leonardo da Vinci's notebooks and the Lindisfarne Gospels, to name but a few. The website contains an extensive database as well as much other useful information of interest to booklovers.

The Morgan Library (www.morganlibrary.org) in New York was originally the private library and museum of Pierpont Morgan. It became a public institution in 1924 and has one of the most important rare book and manuscript collections in the world.

Rare Book Review (www.rarebookreview.com), an online magazine for bibliophiles, has details of auctions, exhibitions, fairs, news, etc.

Information and publications

Entity	Web address	Main location	Email address	Telephone	Category
Bookfinder	www.bookfinder.com	Canada	On site		Information
Book & Magazine Collector	www.collectors-club-of-great-britain.co.uk	Lincolnshire	Through site	01778 391 180	Publication
Book Guide (The)	www.inprint.co.uk	Stroud	On site	01453 759 731	Information
British Library	portico.bl.uk	London	Customer-Services@bl.uk	020 7412 7676	Information
Morgan Library (The)	www.morganlibrary.org	New York	visitorservices@themorgan.org	212 685 0008	Information
Rare Book Review	www.rarebookreview.com	n/a	On site	n/a	Online magazine
US Library of Congress, Catalog	catalog.loc.gov	Washington DC	On site	(202) 707 5000	Information

Books

Publications

Three publications stand out as essential reading for a would-be investor in the book field.

Book and Magazine Collector is a monthly publication that contains a range of interesting articles on various aspects of book collecting. Of interest to collectors is a large classified section at the back of each issue where dealers advertise their current stock (with information on condition and price) and books they are seeking for clients. The publication is available from leading newsagents.

Rare Book Review is a monthly publication with articles of general interest to collectors. It has no classified section, but does contain detailed listings for fairs and auctions.

Scottish Book Collector (www.essbc.demon.co.uk) is published four times a year and can be subscribed to online. The magazine features interviews with major authors, information on rare and collectable books, reviews, salesroom reports and a section on Scottish history. A list of reasonably priced second-hand Scottish books is issued to subscribers.

Books about books

Breese's Guide to Modern First Editions, by Martin Breese (Breese Books, 1999)

This is a resource for collectors of British first editions with profiles of authors and values at the time of writing.

Collecting Children's Books, by the *Book and Magazine Collector* (2003)

The book contains references to 12,000 titles by 330 children's authors and illustrators with current values.

Guide to First Edition Prices 2008/9, by R. B. Russell (The Tartarus Press, 2007)

The title speaks for itself.

Book Finds: How to find, buy, and sell used and rare books, by Ian C. Ellis (Perigree, 2006)

This book mainly deals with first editions of modern books. The various chapters include buying and selling on the internet, auctions, catalogues and avoiding beginner's mistakes.

Miller's Collecting Modern Books, by Peter Selley and Catherine Porter, (Miller's Publications, 2002)

This is a guide to collecting British and American books from the late 19th century to 2002, explaining the factors that influence value. There is practical information on collecting, together with a glossary of technical terms.

The Official Price Guide to Collecting Books, by Marie Tedford and Pat Goudey (House of Collectables, 2008)

This book contains values for thousands of collectable books in all genres with prices in US$. Information is also included on topics such as the care and repair of books, a look at the book trade, what to collect and a review of the book market.

Used and Rare: Travels in the Book World, by Lawrence and Nancy Goldstone (Griffin Trade Paperback, 1998)

A readable and well-written book, which tells the tale of how an American couple's search for a hardcover version of *War and Peace* led to a lifelong passion for book collecting. The pleasures and pitfalls of collecting are narrated along the way.

BALDWIN'S
The Name for Numismatics

A Potential Hedge Against Inflation

The best investments come about through a trusted relationship with your advisor. We pride ourselves on the personable and professional service we have provided collectors and investors since 1872.

With over 200 years combined experience in all areas of numismatics, Baldwin's is ideally placed to assist you with information about market trends, upcoming auctions, available stock and a range of other aspects of coin and medal investments. Our specialists are world renowned experts in their fields.

- Historical figures show compound returns of over 10% in the mid-long term
- An attractive and enjoyable diversification away from traditional investment
- Higher mid-long term returns than other alternative investments
- An affordable investment at any level
- Tangible assets with over 2000 years of historical resonance
- An honest, transparent and global market

Baldwin's is a *Noble Investments (UK) PLC* company and is the only numismatic house to be listed on a London Stock Exchange

For more information:
contact Ian Goldbart, ian@baldwin.co.uk
or call our London showroom on
+44 (0)207 930 6879
to make an appointment with our specialists.

For a free guide to coin collecting email AIGC@baldwin.co.uk and quote this advertisement

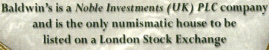

11 Adelphi Terrace, London, WC2N 6BJ
tel: +44 (0)20 7930 6879   fax: +44 (0)20 7930 9450
www.baldwin.co.uk
A Noble Investments (UK) PLC Company

4.

Coins

In the chapter that covers investing in gold, I explain that it's possible to buy gold coins like South African Krugerrands and Australian Koalas. It's simply a way to buy bullion. So if an investor wants to invest in gold coins and those made from other precious metals, it pays to distinguish between bullion coins like Krugerrands, which are minted regularly, and rare gold coins like golden guineas and some sovereigns. Rare coins may have some bullion content, but investors and collectors value them for different reasons – primarily on the basis of their rarity, condition, and aesthetic appearance. In this case, the bullion content of the coin is, if not entirely irrelevant, usually far outweighed by the *numismatic* value of the coin.

Prices are set differently too. Present-day bullion coins have a value that is 99% determined by the value of the weight of metal they contain. That price is set every day. But rare coins, which also include coins other than those made of gold or silver, have a price that varies according to condition and is usually determined by annual coin catalogues, dealers' lists and auction results.

Rather like stamps, those keen to do so can both collect coins and invest in them. The two activities are not mutually exclusive. Some collectors become investors as they gradually upgrade their collections, selling the more common items to buy a smaller number of rare pieces. Some of those who start off as investors may get hooked and develop an interest that goes way beyond mere consideration of investment returns.

Again like stamp investment, assembling a collection of investment-quality coins is a similar process to investing in the stock market. Certain coins move in and out of favour, and, like stamps, demand for coins is broadly linked to the state of the economy and the spending power of the underlying collector base. In both cases the collector base is international. So investors in coins can pick a portfolio of ten or 20 items to avoid undue dependence on any one particular coin, and can buy additional items if they wish as they go along, adding to their portfolio over time.

As is also the case with stamps, the coin dealer can play the role of an advisory broker, drawing attention to possible new portfolio additions, and perhaps highlighting the potential to take a profit in an item that has risen too far in value relative to the rest of the market.

Most experienced stock market investors should be pretty relaxed with this approach, because it is similar to the one that most adopt for stock-exchange investment. Like stamps, coins form an easily understandable, well-researched and documented investment category. The sizeable collector base provides liquidity (although difficult to establish precisely, an estimated 75,000 in the UK and 2 million worldwide would be a reasonable estimate of its size).

Basics

History

Coins were first introduced in Ionia around 650 BC. This long history means there is infinite variety in the types of coins that can be collected for either aesthetic or investment purposes. In turn this means that would-be investors probably need to pick a theme or series of themes around which to base a rare coin portfolio, avoiding those areas that are temporarily fashionable and picking those that have long-term potential.

Coins are split into two broad types: the older hammered variety and the more modern milled type. Hammered coins were produced by hitting two interlocking pieces of iron or bronze (the 'dies'), holding a blank coin within them, with a hammer. On the inside, the bronze or iron dies contained the imprint for each face of the coin, and the hammer blow would imprint the pattern simultaneously on each side (typically the head of the monarch on one side and the coin's denominations and some other pattern on the other). This was clearly a slow and cumbersome way of creating coins, and prone to error and irregularity.

Milled coins, produced in large quantities from the mid-17th century onwards, are machine made. Such coins have much more precise definition and uniformity. The machining of coins also enabled the introduction of milled edges and inscriptions, which prevented the coins being 'clipped'. (Coins were clipped, especially in the days when they were backed by silver or some other precious metal, so that small amounts of metal removed from a number of coins could be used to make another one, thus yielding the clipper a profit.)

We'll come onto the condition of the coins later. This is a separate subject in its own right, and vitally important to the value of a coin.

Collecting themes

Typical coin collectors will look to collect the coins of one country or group of countries, coins from a particular historical era or geographical region (including, for example, ancient Greek and Roman), or else coins that have something unusual about them – either commemorative sets or those with errors, or the same or similar coins with different varieties of die.

A common collecting theme is to collect a set series: one coin of each type for each year the coin was minted during the reign of a particular ruler, and including any design variations that may have been introduced, or those originating from different mints. For example, the silver pennies produced in Anglo-Saxon times in the reigns of rulers like Cnut and Æthelred II were produced at many different mints and in several different designs, producing a large number of different variations for collectors and investors to assemble.

As a general rule, it makes sense to collect and invest in the coins of the country where you live, because the chances are that you will be more aware of its history and better able to judge what makes a particular coin special. From a more practical standpoint, it also makes sense for UK collectors to collect British coins because: it is likely that the biggest volume of coin dealing and the largest number of collectors of this type of coin will also be in their home market.

The goal of having a complete set of, say, the coins of Henry VIII, is within the reach of most collectors or investors: remember that millions of examples of the coins in question were produced, and, unlike stamps for example, coins are much more durable and almost never discarded. So there are no limits on the number of complete collections of this type that can be assembled. Another interesting theme is to attempt a collection of all the coin issues during the years of Victoria's reign. There is plenty of material like this around, and there are also plenty of collectors of it, and hence potential buyers and sellers. (A wrinkle to consider here though is that, for a long-reigning monarch, several different styles of coinage may have been issued, each with a different representation of the monarch, some of which are more collectable than others.)

There are further common variations of collection. Rather than currencies, some assemble sets of commemorative medallions and others have collections of tokens, substitute coinage issued at times when specie was short or introduced for specific purposes by individual businesses to attract trade back to their establishment. There are specialist dealers and collectors in each.

What determines value

This brings us on to the factors that make up the price of a rare coin. The value of a collectable coin depends primarily on its date and design, on its precisely graded condition, on its mintmark, and on the supply and demand for that particular type of coin at any one time. The coin's condition, that is to say its state of preservation, is of paramount importance in determining price and saleability.

One way of making sure that the coins you buy for investment have a scarcity value is to collect only those of monarchs with a short reign, and who are not known to have debased the currency to a greater than normal degree. So, for example, Eadred (946-955), Richard III (1483-85), Edward VI (1547-53), Mary and Philip (1553-58), the Commonwealth (1649-1660) and so on, may make good subjects for coin investment. On the other hand, the chances of finding coins like this in sufficiently good condition to warrant investment may be harder.

Indeed, as is also the case with stamps and many other tangible assets, condition is the single biggest factor governing price. The next section looks in more detail at how to grade the condition of a coin, and how to keep it in that condition once it has been purchased.

Condition

As said, as with many tangible assets, condition is crucial to a coin's value. But it isn't as simple as it might seem.

Coins are sometimes called 'proof' or 'prooflike' if they have particularly sharp definition. This is a special category of coins, collectable in their own right, but not to be confused with the grading that is applied to coins in general. 'Proof' coins are struck from specially-prepared dies as samples of new coinage. They frequently have plain edges, rather than milled ones, and a mirror-like finish that comes from the highly polished dies from which they are struck. 'Prooflike' coins are the first examples of new coins for circulation struck from these dies.

This table shows the variations of condition that are generally accepted for coins in the UK. The US has its own slightly different terminology. At the margin the variations in condition may only be detectable under a magnifying glass, although some will be more obvious. To a degree this terminology of the grading given to a coin is subjective and some dealers are more cautious than others in the grade they give. This argues for going to a reputable and long-established dealer whose gradings are consistent and reliable. Less expert dealers may tend to overgrade coins.

UK grading terms for coins

FDC	'Fleur de coin'. Perfect mint state.
BU	'Brilliant uncirculated'. Used for modern coins. Full lustrous mint condition.
UNC	'Uncirculated'. Some loss of lustre due to exposure to air.
EF	'Extremely fine'. Magnification shows wear on high points, fine scratches.
VF	'Very fine'. Clearly in circulation, but clear detail.
F	'Fine'. Noticeable wear on high points, details faded.
Fair	Worn, but with features and legend clearly distinguishable.
Poor	No value to a collector.

Note: American terms describe 'poor' coins as 'fair', and 'fair' as 'very good'.

The tone of the coin is also important. Tone signifies a coin that has, with time, acquired a colour that is deeper and richer than the original. The importance of toning usually applies to older coins. Most collectors and investors prefer more modern coins to have their full lustre, as though they had just been minted. But a brown or green patina on ancient bronze and copper coins is said to increase their value substantially.

Toning is also evident on old coins made from precious metals. Silver can have a golden tone ranging through to an almost black or plum colour. Tone can also affect the raised parts of the coin differently from the rest. While to some degree the attractiveness of the tone can be subjective, an attractively toned coin could add as much as 40-50% to the value of a coin over and above one that has no tone.

The legend on a coin can have an impact on its value, especially in cases where the monarch's name has been misprinted or abbreviated. This is not uncommon on older coins, where the literacy of those making the coins may not have been high, and occasional mistakes were more likely. Mint marks on the coin, usually a single letter to indicate where it was made, are also a distinguishing feature and can have a significant affect on value.

The edges of a coin are important, too. Edges that have been knocked or damaged in some way warrant a discount, compared with the price of those that don't have this sort of imperfection.

Some dates are much rarer than others. In the UK, a 1933 penny is scarce. The same is true of an 1804 US dollar, an Australian 1919 shilling and a Canadian 1921 50-cent piece. These capture the public's imagination, but the date alone is rarely the basis for a good investment.

Though there is a temptation to do so, coins should not be cleaned. This is because most methods of cleaning will result in some abrasion to the coin's surface, and the removal of what may otherwise have been a valuable patina or lustre. According to dealers, any form of treatment of this sort can more than halve the value of the item, and the risk is just not worth taking. An expert can easily detect treatment of this sort.

Protecting a coin portfolio once acquired is a separate subject in itself. I have already alluded to the need to store coins securely in a safe or safety deposit box if a collection is of considerable value. Insurance is also a good precaution, though sometimes neglected.

Most importantly, investors wishing to keep a collection of high-grade coins in their home are advised to take great care in storing and handling them. Coins are sensitive to moisture, and dropping them will cause damage, and impact their value. Even handling them carelessly will make a difference. Collectors should wear gloves when handling coins. The human finger contains a corrosive salt that will damage copper and bronze coins, and tarnish silver ones.

It is essential as far as possible to store items in an airtight, moisture-free seasoned hardwood box (mahogany is a popular choice). Coins should be stored out of sunlight, in a storage system made from inert material. Items should not be placed in contact with each other or with any other metal object.

The Right Alternative Asset for You?

Investing in coins, as with many of the tangible investment categories in this book, can provide a hedge against inflation. Coin prices tend to rise as the general level of prices rise. This is because, as is also the case with stamps, the general well-being and spending power of the collector base is all-important.

Let's look at the questions that need to be answered to determine whether coins could form a place in a wider portfolio of investments.

A medium to long-term investment?

Investing for the long term is crucial. The May 2003 auction by Spink of the Slaney collection of British coins suggested that the optimum period for investing in coins could be as long as 50 years. The sale of Lord Hamilton of Dalzell's collection in 1979 also contained coins acquired over a 50-year period, and in 2005 Baldwin's auctioned the Boyd collection, formed over 100 years. Holding a portfolio of coins for this length of time may not be necessary to achieve good returns, but the certainty of achieving excellent returns probably increases the longer they are held. There have been many subsequent auctions that have confirmed these numbers, the latest being the three-part so-called (it is called The Diana Collection, we're not sure why it is referred to as 'so-called') Diana Collection, auctioned by Baldwin's.

Capital requirements?

Whether or not investors feel able to afford an investment in coins depends on the scale of their other assets, and what other tangible investments they might be contemplating. However, would-be investors need not be put off by the high headline prices fetched by some coins in the Slaney sale or indeed the subsequent records set in the coin market when the Edward III Double Leopard fetched £460,000, and a rare Catherine the Great '20 rouble' a massive £1.55 million.

These large amounts should not deter would-be investors. One of the attractions of numismatics is that rare coins which are sought out by avid collectors exist at all price levels. Many coin dealers have stock dating from the Edward III era, and earlier, priced at a few hundred pounds. This enables those with modest amounts to invest to assemble a small but diverse portfolio for as little as £5000, much as one might collect investment-grade stamps or Victorian watercolours.

Those with more to invest can have their choice of individual coins ranging into thousands and tens of thousands of pounds. The most expensive coin in the Slaney collection back in 2003 was sold for £138,000. A Henry VIII gold sovereign, topical at present with the recent 500th anniversary of his coronation, might sell for over £22,000, but an equally attractive and sought-after gold angel (one third of a pound) in similar condition might go for £1,450.

What about storage and insurance costs?

As we will see in the later chapter dealing with stamps, it is perfectly possible to hold a coin portfolio physically in the investor's home or office. Coins are high-value small-scale items, and not hard to find space for. But investment in both insurance and security measures is needed. One obvious measure is to install a safe. Safes designed for collectors can cost anything up to £1000 plus VAT, including installation. Unlike stamps, whose value is not readily apparent to the untutored eye, rare coins, especially gold and silver ones, would have obvious value to a thief. This means they probably do need a bit of extra-special protection.

These valuable assets need not be kept on the investor's premises, however. Whether or not an investor wishes to invest in security measures depends on whether or not they intend to have the coins available and on view at home or in their office, or whether they simply have them stored in a bank safety deposit facility or at a dealer's premises. Firms like Spink and Baldwin's offer secure storage facilities for coins bought through them. Fully alarmed safety deposit boxes can be rented for as little as £100 a year in central London. Outside the City, a local branch bank may offer such a facility for less.

The choice between the two of these storage options depends on the size of the collection they wish to build. If the collection is likely to be just a few high-value items that only need to be viewed occasionally, then a safety deposit box may be the best answer. If the intention is to have a larger collection at home for browsing and personal enjoyment, then a fireproof safe large enough to store a coin cabinet is essential.

Portfolio diversification potential?

Prices of rare coins should rise in line with economic growth and inflation. But unlike bullion coins such as Krugerrands, they may not protect an investor's wealth particularly well in the case of a severe economic downturn. In short, they appear to have rate-of-return characteristics similar to some parts of the stock market, but without the volatility normally associated with day-to-day investment in shares. They are not true diversification away from securities in the way that, for example, gold can be. Their prices move in line with, rather than against, the general trend in the stock market.

Paradoxically stamps, though flimsier, may have the edge over coins in this respect. They are less durable; so fewer good examples of top-quality stamps exist. On the other hand, stamp history only goes back to the first half of the 19th century: coin collecting stretches right back to the pre-Christian era.

Numismatics is essentially about history. Enthusiasts would add that it also takes in economics, geography, heraldry, metallurgy, politics, art and military history. Coins are essentially 'pictorial' historical items. They tell us about the conditions of the time they were issued, intimately embodying war, revolution, currency debasement, human corruption, and even engineering prowess. While it is not essential to have an interest in this to buy coins for an investment, it helps.

Returns

Prices of coins are well documented and periodic auctions make it fairly easy to calculate returns. Using the Slaney auction at Spink in May 2003 as a benchmark exemplar, the prices realised by this collection confirmed that there are highly respectable rates of return to be had in long-term quality coin investments.

A selection of 50 coins from the collection, acquired during the 1940s and 1950s at an aggregate cost of £2350, fetched £460,000. If the mid-point of the acquisition period for these items was 1950, this represents a compound return of 10.5% a year over the 53-year period involved.

The most spectacular result from the auction, the sale of a Charles II silver pattern crown from 1663 (known as the Petition Crown) produced a not dissimilar return. This was purchased in 1950 for £450 and sold in 2003 for £138,000, versus a pre-sale estimate of £40,000 to £50,000. The price realised represents a compound return of 11.4% per year. In terms of the price offered, this coin has long since been superseded in terms of the record price paid for an English coin – but it was an impressive figure nonetheless.

The sale of Lord Hamilton of Dalzell's collection in 1979, again built up over a 50-year period, appears to have resulted in a return of something in the region of 8.7% per annum.

By any judgement these are respectable returns, but many investors will not want to wait for that length of time before cashing in their investment. Using the 1996 prices from the Seaby's (now Spink's) coin catalogue edition as a proxy for 1995 levels (see the end of this chapter for more details on this invaluable publication) and the latest edition (2009) for 2008 prices, we can see how the prices of a selection of 'extremely fine' and 'uncirculated' coins have increased over this period. The tables also calculate returns for English coins in gold, silver and bronze/copper categories over the same period.

Returns from rare English coins over time (based on a sample of 50)

Type	1996	1999	2002	2005	2008	2009	CAGR %
Gold	100	136	154	269	300	325	10.3
Silver	100	127	168	303	381	396	12.2
Bronze/copper etc.	100	149	171	395	451	455	13.5
Total	100	134	158	285	330	351	11.1

Performance of randomly selected coins over the same period

Type	1996	1999	2002	2005	2008	2009	CAGR %
Gold							
George I Guinea	1714	2000	2,300	2,750	5000	5,500	7.7
Edward III Noble	600	750	1000	1,650	2000	2,250	10.8
James II 5 Guinea 1687	3,600	4,850	5,500	9,750	12,500	12,500	10.7
George VI Sovereign 1937	350	400	400	950	1,350	1,550	13.1
Silver							
George I Shilling 1723	75	85	150	300	225	225	10.5
Newark Shilling 1645	385	575	750	1,200	1,600	1,500	11.3
Victoria Gothic Crown 1847	850	1,250	1,750	2,500	2,750	2,750	10.3
George V Crown 1934	950	950	1,500	2,250	3,900	4,350	12.6
Copper/bronze etc.							
George III Twopence 1797	95	150	200	325	375	375	13.3
Victoria Penny 1844	80	80	90	185	225	275	9.9
Anne Farthing 1714	350	375	450	800	950	950	9.5
James II Halfpenny 1685	550	800	1000	3000	3,250	3,250	17.5

The tables demonstrate the degree to which individual coins can have fluctuations in returns, and also show that high-priced coins are not necessarily the best performers at any given time. It is also clear from this that a modest portfolio of coins can be assembled without the hefty outlay that recent spectacular and well-publicised auction results might indicate, but without sacrificing anything in terms of performance. Above all, the reliable returns generated by a diversified portfolio of coins can easily be gauged.

How to Invest

As with most of the categories in this book, there are a number of different ways to buy coins for long-term investment purposes.

While those collecting for the purposes of a modest pastime may be content to buy smaller value coins by mail-order or from dealers at fairs, those who are approaching the task from the standpoint of a serious tangible asset investor need to be more cautious. Buying 'sight unseen' is absolutely not recommended. It is safe enough if you buy from an ultra-reputable dealer like Spink or Baldwin's. But that is not the issue. Even then, it is surely important to view the coin before buying, especially if the resulting purchase is then going to be locked away in a safety deposit box.

Coin exhibitions are a good way of meeting a number of dealers clustered in the same place, and the competition helps to keep prices fair. Coinex, which takes place each year in October in London, is a good place to start. Auctions of antiques, country house sales, flea markets, craft fairs and the like may be a source of material, although it is often the case that coins displayed in sales like this are overgraded, sometimes unintentionally and sometimes deliberately. Some dealers use sales like this to sell problem coins to uninformed buyers. Items on display at antique shops need careful examination for the same reason. A reference guide, as well as a magnifying glass, is an essential accompaniment to any purchasing process.

The ideal way to buy is through a trusted and highly reputable dealer with whom the individual has, or can build up, a good relationship. If there is some serious intent about establishing a portfolio of coins, the dealer will realise that the investor/collector will be likely to represent a considerable source of future business and treat them accordingly. Purchasing coins over the web falls foul of the strictures over being able to inspect the coins, although it is useful as a way of making contact with other collectors who have coins they wish to sell. The investor can then arrange to meet in person to view the coins and make a trade. I deal elsewhere in the book with the advantages and disadvantages of using online auctions like eBay.

Would-be coin investors should note that some well-known auction houses now incorporate internet bidding at coin auctions. This is now widespread and though, in the first edition of this book, I viewed it as something of a last resort, the technology is now such that internet bidding can come quite close to the feeling of being in the saleroom and gauging the right level to pitch a bid.

Selling a collection to harvest investment returns may be the last thing on the investor's mind at the outset. Depending on the strength of the market, the auction is probably the most favoured exit route, since it will attract a considerable number of buyers and potentially allow competitive bidding to drive the price up to an optimum level.

Setting realistic reserve prices (or even no reserve at all) is also very important, and bear in mind that any realisation will also be net of the saleroom commission. Getting a realistic estimate of a portfolio's value before submitting it to auction is also a good idea. Setting a reserve price can cost extra. Issues like this need thrashing out with the auction house before any commitment to consigning items to an auction is made.

The next table sets out a list of coin dealers and auctioneers.

Where to Go for More Information

As with many other areas of alternative-asset-investing, the web has made a considerable difference to the business of coin dealing. The changes are arguably less marked than with stamps or books, since the three-dimensional nature of a coin is harder to render on a web page than a two-dimensional stamp. Nonetheless, dealers provide information and price lists on the web, online bidding is now a feature of coin auctions, and considerable coin dealing is still done by mail-order, notwithstanding the importance of seeing and examining coins before buying.

The following are some useful web-based sources of information and print publications that can help with background information and prices.

Dealers

Baldwin's (www.baldwin.co.uk), established in 1872, is a coin dealer based in London, now part of Noble Investments (UK) plc, which also owns Apex Philatelics. An online stock list is featured on the Baldwin's site and fixed-price lists are produced bi-annually. Baldwin's auction department holds auctions in London, Hong Kong, the Gulf states and New York. Forthcoming auction catalogues and prices realised are both on the site and coins can be purchased directly from them online. Online bidding is available in most auctions.

Bonhams (www.bonhams.com), incorporating Glendining's, sells all types of coins from Ancient Greek and Roman up to present day issues.

Coincraft (www.coincraft.com) is a family firm based in the Bloomsbury area of London. The site has information on collecting as well as detailed information about the available stock. The *Phoenix* newspaper/catalogue is published monthly and contains a list of items for sale. This publication includes banknotes as well as coins. Special mailings are sent to favoured collectors.

Coins

Dealers & Auctioneers

Entity	Web address	Main location	Email address	Telephone	Category
Baldwins	www.baldwin.co.uk	London	On site	020 7930 6879	Dealer
Bonhams (Glendinings)	www.bonhams.com	London	coins@bonhams.com	0207 393 3914	Auction house
Bowers and Merena	www.bowersandmerena.com	California	info@bowersandmerena.com	949 253 0916	Auction house
Coincraft	www.coincraft.com	London	info@coincraft.com	020 7636 1188	Dealer
Colin Cooke	www.colincooke.com	Altrincham	coins@colincooke.com	0161 927 9524	Dealer
Dix Noonan Webb	www.dnw.co.uk	London	auctions@dnw.co.uk	020 7016 1700	Auction house
Dr. Busso-Peus Nachf.	www.bussopeus.de	Frankfurt	info@peus-muenzen.de	49 69 959 6620	Dealer
Dorotheum	www.dorotheum.com	Vienna	coins@dorotheum.com	43 1 515 60 298	Auction house
Forum Ancient Coins	www.forumancientcoins.com	North Carolina	Through site	252 646 1958	Dealer
Hess Divo	www.hessdivo.com	Zurich	mailbox@hessdivo.com	41 (0)44 225 4090	Auction house
London Coins	www.londoncoins.co.uk	Kent	info@londoncoins.co.uk	01474 871 464	Dealer
Monetarium	www.monetarium.com.au	Sydney	info@monetarium.com.au	(61) 02 9588 7111	Dealer
Morton and Eden	www.mortonandeden.com	London	info@mortonandeden.com	020 7493 5344	Auction House
Nomos	www.nomosag.com	Zurich	info@nomosag.com	41 44 250 5180	Auction House
Numismatica Ars Classica	www.arsclassicacoins.com	London	info@arsclassicacoins.com	020 7839 7270	Auction House
Ponterio	www.bowersandmerena.com	California	info@bowersandmerena.com	as above	Auction house
Simmons Gallery	www.simmonsgallery.co.uk	Leytonstone	simmon@simmonsgallery.co.uk	020 8989 8097	Online dealer/auction
Sixbid	www.sixbid.com	Stuttgart	service@sixbid.com	n/a	Online auction platform
Spink	www.spink.com	London	info@spink.com	020 7563 4000	Dealer
Stack's	www.stacks.com	New York	Through site	212 582 2580	Auction house
Varesi	www.varesi.it	Pavia Italy	segreteria@varesi.it	39 0382 570685	Auction house
Warwick and Warwick	www.warwickandwarwick.com	Warwick	richard.beale@warwickandwarwick.com	01926 499 031	Auction house

Colin Cooke Coins (www.colincooke.com) is based in South Manchester and deals in British, foreign and ancient coins.

CNG (Classical Numismatic Group) (www.cngcoins.com) a dealer and auctioneer in ancient, medieval and British coins. CNG operates from two locations, one in Pennsylvania, USA and the other in London (formerly Seaby Coins).

Dix Noonan Webb (www.dnw.co.uk), a London-based specialised auctioneer and valuer of coins and medals, holds four traditional sales a year plus internet-only sales. Online valuations can be requested. For those who prefer more traditional sales methods, DNW also handles high value private treaty sales.

Dr. Busso-Peus Nachf (www.bussopeus.de) is an old established dealer and auctioneer based in Frankfurt.

Hess-Divo (www.hessdivo.com), based in Zurich, holds two to four auctions per year.

The dealer and auctioneer London Coins (www.londoncoins.co.uk), despite the name, is now situated in New Ash Green in Kent.

Monetarium (www.monetarium.com.au) is based in Sydney with offices also in Adelaide and Singapore. The firm sells rare Australian coins. The site has a number of numismatic articles, market updates and research notes.

The auction house Morton & Eden (www.mortonandeden.com) was set up in 2001. Its principals are two former Sotheby's directors. It still maintains a close association with Sotheby's. Catalogues of forthcoming and past sales are available on the site.

Nomos (www.nomosag.com) is a Zurich-based dealer and auctioneer.

Numismatica Ars Classica (www.arsclassicacoins.com), a dealer and auctioneer founded in 1988, has offices in London, Zurich and Milan.

Ponterio, a division of the auctioneers Bowers & Merena (www.bowersandmerena.com), is based in California. They have handled four of the five most valuable United States coin collections ever sold.

Simmons Gallery (www.simmonsgallery.co.uk) are online dealers and auctioneers. They have run the London Coin Fairs for the last thirty years.

They specialise in coins from South East Asia, the Indian Sub-Continent and Latin America.

Sixbid (www.sixbid.com) is an internet platform for numismatic auctions. It represents a number of major auction houses, all of which are listed on the site together with information about their forthcoming auctions. The site also has a database of completed auctions with prices realised through a link to www.coinarchives.com.

Spink (www.spink.com), based in Bloomsbury, was founded in 1666 and has been dealing in coins, as well as banknotes, medals and stamps, since 1703. The *Spink Numismatic Circular* is published six times a year and has details of coins for sale and articles on various numismatic topics. The website also has numerous links to societies and museum numismatic collections, plus information on buying and selling at auction.

Stack's (www.stacks.com) is a leading American numismatic auctioneer based in New York. Coins can also be bought online.

Varesi (www.varesi.it) is a leading Italian numismatic auction house based in Pavia.

Warwick & Warwick (www.warwickandwarwick.com), established in 1958, holds coin auctions six times a year in Warwick. It also deals in banknotes and stamps.

Information

The British Museum (www.britishmuseum.org) houses one of the world's finest numismatic collections, with coins from 7th century BC to the present day, although only a limited number are on display at any one time. As well as a brief summary of the collection, the site also features a history of coinage and information on forthcoming exhibitions.

The Coin Dealers Directory (www.numis.co.uk) is a list of coin dealers in the British Isles and has information on magazines, associations, clubs and other resources. The site includes a useful section on how to identify and value coins. The site is operated by coin and bullion dealer Chard.

Coin News (www.tokenpublishing.com) publishes three yearbooks and two monthly magazines, respectively on coins and medals, together with a range of other titles. *Coin News* features a 'what's on' section with details of fairs, societies, and auctions. The magazine also has saleroom reports and book reviews. Subscribers can opt to receive their copy by PDF in addition to the print version.

Coin Resource (www.coinresource.com) is a US site with a 'Coin Encyclopedia' of American coins containing facts, photographs and history. Among the site's many other features are a beginner's guide to collecting, articles on coins and numerous links.

Coin News (www.coinnews.net) is an American online magazine site, with news and useful information for collectors. Not to be confused with the UK-based magazine published by Token Publishing.

Cornucopia (www.cornucopia.org.uk), run by The Museums, Libraries and Archives Council, has a searchable online database of museum, galleries, archives and libraries in the UK.

The Royal Australian Mint (www.ramint.gov.au), the supplier of Australia's circulating currency, has links to numismatic dealers throughout Australia.

The Royal Mint (www.royalmint.com) situated in Llantrisant, South Wales, has information on collectable and present-day coins. Although its primary purpose is to provide UK coinage, more than 100 countries have entrusted the striking of their coinage to the Royal Mint, such is its reputation. Coins can be purchased online.

Coins

Information and publications

Entity	Web address	Main location	Email address	Telephone	Category
Ashmolean Museum	www.ashmolean.org	Oxford	coin-room@ashmus.ox.ac.uk	01865 278 058	Information
Athens Numismatic Museum	www.nma.gr	Athens	Through site	30210 3612 519	Information
British Museum	www.britishmuseum.org	London	coins@britishmuseum.org	020 7323 8000	Information
Classical Numismatic Group	www.cngcoins.com	London	cng@cngcoins.com	020 7495 1888	Information
Coin Dealers Directory	www.numis.co.uk	Blackpool	contact@numis.co.uk	01253 343 081	Information
Coin News	www.tokenpublishing.com	Honiton Devon	info@tokenpublishing.com	01404 46972	Publication
Coin News	www.coinnews.net	San Antonio Texas	Through site	n/a	Online publication
Coin Resource	www.coinresource.com	Texas	info@coinresource.com	n/a	Information
Cornucopia	www.cornucopia.org.uk	London	Through site	n/a	Information
Digital Coins Network	www.digitalcoins.org	USA and London	Through site	n/a	Information
Fitzwilliam Museum	www-cm.fitzmuseum.cam.ac.uk/dept/coins	Cambridge	fitzmuseum-coins@lists.cam.ac.uk	01223 332 900	Information
Hellenic Numismatic Society (The)	www.coins.gr/hellenum	Athens	hellenum@hotmail.com	30 210 672 1542	Information
Hunterian Museum	www.hunterian.gla.ac.uk	Glasgow	hunterian@museum.gla.ac.uk	0141 330 4221	Information
Islamic Coins Group	www.islamiccoinsgroup.50g.com		Through site	n/a	Information
Medieval Coins Group	www.medievalcoins.50g.com		Through site	n/a	Information
Royal Australian Mint	www.ramint.gov.au	Canberra	Through site	612 6202 6800	Information
Royal Mint	www.royalmint.com	South Wales	Through site	01443 222 111	Information
State Hermitage Museum	www.hermitagemuseum.org	St Petersburg	Through site	812 710 9629	Information

Numismatic associations

The American Numismatic Society (www.numismatics.org) has an online collection database of over 800,000 coins and related items plus a library catalogue. The site also hosts the Digital Coins Network (www.digitalcoins.org), which promotes the effective use of information technology in the collection, publication and exchange of numismatic data. This was originally conceived, established and funded by the UK Arts and Humanities Research Council. The site features links to online numismatic databases and digitalised literature.

The British Association of Numismatic Societies (www.coinclubs.freeserve.co.uk), known as BANS, is based at the Manchester Museum. It is the national organisation for numismatic societies throughout the UK. Apart from links to societies the site has details of publications and video lectures by prominent numismatists, together with details of conferences and lectures.

The British Numismatic Trade Association (www.bnta.net) has more than 60 members throughout the British Isles, all of whom are listed on the site. The BNTA organises Coinex, the London coin fair, which takes place each October.

The Oriental Numismatic Society (www.onsnumis.org) serves collectors of all types of oriental coinage, from North Africa to the Far East. The society publishes a newsletter four times a year with information and articles about individual coins, problems of dating them, and several other topics.

The Royal Numismatic Society (www.numismatics.org.uk), based at the British Museum, is a leading academic numismatic society. Meetings are open to all. The library, housed in the Warburg Institute in Woburn Square, has over 7000 volumes plus many auction catalogues and periodicals. The site has links to museums with numismatic collections and other societies and organisations.

Also based at the Warburg Institute is the British Numismatic Society (www.fitzmuseum.cam.ac.uk/coins/britnumsoc), which promotes the study of coinage, banknotes, medals and tokens from the British Isles and former British colonies.

Fairs

The Chicago International Coin Fair organised by *World Coin News* (www.worldcoinnews.net) takes place each year in April.

Coinex, organised by BNTA (www.bnta.net), takes place in October in London. (There are no plans for a show in Cardiff.)

Numismata (www.numismata.de), the International Numismatic Convention, is held in the following cities:

- Munich – March
- Vienna – May
- Berlin – October
- Frankfurt – November

The Taisei Hong Kong International Coin Show is held twice yearly in April and August (The Taisei group was disbanded some years ago, this is now called the Baldwin's – Ma Tak Wo Hong Kong International Coin Convention but still held twice annually in April and August.)

The World Money Fair (www.worldmoneyfair.ch) is held in January in Berlin.

Associations and fairs

Entity	Web address	Main location	Email address	Telephone	Category
American Numismatic Society	www.numismatics.org	New York	On site	212 571 4470	Association
Ancient Coin Collectors Guild	www.accg.us	Missouri	director@accg.us	417 679 2142	Association
British Association of Numismatic Societies	www.coinclubs.freeserve.co.uk	Manchester	Through site	0161 275 2643	Association
British Numismatic Society	www.fitzmuseum.cam.ac.uk/coins/britnumsoc	London	secretary@britnumsoc.org	n/a	Association
British Numismatic Trade Association	www.bnta.net	East Sussex	bnta@lineone.net	01797 229 988	Association/fair (Coinex)
Chicago Coin Fair	www.worldcoinnews.net	Chicago	On site	n/a	Fair
New York International Numismatic Convention	www.nyinc.info	New York	kfoley2@wi.rr.com	n/a	Fair
Numismata	www.numismata.de	Germany	numismata.modes@t-online.de	49 (0) 89 26 83 59	Fair
Oriental Numismatic Society	www.onsnumis.org	UK	On site	n/a	Association
Royal Numismatic Society (The)	www.numismatics.org.uk	London	info@numismatics.org.uk	n/a	Association

Books

Coincraft's Standard Catalogue of English and UK Coins, by Richard Lobel et al, (Standard Catalogue Publishers)

This is a handbook of English and UK coins from 1066 to the present, with historical information, prices, a section on hammered and milled patterns, and collecting tips – plus other detailed information. It is printed in large size (A4) format with over 740 pages.

Coins & Investments: A Consumer's Guide, by J. Pearson Andrew (Seaby, 1986)

This is a useful book covering all aspects of coin collecting from an investment point of view. Areas discussed include the various factors that determine the price of a coin, the coin market past and present, forgery, and a dictionary of coins and their history.

Coin Yearbook, eds. John W. Mussell, Philip Mussell (Token Publishing)

This is a price guide and collector's handbook for UK coins. Articles include valuation for UK coins, a collector's review of the previous year, a guide to the latest auction prices, the storage of coins and other useful information.

Standard Catalogue of British Coins (Spink)

This book is considered by many to be the 'bible' for coin collectors. It has been published regularly since 1929 and is a complete catalogue for British coins, providing an invaluable tool for collectors. The book also contains a useful beginner's guide to coin collecting, with advice on buying and selling coins and detailed information on minting processes and condition. It is universally called 'Seaby's', after the original publishers, even though it has been owned and published by Spink for a number of years.

Standard Catalog of World Coins, eds. various (KP Books)

Published annually, this has complete coverage of coins from 1601 to the present day, in four volumes, each covering a century. Each volume is lavishly illustrated and the four volumes in total comprise nearly 6000 pages. Coins are priced in five grades of condition and include the mint number and date. The book also includes a guide to identifying coins, a coin sizing chart and much more. As this is a US publication, prices are given in US$.

Investments That Stand The Test of Time

Since time immemorial, diamonds have been valued as objects of wealth and prosperity.

In today's uncertain markets, investment diamonds continue to impress as a truly versatile alternative asset class.

Fusion Alternatives is a boutique investment advisory firm specialising in investment-grade polished diamonds.

We provide superior purchasing and investment expertise combined with second-to-none client services in this emerging market.

- Managed Accounts
- Bespoke Diamond Buying Service
- Diamond Investment Vehicle

Contact our advisors for more information
Tel.: +44 (0)20 7183 0244
Email: info@fusionalternatives.com

Visit us at www.fusionalternatives.com

5.

Diamonds

Diamonds are the ultimate form of portable wealth. At a price in September 2009 of $25,000 per carat for a stone of the highest quality, a million dollars can be transported, in the form of 40 high-quality one-carat stones, in a container the size of a small paperback book.

Stones like this, which weigh around 200mg and have a width of approximately 6.5mm, are extremely rare. One estimate suggests that only 750 a year are produced, and that to extract them the mining companies have to dig up some 8000 tonnes of kimberlite (the diamond bearing ore).

On average 100 tonnes of kimberlite produces 70 carats of rough diamonds, of which less than 20% is usually considered to be gem quality. Only 40-50% of this weight is retained once the diamond is cut and polished. However, this is only an average. Diamond mines differ considerably in terms of carats produced per tonne of ore and high-quality diamonds are produced irrespective of the grade of mine.

Diamonds are considerably scarcer than gold. Fewer than 1000 tonnes of gem quality diamonds have ever been mined. There are only 20 years of known diamond reserves left, and no new discoveries have been made since the early 1990s, despite a boom in exploration. Many existing diamond mines are in the phase where production is declining and new mines are generally small. Production is forecast to decline for the next decade (2010-2020) to significantly lower levels than that seen recently.

All this contributes to scarcity and underpins prices in the long term. Apart from a peak in 1979, which coincided with speculation in a range of other areas from stamps to gold, and which was followed by a collapse in prices back to the long-term trend line, growth in the price of the best quality one carat diamonds has been steadily upwards, reinforced by their increasing scarcity. In 1979, the previous peak, the price reached $18,000 per carat, below the current price. Buying and selling diamonds requires skill, patience and precautions, because each diamond is unique in terms of size, colour and clarity. There is no homogeneous price as there is with gold, and making sure a diamond is authentic, correctly valued at the time of purchase, and with a guarantee of liquidity should an investor wish to sell, are the keys to investing.

Basics

The popularity of diamonds has increased steadily since the 19th century, largely because of highly successful advertising. There is, according to industry sources, proven continuous and steady historical growth in demand for polished diamonds, even in times of economic contraction. The industry went through a period where supply increased sharply, but this is now not the case. Lead-time for new mines is around eight years, and the credit crunch has caused exploration activities to be cut back. Indeed extracting diamonds is extremely costly and difficult, and the demand for stones is now quickly outstripping supply to such a point that some industry sources suggest that the supply of gem quality stones will be mostly exhausted inside of 20 years.

The investment case for diamonds is not dissimilar to that for gold. The essence of the appeal of diamonds, aside from the portable wealth argument, is that they are a long-term store of value and in particular an effective hedge against a diminution in the value of the dollar, much as is the case for gold. Research suggests that diamonds are already being used in this way by high net worth individuals in Russia and India. The US remains the largest consuming country, followed by Japan, Europe, China and the Middle East. New wealth in China may lead to increased demand for polished stones, as it has in India.

But diamond investing is much more complex than some other areas, partly because of the individuality of each stone and partly because there is an essential and subjective aesthetic component to their value. Each diamond is different and its value is partly determined by fashion and the opinion of those grading it. Equally, value per unit of weight is not linear. Larger diamonds are considerably scarcer and command a proportionately higher per carat value.

Liquidity is a difficult subject. Dealers will offer to buy back diamonds from existing customers, but the bid-offer spread will be a hefty one. The auction route is possible, but tends to be reserved for the more expensive and 'important' stones. Even then, as with other alternative assets, going down the auction route also involves hefty costs.

Carat, colour, clarity and cut

The value of a diamond is determined by a range of characteristics, namely its carat value (size and weight), colour, clarity and cut. The underlying value is determined, other things being equal, by the size and weight of the diamond; that's to say, its carat value. Diamonds are typically priced on a per carat basis, in US$, although as noted earlier, larger stones tend to be proportionately more expensive. Two half carat stones would not sell for the same price per carat as a single one carat stone. This means – together with the subjective factors mentioned below – that there is no single universally recognised price for diamonds. That is in marked contrast to gold, which has a price that can be easily determined, and which can be sold anywhere. Other than relatively small differences in the premium charged for coins or bars, there is a direct linear relationship between weight and price, and no subjective factors involved.

Carat weight and relative size

Carat size	Width (mm)
0.1	3
0.2	3.8
0.25	4.1
0.33	4.4
0.5	4.2
0.65	5.6
0.75	5.9
0.85	6.2
1.00	6.5
1.25	7.0
1.5	7.4
1.75	7.8
2	8.2
2.5	9.0
3	9.3
4	10.2
5	11
6	11.7

Source: Ajediam

Carat weight and relative price

Weight group	Price per carat (as % of one-carat price)
0.19 to 0.29	26
0.3 to 0.40	33
0.5 to 0.59	44
0.6 to 0.99	58
1 to 1.49	100
1.5 to 1.79	138
1.8 to 1.99	191
2 to 2.49	191
2.5 to 2.99	321
3 to 3.49	350

Source: Diamond Price Guru

Note: Implied price change is non-linear. A three-carat stone is three times more expensive *per carat* than a one-carat stone. All figures are approximate for stones of similar grade and colour.

In addition, diamonds vary in colour and clarity, and the way in which they are cut also has a bearing on value and how a diamond will be graded. Colours can range from white to yellow, with various gradations in-between detectable by an expert. In broad terms these range from exceptionally white, through rare white, white, tinted white, faint yellow and very light yellow. In all there are around 16 different gradations of colour detectable by experts (see following table).

Colour-grading for 'white' diamonds

Letter	Colour term	Subsidiary term
D	Exceptional white +	River
E	Exceptional white	River
F	Rare white +	Top Wesselton
G	Rare white	Top Wesselton
H	White	Wesselton
I	Slightly tinted white	Top Cristal
J	Slightly tinted white	Top Cristal
K	Tinted white – faint yellow	Top Cape
L	Tinted white – faint yellow	Top Cape
M	Faint yellow	Tinted Cape
N	Faint yellow	Tinted Cape
O	Faint yellow	Tinted Cape
P	Very light yellow	Tinted Cape
R	Very light yellow	Tinted Cape
S	Very light yellow	Tinted Cape
Z	Very light yellow	Tinted Cape

Source: Ajediam

Clarity is a measure of the degree to which a diamond is free from any internal or external flaws. A completely flawless diamond is termed 'internally flawless/loupe clean', sometimes abbreviated to IF/LC, which means that an experienced grader can detect no internal or external flaws having examined the stone with a loupe (a magnifying glass held close to the eye) with a magnification of 10x.

Terms then range from VVS (very, very small inclusions), through small inclusions detectable only under magnification, through to obvious flaws and spots visible to the naked eye. Some of the more obvious flaws and inclusion can affect a diamond's clarity and brilliance, but, in most cases, flaws and inclusions will only be visible under magnification. Grading terms related to clarity are shown in the table.

Diamond clarity – grading terms

Grading term	Meaning	Description
LC/IF	Loupe clean / internally flawless	No internal or external visible flaws under 10x magnification
VVS1	Very very small inclusions (1st degree)	Very very small flaws extremely difficult to detect with 10x magnification
VVS2	Very very small inclusions (2nd degree)	Very very small flaws extremely difficult to detect with 10x magnification
VS1	Very small inclusion (1st degree)	Very small flaws difficult to detect under 10x magnification
VS2	Very small inclusion (2nd degree)	Very small flaws difficult to detect under 10x magnification
SI1	Small inclusions (1st degree). Eye clean	Small flaws detectable under 10x magnification but not to naked eye
SI2/3	Small inclusions. Sometimes eye clean	Small flaws detectable under 10x magnification and sometimes to naked eye
I1/P1	Inclusions, flaws and spots	Flaws easily detectable under magnification and to experienced naked eye
I2/P2	Inclusions, flaws and spots	Flaws visible to naked eye
I3/P3	Inclusions, flaws and spots	Obvious flaws, easily visible to naked eye and affecting transparency and brilliance

Source: Ajediam

The way a stone is cut can also affect its value. Diamond cutting changes a rough diamond into a faceted gem. There are several classic shapes and styles for a cut diamond ranging from round, square, cushion and emerald, to oval and several others. The basic shape is distinct from the cut, although there are standard numbers of facets, angles and proportions for each shape. Each aspect of a cut can be graded separately, namely its proportions, polish and symmetry. Grading in this area is normally: excellent, very good, good, fair, poor or unusual. Too shallow or too deep a cut and brilliance will be lost. Diamonds are polished after cutting to remove all imperfections, abrasions and scratches.

For a standard pattern, a number of proportionate dimensions are usually followed by convention. These relate to the size of the 'table' – the flat part of the diamond – as a percentage of its overall width at the 'girdle', the widest point (this percentage is normally between 52% and 63%). Girdle thickness is also important and should be as small as possible (typically 2% of overall depth), without being so small as to risk the diamond being chipped.

Other conventions cover total depth as a percentage of width (usually around 60%) and also the angles at which the facets are cut above and below the girdle (respectively the 'crown' and 'pavilion' angles) and the thickness of any points. Patterns, such as hearts arranged in a circle around a central point, and an arrow effect, can add to the price of the finished stone. Buyers looking for premium stones will demand a cut of this type and one that rates as excellent in terms of the proportions of the cut, its polish and its symmetry.

The tables show the proportions, etc. expected for different grades of cut stone.

Typical diamond shapes when cut

Term	No. of facets	Description
Round brilliant	57-58	Circle
Princess	53-54	Square
Brilliant modified	57-58	Cushion
Asscher	48-49	Rounded square
Emerald	49-50	Rounded rectangle
Heart	57-58	Heart
Marquise	55-56	Rugby ball
Oval	55-56	Oval
Pear	56-57	Teardrop
Radiant	53-54	Rectangle – slightly rounded corners
Trilliant	40-41	Rounded triangle/shield

Source: Ajediam

Approximate ideal proportions for 'fancy' shapes

Cut	Length	Width
Oval	1.3 to 1.68	1
Marquise	1.75 to 2.25	1
Princess	1.0 to 1.1	1
Pear	1.5 to 1.75	1
Heart	1.0 to 1.1	1
Emerald	1.5 to 1.75	1

Source: Ajediam

Typical dimensions for different grades of cut diamonds

	Total depth %	Table %	Crown %	Crown angle (deg)	Pavilion %	Pavilion angle (deg)	Girdle
Excellent	58.0 to 63.5	52 to 63	12 to 16.5	31.5 to 36.5	42 to 44.5	40 to 41.7	Thin to slightly thick
Very good	55 to 65.5	52 to 66	10 to 17.5	28.5 to 38	41.5 to 45	39.7 to 42.3	Very thin – up to thick
Good	53 to 69	50 to 70	8.5 to 19	26 to 40	41 to 46.5	39.4 to 42.9	Extremely thin to very thick
Fair/poor	Less than 53	Less than 50	Less than 8.5	Less than 26	Less than 41	Less than 39.4	Other

Source: Ajediam

It is, however, important to stress at this point that while carat weight can be determined accurately, the three remaining factors in determining value – cut, colour and clarity – are subjective and based on the opinions of graders. There is also no real order of importance as far as these three factors are concerned, as likes and opinions may differ over time and between different buyers and different markets.

Coloured diamonds, for example, are currently considered fashionable and hence are markedly more expensive. But until recently diamonds like this were considered to be inferior. However, coloured diamonds are much rarer than conventional 'white' ones, and hence are likely to attract buyers more readily.

It is important to bear in mind that the whole business of grading and pricing diamonds is comparatively recent. A comprehensive grading system for diamonds was only introduced in the 1950s and price guides only became available for white diamonds in the 1980s.

One central point often alluded to by dealers is that rarity must play a role in the decision to invest. Beauty – related to clarity and cut – is one of the key factors driving price, but the other important factor is rarity, which for diamonds really equates to a combination of size (in terms of carat value) and colour. One commentator suggests that beyond a certain size, rarity drives prices substantially higher.

Beware: scams and dirty tricks

Scams are as prevalent in the diamond and gem trade as in any other. A wide variety exist.

Stones may gain in value, but certain sections of the market are susceptible to fraud and dishonesty in their pricing. As with other alternative assets, one simple con is to overcharge for genuine stones. Some professional dealers have been known to make a handsome profit on the mark-up on stones and jewellery shown in shop windows, particularly when specialised lighting is used to enhance the brilliance and whiteness of a diamond in such conditions. Additional mark-ups can be as much as 50%-100% of the intrinsic value.

Other dirty tricks involve marketing poorly-cut diamonds (known as off-makes) at prices that would normally only be commanded by perfectly-cut ones. Fake certificates of authenticity are also sometimes used by online sellers and some tourist shops, while certificates for a diamond of a higher grade are sometimes substituted to allow the dealer to charge a higher price. Diamonds with excessively thin girdles (see above) can break and chip, command lower prices, and are best avoided.

There are other tricks too. One is the selling of doublets, which are composites of a diamond but with a zircon, or some other diamond substitute, forming the bottom two-thirds of the stone (which is not usually displayed to the buyer).

Treating, particularly heat-treating average diamonds, to enhance their brilliance and hence their price, is also a common trick, although it makes the diamond brittle. There is also the practice of irradiating diamonds to create an unusual colour, and diamonds where fractures in the stone have been artificially filled and which are sold as perfect and genuine articles by the unscrupulous.

Outright fraud also exists. Some investors have been persuaded to buy stones that they are told will sell for a profit of several hundred per cent at a later date at an auction, possibly in another country. All too often the auction never takes place and the company is wound up. To add insult to injury, the original scam company sells its list of gullible investors to a second company. This company then approaches the investors and explains that for a further investment they can find a buyer for the gemstones.

Another pitch has been to send diamonds to investors in sealed packets with a microfilm guarantee, but a rider that breaking the seal on the packet will invalidate the guarantee. This is done to avoid investors seeking independent appraisal.

Like a number of collectables and gold bullion, diamonds and gemstones are not regulated as investments by the financial regulators like the UK's Financial Services Authority. Dealing firms are not vetted and there are no investor protection rules. Dealing with reputable firms based in traditional diamond-selling areas like London's Hatton Garden or Antwerp, and seeking bona fide guarantees, provides the best chance of avoiding fraud.

The Right Alternative Asset for You?

Most investors with a substantial portfolio of assets invested in the stock market might look at diamonds as a reasonable alternative asset, perhaps on a par with gold as a store of value but with the advantage of extreme portability. But investing in diamonds needs to be undertaken with extreme care. It requires investors to have positive answers to a number of crucial questions.

A long-term investment?

Aside from a pronounced bubble in the late 1970s, top-quality diamond prices have generally shown a steady upward progression for the last 60 years – although prices have been soft of late. One estimate put diamond prices in late 2009 at similar levels to those seen in 2005, which contrasts with much more robust price action seen in the price of gold over the same period.

Market conditions are not uniform, however, and the grading of diamonds is subjective. Demand, as noted earlier, is subject to the whims of fashion. Transaction costs can be high. Dealers operate on the basis of a wide bid-offer spread (30% and upwards) for the widely offered buyback policies and the alternative route to liquidity, through the auction market, entails substantial transaction costs. As with other areas covered in this book, the best returns will only be garnered if investors avoid buying in bubble conditions and if the investment is held for a lengthy period of time, perhaps up to ten years as a minimum.

Capital requirements?

Investment-grade diamonds command premium prices. A top-quality D-grade one-carat stone rated loupe clean and internally flawless will, according to latest prices from Ajediam, command a price in the region of $25,000. Some sources suggest that the price per carat for larger stones could be up to three times this level. Larger stones and those with unusual colour typically attract more attention than smaller-sized 'white' diamonds and are therefore easier to sell to dealers and through auction houses.

Investors, as with other categories in this book, need to buy the best stones they can afford above an absolute minimum of one-carat category D LC/IF. It is sometimes said that stones can be purchased slightly more cheaply immediately below the move to a new carat bracket. In other words a stone of 2.49 carats identical in all other respects to one of 2.50 carats could be disproportionately cheaper than the small difference in weight might justify.

What about storage and insurance costs?

Rather as with gold, if an investor wishes to hold diamonds physically on his or her own property, then investment in both insurance and security measures, such as installing a safe in which to keep it, is needed. The alternative is to trust holdings in diamonds to a bank safety deposit box. Unlike gold, it is not possible to buy an entitlement to diamonds in the form of an exchange-traded fund (ETF) which is, in any event, an indirect means of ownership that relies on the integrity and permanence of the issuing institution.

Since the essence of diamonds (and gold) is their store of value characteristics in the event of a cataclysm such as financial meltdown or hyperinflation, physical possession is of the essence, notwithstanding the costs involved.

Portfolio diversification potential?

Diamonds demonstrate a similar price pattern to gold, similar returns and, like gold, relatively high price volatility as measured by standard deviations over time. The pattern of diamond price movements over time also has echoes of similar movements in the price of high-quality investment-grade stamps. Although few formal statistical studies have been performed on diamond prices over long time periods (largely owing to the absence of consistent data) it seems reasonable to suppose that diamonds, like gold, have a negative correlation with most other financial assets, and particularly with stocks and bonds. This makes them a good way of diversifying away from traditional paper assets.

Unlike gold, art and wine, there has also, to date, been little investment activity in diamonds from either professional or private investors. This may change in future, as market developments may open up liquidity and the supply and demand balance is seen as tightening significantly.

Returns

Calculating returns from investing in diamonds is much less easy than for gold, largely because of the subjective factors involved, the swings in fashion and opinion, the premium per carat price commanded by larger, rarer stones, and the lack of any homogeneity in the market. This factor contributes to wide differences of opinion about the returns from diamonds over the long term.

According to the international diamond wholesaler Ajediam, prices for diamonds have increased at a compound annual rate of 15% since 1949. More recent studies from Emotional Assets Management & Research (www.emotionalassets.com) suggested that, over the last 30 years, returns on a standard index (the HRD Carat D Flawless Index) had been of the order of 4.4% a year, with a standard deviation of close to 20%, while over 20 years the numbers were 2.5% a year and 10% respectively. Standard deviation measures volatility and therefore risk.

According to one observer, the returns have been better than this. In 1968, a one-carat D Flawless round brilliant sold at wholesale for $1,400, a price that had risen to $7,600 by 1976. The current price of a stone like this is in the region of $20,000, a return over a 40-year period of around 7.6%.

Some recent diamond prices per carat

Weight (ct)	Colour	Clarity	Make	Price/carat ($)
0.3 to 0.39	D	VS2	VG	1,534
0.3 to 0.39	E	SI1	X	1,140
0.3 to 0.39	G	VS1	X	1,320
0.3 to 0.39	H	SI1	X	885
0.4 to 0.49	E	VVS1	X	2,340
0.4 to 0.49	F	IF	XX	2,478
0.4 to 0.49	I	SI1	XX	976
0.5 to 0.59	D	VS2	VG	2,419
0.5 to 0.59	E	VVS2	X	3,060
0.5 to 0.59	F	VS2	X	2,100

Source: DODAQ

Relatively low long-term returns and relatively high volatility is characteristic of gold too, although in its case the numbers are less extreme. In recent years, collectables like books, stamps, rare coins and other such items have shown measurable annual returns in high single digits and low double digits, with much lower volatility than is the case for diamonds (with which they can to some degree be compared because of the different gradations of rarity involved, and the high element of subjectivity involved in determining their value).

The placing of diamonds alongside other collectables and indeed alongside gold is confirmed by the fact that like gold and also like, for example, stamps, diamond prices hit a peak in the late 1970s – reaching a high point at that time which they have only recently surpassed.

Between October 2008 and September 2009, diamond prices, as measured by the IDEX Diamond Index, fell by around 14%, reflecting depressed consumer demand, forced sales and a shortage of credit that affected the efficient functioning of the diamond trade. All of the fall occurred between October 2008 and March 2009. Some sources suggest that diamond prices in general are currently around levels seen in 2005, in sharp contrast to the upsurge in the gold price over the same period.

How to Invest

Traditionally secretive, with deals sealed face-to-face with a handshake, and limited price data available, diamonds might seem a difficult and illiquid market for private investors to access. However, a number of recent developments have been opening up the market to new influences.

For almost all its history, buying and selling polished diamonds – a trade with an annual value estimated in the region of $20 billion – has not been done in a centralised marketplace. Several trading centres exist, in Antwerp, Mumbai, New York and Dubai for example, but in general trading was fragmented. This is changing slowly, with the advent of marketplaces that employ new technology as well as the creation of collective-investment vehicles for diamonds.

Physical buying of diamonds requires guarantees of authenticity from one or other of the leading gemological institutes, in order to ensure that the genuine article, of a recognised grade, is being purchased.

Buying through reputable dealers is a possible route. Most reputable dealers will offer a money-back guarantee if a purchaser is not satisfied or has second thoughts within a limited time of purchase. Dealers also offer buyback guarantees, although those taking advantage of them will suffer a considerable 'haircut' in the form of sizeable percentage discount on the underlying value of the stone. In this respect, this practice is not that dissimilar from what happens in assets such as stamps and coins, where the bid-offer spread can be as much as 30-40%.

Some dealers also offer co-investment/shared-profit arrangements, as is also the case in some instances with stamps, although it seems reasonable to suggest that these will work in large measure to the benefit of the dealer given the opaque nature of diamond pricing. The perennial problem is that it is hard for investors to buy good quality material at less than the 'retail' price, although some dealers will offer discounts to encourage regular custom.

Buying through auction depends on the capital available to be committed to this area. Only the best and more unusual stones attract interest at auction – typically with price tags in the hundreds of thousands of US$. In this instance, however, costs, in the form of buyer's premium and seller's commission, amounts to a substantial spread between the effective bid and offer price.

A recent initiative is DODAQ (Dealers' Organisation for Diamond Automated Quotes). This is an electronic exchange set up in Antwerp for trading standardised certified and graded stones on a willing buyer/willing seller basis, with all transactions being free of sales taxes. Transactions are settled instantly in cash through ABN Amro and all diamonds bought, held and sold, are stored by Malca-Amit, a well-known provider of such services to the diamond industry.

Price quotes displayed on the DODAQ system suggest that the stones available to be bought and sold appear to be the smaller ones (less than one carat) and with a mixture of grades, including some lower graded stones that would arguably not be regarded as investment-quality. Nonetheless, the platform represents a liquid entry and exit point for would-be diamond investors and its scope may well increase in due course.

It is also possible to access the diamond market through the AIM-listed fund, Diamond Circle Capital. The fund buys high-grade polished diamonds, including coloured stones and large white diamonds, with average purchase prices in the £3-£5 million range. The fund in Q4 2009 was 90% invested and stood at a discount of around 30% to NAV (net asset value). Net assets have dropped by around this amount since launch, but the fund has halved in value since issue in mid-2008. It does, nonetheless, represent a relatively easy way to take advantage of any long-term growth in diamond prices and burgeoning demand for hard assets from emerging markets.

Where to Go for More Information

Investing in diamonds retains a considerable mystique for the average investor, and this is reflected in the relatively limited number of sites that have user-friendly information. The following brief outlines suggest some of the more obvious ports of call for information.

Ajediam (www.ajediam.com), based in the Antwerp World Diamond Centre, is a leading manufacturer, polisher and supplier of diamonds. The site has a buying guide, including information on cut grading, sizing, colour grading, and a range of other topics. The site is one of the most helpful from the standpoint of providing basic information about diamond investing.

The Antwerp World Diamond Centre (www.awdc.be) is the coordinating body and official representative of the Antwerp diamond sector.

The De Beers (www.debeers.com) retail site is part of an independently managed 50-50 joint venture between the De Beers Group and LVMH (Moet Hennessy Louis Vuitton). Their flagship store is in Old Bond Street in London, with further stores in Japan, Paris, Dubai, Kiev and various locations throughout the USA. The site has useful information on the four Cs – cut, clarity, colour and carat – the grading standards largely devised by De Beers some 70 years ago. The new standard of 'brilliance' is a more recent addition.

IDEX (www.idexonline.com), an online international diamond exchange, is designed for professional dealers and jewellers and as such much of its information is restricted to members. However, free content includes diamond industry news, diamond prices and links to dealers worldwide.

Based in Antwerp, DODAQ (www.dodaq.com) is an automated exchange for trading standardised and certified diamonds and can be used by private investors. The site has a range of information on the diamond market generally, as well as price lists for its most popular categories of diamonds.

The Israel Precious Stones and Diamonds Exchange (www.ipsde-il.com) has a list of members, together with their contact details.

The *Rapaport Diamond Report* (www.rapaportdiamondreport.com) is published weekly and is the primary source of diamond price information for the diamond industry, providing news, market analysis, market data and statistics. Information is only available on subscription, which at the time of writing was $250 per month for international subscribers.

Diamond-related websites

Entity	Web address	Main location	Email address	Telephone
Ajediam	www.ajediam.com	Antwerp	janhuts@ajediam.com	32 479 28 1213
Antwerp World Diamond Centre	www.awdc.be	Antwerp	diof@awdc.be	32 3222 0531
De Beers	www.debeers.com	London	clientservices@debeers.com	1 888 376 9230
DODAQ	www.dodaq.com	Antwerp	enquiries@dodaq.com	32 (0)3 289 8665
International Diamond Exchange (The)	www.idexonline.com	New York	customersupport@idexonline.com	1212 3823 528
Israel Precious Stones and Diamond Exchange	www.ipsde-il.com	Israel	info@ipsde-il.com	03 575 1177
Rapaport Diamond Report	www.rapaportdiamondreport.com	USA	info@diamonds.net	1 702 893 9400
Sotheby's Diamonds	www.sothebysdiamonds.com	London	On site	020 7293 6430
Steinmetz	www.steinmetzdiamonds.com	Geneva	info@rstei.com	1 212 398 1399
World Federation of Diamond Bourses	www.wfdb.com	Antwerp	Info@worldfed.com	32 03 234 9121

Steinmetz (www.steinmetzdiamonds.com) has diversified interests in the diamond industry, supplying rough and polished diamonds, as well as manufacturing, cutting and polishing. The company has entered into a partnership with Sotheby's (www.sothebysdiamonds.com) to sell individually crafted diamonds and jewellery. These are available for purchase in New York, London and Hong Kong, as well as through exclusive selling exhibitions and Sotheby's worldwide offices.

The World Federation of Diamond Bourses (www.wfdb.com) was founded in 1947 and sets the common trading practices for its 28 member diamond bourses. The site has links to members and news on the diamond industry.

The Biofore Company **UPM**

WATCH YOUR PROFITS GROW

Getting the best possible return from your woodland is vital. Timber harvested from well managed plantations can generate a substantial income.

UPM Tilhill provides a unique seedling to harvester management service to help you maximise the best value return on your forest. We have access to all the UK's high value markets, including the rapidly expanding biomass sector.

Get the most from your investment. Call us today or visit our website and find out how UPM Tilhill can help you.

Freephone 0800 328 2128 quoting **HAA**
or visit **www.upm-tilhill.com**

UPM – The Biofore Company
UPM leads the integration of bio and forest industry into a new, sustainable and innovation-driven future

UPM TILHILL

6.
Forestry

Forestry has been an investment medium for private individuals for about fifty years. But it is surrounded by misconceptions – not least that it is only for the very wealthy. Many wealthy individuals *have* invested in woodland because of its tax benefits; in recent years, however, the interest in it has widened. To cater for this, some collective investment plans have been devised to appeal to those investors who wish to invest modest amounts.

The basics of forestry as a long-term investment are pretty easy to understand. They centre on one simple fact: trees grow, and become more valuable the larger they get. Buy a parcel of young forestland, and if you sit on it for long enough the trees on it will increase in size and its value should go up. Eventually you will be able to harvest some of the trees and sell the timber. Or you can buy an already mature plantation and harvest the crop from day one.

The attractions of forestry as an investment are enhanced (in the UK at least) by the tax advantages it possesses, which will be covered later in this chapter. Suffice to say at this point that forestry can be used to mitigate inheritance tax, and also to generate tax-free income and capital gains. It is effectively a tax-free investment.

In the rest of the chapter we'll look in more detail at the basics of forestry and why it can be a valid alternative investment, its tax advantages, the long-term returns that can be made from it, and some of the pitfalls that investors need to avoid.

Basics

The UK was once covered with forests, but the industrial revolution and subsequent eras led to wholesale clearance of forestland. This proceeded to the point where, at the turn of the 20th century, only about 5% remained under woodland. The figure now is around 12%. Much of this reforestation has occurred since World War II, as successive governments have tried to encourage the commercial timber industry. The state-owned Forestry Commission dates from 1919.

Most of the private sector forestry established since the war is in Wales, Northern England and Scotland. It is predominantly of Sitka spruce, a perennially productive and hardy species. The outlays of that period were made because investment in forestry then attracted an immediate income tax deduction, rather as do Enterprise Zone Trusts and Enterprise Investment Schemes now. This concession ended in 1988, although sizeable tax benefits remain. These include grants originally designed to compensate investors for this loss of income tax relief. The size of the forest market potentially available for outside investment was also boosted from 1980 onwards when some Forestry Commission properties were sold off, although this source of supply has now dried up.

The current UK figure of 12% for forest coverage compares with an average of 31% forestation across the EU and much higher percentages (around 60%) in countries like Finland and Sweden. The EU currently produces only 25% of its timber requirements, compared to abundant self-sufficiency in food, although the enlarged 25-member EU will be 95% self-sufficient. The EU and individual member governments support the forestry industry with tax breaks and grants, recognising that there is both an economic case for supporting forestry and to encourage its role of sustaining rural development. Interestingly, forestry falls outside the scope of the Treaty of Rome: most EU grants derive from the environmental benefits conferred by forestry, or from taking land out of conventional farming.

Scandinavia is indelibly associated in people's minds as the home of forestry, but in fact the climate for growing trees in the UK is superior to Scandinavia and among the best in the world. It is on a par with Chile and bettered only by New Zealand. Trees in Scotland, for example, on average put on 16 cubic metres of growth per hectare per year, compared with around five cubic metres in Russia and Canada and seven or eight in Scandinavia and the USA. It is this strong growth that underpins any investment in UK forestry. It does, of course, also underline that forestry is a naturally renewable resource.

The returns investors can earn from forestry as an alternative investment are therefore reasonably predictable. They are a function of the maturity and quality of the woodland you own, timber prices, and the tax breaks and grants available. Commercial timber in the UK takes about 40 years to mature fully. Where, in this cycle, an investor might buy in, governs the price paid per hectare, as well as the timing and scale of the income that can be extracted. Whether an investor buys an immature plantation or a mature forest depends on the desired time horizon and investment objectives. Forests are normally divided into four categories: young (up to ten years old); mid rotation (11-20 years old); semi mature (21-30 years old) and mature (31 years and older). They are also split into different yield classes. The yield class measures their general productivity in terms of the incremental growth per year and their consequent income-earning potential. Yield class in turn depends on species, soil fertility, rainfall, the topography of the site, and several other natural influences. Because it is hard to predict early in their life how productive a particular new plantation is going to be, there is sometimes the opportunity to buy young potentially high yielding crops at 'average' prices. The investor may then benefit from an uplift in values as the yield class of the woodland becomes more evident.

Other factors affect the price of forests. The larger a forest, the cheaper it will tend to be per hectare. A typical difference might be £2000 per hectare for a parcel under 50 hectares, but perhaps £1600 per hectare for a forest of more than 200 hectares. Small woodlands, classified as being less than 25 hectares (around 60 acres), tend to be valued also for their amenity value and sometimes for their sporting potential. Prices of small woodlands vary considerably by region. In the UK, for example, prices are highest in the South East and Central England and lowest in South Wales. Location and proximity to large markets also has a significant impact on the price of larger forest properties. Again in the UK, the West Country, the Welsh Marches, Northumberland and Southern Scotland are favoured areas. Finally, tree species go in and out of fashion. So investors need to make sure that the forest they buy contains timber that the market will want when harvested. Sitka spruce, Douglas fir and larch are perennial favourites.

UK Tax Benefits From Forestry

The heyday of UK investing in forestry was between the end of World War II and 1988. During that period higher rate taxpayers received an immediate tax deduction for investment in forestry, which made it highly attractive. The benefit was similar, as said, to the tax concession that applies at present to investment in Enterprise Investment Schemes (EIS). But forestry then was more attractive than EIS is now, because returns from it were essentially more predictable. The abolition of the Schedule D/Schedule B system in 1988 removed this benefit, but despite this forestry can be an extremely tax-efficient investment.

The current benefits from forestry investment come in several different areas.

Income tax

Income from sales of standing or felled timber, and grants received from the Forestry Commission under the Woodland Grant Scheme, are currently free from income tax. Grants can be awarded for the maintenance and restocking of woodland as well as other activities such as deer control, recreational development and community work. What this means is that forestry can generate significant tax-free income. Moreover, because of the flexibility inherent in forestry (more trees can be cut down one year, and fewer the next), this income can be used to form part of wider tax planning goals.

Capital gains tax (CGT)

Any increase in the value of standing timber in commercial woodlands is not subject to capital gains tax, although the land on which it stands, and any building in the property, does fall into the normal CGT regime. There may, however, be opportunities for rollover relief if new planting is being contemplated.

Inheritance tax (IHT)

For many investors the biggest draw to investing in forestry is the exemption from inheritance tax. This arises because woodland managed on a commercial basis is eligible for 100% Business Property Relief from inheritance tax provided it is held for more than two years. Amenity woodland not managed on a commercial basis may attract Agricultural Property Relief, although the scale of this relief depends on circumstances and could be as little as 50%. This particularly attracts present-day investors because the rise in the value of residential property has brought many more ordinary individuals into the inheritance tax bracket for the first time, and so prompted a search for inheritance tax planning options that allow them to pass on their assets, untaxed, to their children. While benefits like this are a potent attraction, it is also important that individual investors do not get completely carried away by them. Other simpler means, such as trusts, can be used to minimise or eliminate IHT for those with relatively modest estates. It is an old investment adage that you should not let the tax break drive the investment decision. In other words, if an investor is thinking about forestry as a potential investment, the decision should be based on its attractions as an alternative asset and the returns it can make. Any tax breaks should be treated as an additional bonus.

A forestry investment needs to make sense in the context of the size of an investor's other assets and the size and asset allocation of the rest of their portfolio. A direct investment in forestry can demand sizeable capital and it should not form a disproportionate percentage of an overall investment portfolio simply because the tax treatment is favourable. Rather like property, forestry has the drawback that it is a 'lumpy' asset and one that lacks immediate liquidity. This is much less true of some other categories of alternative asset, such as coins or stamps, which can be sold through a dealer relatively quickly if there is an urgent need for an investor to raise cash. Investors should bear in mind also that tax benefits can be changed over time. Although governments have consistently wished to foster forestry through the use of tax concessions, there is no guarantee that arrangements will remain precisely as they are over the time-horizon demanded by an investment of this sort. It is also true that a later removal of a tax concession might affect the demand for the type of forest which an investor may have acquired, and therefore have a subsequent adverse impact on its value. Having said that, the beauty of a forestry investment is that the ultimate exit route could simply be to fell the timber and sell it. And it's worth remembering that the IHT tax concession is not specific to forestry but relates to relief given on business properties as a whole, which it is most unlikely any future government would remove entirely.

Remember that the tax benefits in the main apply only to woodland that is operated on a *commercial* basis. Buying a few acres of woodland from your local farmer for amenity reasons will not produce the tax benefits described earlier. To derive the benefits, an investor needs to demonstrate that it is a commercial operation, by having it professionally managed, keeping proper records, applying for and receiving grants, and registering for VAT. All of this means that the capital outlay required to buy an appropriately sized parcel, and the administrative complexities of dealing with it, may be more than some investors want to commit. It may entail an investment that is too large, relative to their other assets and investments, to be a prudent diversification. Only the individual investor and their advisors can make the decision on whether or not this is the case.

The Right Alternative Asset for You?

Alternative investing is, as I have said elsewhere in this book, very much a matter of finding categories that suit an individual investor, their interests, their appetite for risk, the returns they seek and (in some cases) their tax position. Forestry is no different. Much of the early private investment in forestry was driven by the generous tax breaks available. Though these have lessened somewhat, this remains the case. But if an investor is contemplating an investment like this, it helps to have an appreciation of woodland as an amenity, and an interest in conservation, to derive full satisfaction from it. The economics of the timber industry and the outlook for timber prices are important, if more mundane, considerations.

We can look at all of these aspects in a bit more detail before moving on. It is also important to look in detail at the supply and demand background underpinning forestry investment, and at the mechanics of how to invest. For now let's take a look at the basic requirements investors must consider in evaluating if forestry investment is worthwhile.

Capital requirements

Adequate capital is a must. While it is possible to invest in some collective investment schemes that have a small minimum investment level, most serious forestry investors buy a direct interest in a forest. Broadly speaking, investors get what they pay for: an income generating forest will be worth more per hectare than an immature one, where the trees have several years to go before some can be harvested. Location, access and soil fertility govern value as well. Forests can be bought for as little as £30,000 but prices of worthwhile investments are often much higher than this. Investors have to bear in mind too that there are annual running costs to meet, although these are modest as a percentage of the total value of the investment.

Calculating the amount an investor might have available to invest in this way depends both on the size of his or her conventional investment portfolio, and also on the amount they might wish to put into other alternative investment areas. As always, investors should aim for diversity, and not to have one category dominating all the others. If an investor had an investment portfolio of £1 million, then a forest worth £100,000 might be a sensible investment. If the total portfolio was worth less than £1 million, then it might be necessary to look to collective investment to get a stake in forestry, or indeed avoid it altogether.

The current cyclical position of forestry

A large part of the return investors get from a forestry investment can depend on the movement in timber prices. In general terms, timber demand usually exceeds supply on a global scale. Much of the UK demand for timber is satisfied from imports. Economic growth increases the demand. It follows that the price of good quality timber, an area in which the UK excels, should rise in the long term. This is crucial. Investors need to have confidence that timber prices can increase over the longer term. This is not an investment that can be made simply to take advantage of a short-term imbalance between demand and supply. If an investor commits to an investment in forestry, it has to be for the long haul, and an absolute minimum of five years.

Using the tax breaks

With the proviso that the investment must be held for two years, for UK taxpayers putting assets into forestry and keeping them there means that they will not be counted as part of their taxable estate on their death. For an investment in forestry to be worthwhile from this standpoint, UK investors need to have, or expect to have when they die, an estate of at least £300,000 (£600,000 for a married couple or widow/widower), including the value of their house and any other stock market and tangible investments. Investing capital in excess of this figure in forestry in effect enlarges the exemption limit and minimises any future inheritance tax liability for the next generation. It is important to get professional advice regarding your tax siuation.

Forestry can in certain circumstances also satisfy a requirement for tax-free income. This may be important if a UK investor is in, or close to, the highest rate tax band already. Forestry can also yield grant income, which is tax-free, for maintenance works. The grant system is complex and differs by UK region. In general, grants are available for restocking, for opening up forests for public use, and for conservation.

Interested in woodland as an amenity?

Forestry is a great investment for those interested in conservation. There are few things more satisfying than planting trees and watching them grow. Trees absorb carbon dioxide, which makes them a satisfyingly 'green' investment. Would-be investors probably need to have a feel for, and interest in, these aspects to get the most out of an investment in forestry. The satisfaction of an investor being able to visit and walk in their own piece of woodland should not be underestimated. It is tangible evidence of the quality and durability of the investment.

Negative factors

High winds and forest fires can devastate woodland, although both of these can be insured against and are rare. Pests (such as the pine weevil, which attacks young trees) can be a problem, although attentive management of the woodland can minimise the risk of infestation. Most foresters will spray against pine weevil as a matter of course. If forests suffer storm damage there is no statutory obligation to restock. But if an investor-owned forest suffers a fire, restocking is obligatory; and if the forest is not properly insured, the investor will need to provide funds to cover this.

Annual costs

There are also ongoing costs to fund in the form of annual management fees to cover the services of a forester, and the aforementioned insurance. Management fees are generally in the region of £10 per hectare per year, but other maintenance costs can add a further £30 to £40 per hectare per year. Any planting costs may be offset by grants. Typically, a 100-hectare, 25-year-old forest might cost £4500 a year for management, insurance and routine work.

Prices

Timber *prices* are a big factor in the returns from an investment in forestry. Having a forest that produces a decent amount of tree growth year by year is only one side of the equation. What an investment can realise from selling harvested trees depends ultimately on timber prices. This governs the cash yield from a forest property and in turn the value of the property as a whole. Since there are many areas around the world where timber is grown commercially, this is a function not only of supply and demand but also of sterling's value in the foreign currency markets, especially versus the currencies of other producing countries, such as the euro, the Swedish krona and Canadian dollar. One big problem that forestry investors faced until a few years ago was that timber prices in sterling terms had been very soft. One reason for this is the disintegration of the Soviet Union. This placed many forests in the Baltic States, that were formerly in public ownership, back in private hands, with a very low historic book cost. Forestry in countries like these had also benefited from low labour costs, so actually extracting the timber and getting it to market was cheaper than in the UK. The result was that these countries, desperate for foreign currency, encouraged forest owners to harvest and sell this high-quality timber without being too worried about the prices they realised. The resulting glut of timber meant that timber prices declined for several years. Relative strength of sterling in the foreign currency market didn't help either. In turn, these two factors adversely affected the value of forestry plantations in the UK and elsewhere.

Timber prices did, however, put on something of a spurt from 2005 to 2007, although some of this movement appears to have been due to exchange rate influences, timber prices softening when sterling strengthened and vice versa. Current estimates suggest that sawn timber prices remained stable in the course of 2009, thanks largely to exchange rate movements favouring the home-produced product, although prices of logs have been more affected by influences from the economy after a strong 2008. It is a moot point whether there will be much recovery in either category in 2010. The main bright spot in the demand picture is the market for wood as a biofuel, which has been growing very sharply.

Investors in forestry who plumped for this category of alternative investment at the time of the first edition of this book would have done well. In that publication I suggested that a return to the best levels for timber prices seen in the last six to eight years would provide an uplift of 50-60%, boosting forest freehold prices. This did not prove to be quite the case (prices rose by around 25% between 2004 and 2007). But prices of plantations rose very sharply indeed. This has produced a welcome recovery in total returns from forestry investment. Historically these reached a peak of around a weighted average of 10% in the 1993-96 period and then declined and started to show negative returns for successive three-year periods from 1996 onwards. The 1990s was a particularly bad period. Since then, however, there has been something of a renaissance. According to a report from Tilhill, produced at the turn of 2009, average plantation prices had more than doubled in five years and increased by 52% between 2006 and 2008. Five-year capital growth from existing forests was put at between 125% and 150%. Average prices increased by more than 100% between 2003 and 2008, and when the 5% a year biological growth is added this produces the returns indicated. Activity in the market slowed in 2008, partly due to the absence of a few large transactions in previous years, and also perhaps because forestry was seen as a highly secure income-producing investment. This shortage of property may have had some effect in pushing up prices. There was, however, more woodland coming onto the market in the second half of 2008 and this, together with the sharp fall in timber prices, may have an effect in depressing prices somewhat, as may sales from the Forestry Commission portfolio in both England and Scotland.

Total returns from forestry and timber price movements

	Total return index	Timber price change %	Timber price index
1993	95.5	11.3	111.3
1994	104.9	21.1	134.8
1995	113.8	-5.6	127.2
1996	126.7	-7.5	117.7
1997	131.6	-14.9	100.1
1998	129.7	-37.9	62.2
1999	115.1	-2	61.3
2000	111.7	-9.4	55.5
2001	110.5	-4.4	53.1
2002	105.3	-22.9	41
2003	106.7	-2.1	40.1
2004	116.5	9.2	43.8
2005	133.3	15.1	50.4
2006	160.7	11	55.9
2007	211.4	56.6	87.6
2008	226.2	-28.5	62.6

Source: IPD

Returns

There are no guaranteed returns from forestry, despite the hints dropped by those seeking to sell collective investments based around it.

There have also been big variations in returns between types of property. IPD, for example, quotes variations in return over some three-year periods as ranging from -7% for semi mature forests to +7% for young plantations. That gives an idea of the variations that can exist within what is supposedly thought by many to be a relatively homogeneous investment. The reason for this is the drag effect that falling timber prices have on the older properties that have reached maturity. Similar factors can apply if timber prices rise sharply, as they did in the period to mid 2008 (although they have since fallen back sharply).

As they reach maturity the normal process is for the standing timber to be felled and replaced. The most mature properties are therefore locked into the prevailing timber prices when the time comes to fell it. With younger plantations this 'lock-in' price factor has a much less influential effect on the value of the forest property concerned.

Some investment illustrations about forestry as an investment assume long-term returns in the region of 6% to 8% in real terms. Allowing for inflation at 2% a year suggests money returns in the region of 8-10%. In the past, most forestry experts would have regarded returns such as this as wildly optimistic, although recent experience, which has seen prices rise sharply over a comparatively short period, represent the other side of the coin. Over the longer term, therefore, projected returns of this nature might not be too far away from this target, particularly bearing in mind the underpinning provided by the physical growth in timber (approximately 5% a year) which is also part of the equation.

The central point is that the return an investor makes is dependent to some degree on the timing of a purchase and sale. Prices of forests have been buoyant recently, but timber prices have been in a savage downturn for many months, and this may well work through to plantation prices in the fullness of time.

This table shows the three-year rolling annualised returns from forestry.

Three-year rolling annualised returns from forestry

Period	Weighted average	Top 5%	Bottom 5%
1992-95	4.4	17.2	-7.8
1993-96	9.9	22.5	-5.6
1994-97	7.9	19.3	-3.7
1995-98	4.5	9.9	-6.9
1996-99	-3	6.4	-11.3
1997-00	-5.2	3.9	-13.8
1998-01	-5.1	3.5	-15.4
1999-02	-2.9	7.8	-13.7
2000-03	-1.5	10.7	-11.8
2001-04	1.8	21.6	-8.3
2002-05	8.2	29.2	-4.1
2003-06	14.6	32.4	1.1
2004-07	22	36.7	5.2
2005-08	19.3	35.2	0

Source: IPD

In practice returns like this would be received partly in the form of receipts from harvested timber and partly from an increase in the capital value of the standing timber itself. Income need not be taken if not required, or only enough taken to offset management costs, leaving the rest to benefit from higher timber prices in the future, if that is what is being assumed. Either way, income is not in regular 'lumps' and, with old crops, there is limited flexibility in how it is taken.

A long-term nominal return of 7%, reinvested at the same rate and compounded over 10 years, would produce something in the region of a 100% increase in value.

Returns like this are better than can realistically be achieved in many conventional investments, particularly when the tax advantages are taken into account, although it is worth bearing in mind that while returns at this rate have been seen in the last five years, this cannot be guaranteed to continue into the future given the cyclicality in the price of the underlying product.

How to Invest

There are two options for would-be forestry investors. One is buying direct; the other is owning a stake in forestry through a collective investment scheme.

Buying direct

Forestry is no more and no less than a specialised part of the property market. The process of buying or selling a forest property is essentially no different to buying and selling a house, with similar characteristics at play – the liquidity of the market, for instance, and the time taken to complete legal checks and transfer title. Having said that, there are far fewer forest properties sold each year than is the case in the residential property market. In 2008, the latest period for which figures are available at the time of writing, there were 50 recorded transactions valued in aggregate at some £25 million, according to a report from Tilhill and Savills. The average size of property sold was 135 hectares and the average value per transaction was some £485,000. It should be pointed out that the number of transactions was relatively low in 2008, possibly because forestry was, at a time of financial crisis, seen as a secure investment worth retaining.

The average sale in 2008 was at a price 22% above the guide price set by the agent, suggesting a market with restricted supply. The sale time for a forest property is generally not dissimilar to a conventional residential property, around 15 weeks from initial marketing to completion. The average time taken in 2008 was four months. Stamp duty and agents fees are a fact of life when buying and selling a forest property, just as they are in the residential property market. Agents charge around 2%. Purchasing costs, including legal fees, are generally reckoned at around 4% in total depending on the level of stamp duty to be paid.

The tables later in the chapter show details of the specialist estate agents involved in buying and selling forest properties and those involved in collective investment schemes in forestry.

Forestry-investment schemes

Collective investment schemes that invest in forestry have been designed to permit individuals with smaller amounts of capital to invest in forestry. In total they represent about 20% of the money invested in forestry each year. The idea is that a pool of money is raised from investors and put to work purchasing a range of forest properties. These are managed over the life of the scheme, typically ten years, after which time the scheme is wound up, and the proceeds of the sale of the assets returned to shareholders.

While schemes like this represent a more affordable alternative for many investors, they have some drawbacks not borne by those who choose the direct investment route. The most obvious of these is that ownership is diluted, and you have little or no control over your investment. As a shareholder in a scheme like this, all you own is a share in an unlisted company. The company owns the forest properties. Another issue is that of initial charges involved in setting up the scheme. One scheme of a few years ago had initial charges including commission to intermediaries, professional fees and marketing costs that amounted to 6% of the money raised. Projected returns from schemes like this are not guaranteed and may not be based on realistic assumptions. One scheme that closed recently in the UK projected a nominal return in excess of 8.7% per annum, which seems unrealistically high at least for normal times. Part of the reason was that the illustration was based on assuming an average inflation rate over the period of 3.9%, appreciably higher than the current rate.

The other difficulty with collective investment schemes is that while income can seemingly roll up inside the scheme tax-free, when the scheme is wound up the proceeds fall within the capital gains tax regime as far as the shareholder in a scheme is concerned. Gains may possibly be sheltered by the normal annual exemption and by taper relief, which would amount to 40% if the investment were to be held for the full ten years, but this tax aspect does reduce the attractiveness of schemes like this relative to direct ownership.

There are also schemes that are offered occasionally which involve investing in forestry outside the UK, notably in Ireland. These have suspiciously high projected returns and low minimum investment levels and promise a tax-free lump sum at the end of the investment period. This is despite the fact that forestland prices are much higher in Ireland; roughly five times the UK norm. It doesn't seem to add up. The reason is that Irish forestland prices have been boosted because of entitlement to EU subsidies.

Projected returns from offshore schemes can be a little fanciful. A recent scheme, for example, had a projected rate of return in excess of 9%, but a minimum investment level of €750. UK residents need to beware of schemes like this, because if income or capital distributions are brought onshore they will be assessed for tax.

If an individual is thinking of investing in collective investment schemes related to forestry, it will be necessary to check out the tax consequences of an investment like this with a professional advisor. Remember that, because schemes like this are largely unregulated (although promoters need FSA clearance), independent financial advisors are not allowed to actively promote them.

US forestry REITs and listed timber funds may represent an alternative way in, albeit with hefty upfront charges, although such investments are subject to the vagaries of the stock market and hence do not really represent true alternative investment mediums within the scope of this handbook.

Where to Go for More Information

The following is a summary of the main places where investors can find useful information about forestry investing on the web. The sites are grouped according to the main themes covered in previous sections.

General (including investment)

Bidwells (www.bidwells.co.uk) provides a whole range of services, including the purchase of woodland and investment appraisal.

CKD Galbraith (www.forestry-scotland.co.uk) is an independent property consultant operating throughout Scotland. The forestry department has a list of forests for sale, which can be accessed by emailing the site.

Ethical Investments (www.ethicalinvestments.co.uk) is aimed at the smaller investor. It will assist with the establishment and management of co-operatives and Limited Liability Partnerships for forestry both UK and worldwide.

Forest Enterprises Limited (www.forestenterprises.co.nz), established in 1972, has investment opportunities available on the East Coast of New Zealand's North Island. The site contains a great deal of useful information on forestry investment for new investors.

Forestry Investment Management (www.fimltd.co.uk) has a list of woodlands available for purchase either through direct ownership or unregulated collective investment schemes (UCITS). The company offers a full investment management service, as well as maintaining lists of properties available for direct purchase.

Fountains Forestry (www.fountainsforestry.co.uk) provides advice, consultancy, management and brokerage services in the UK, the USA and internationally.

Agents and advisors

Entity	Web address	Main location	Email address	Telephone	Category
Bidwells	www.bidwells.co.uk	Cambridge	Through site	01223 559210	Agent
CKD Galbraith	www.forestry-scotland.co.uk	Scotland	On site	01463 245387	Advisor
Ethical Investments	www.ethicalinvestments.co.uk	Sheffield	dav@ethicalinvestments.co.uk	0114 2368 168	Agent
Forest Enterprises	www.forestenterprises.co.nz	NZ	pinemail@forestenterprises.co.nz	64 6 370 6360	Agent
Fountains	www.fountainsforestry.co.uk	Banbury	alan.guy@fountainsforestry.co.uk	01295 750 000	Agent
Savills	www.savills.co.uk	UK	On site	01356 628 600	Agent
Greenwood	www.greenwood-management.com	Ireland	info@greenwood-management.com	353 1452 0326	Agent
Highfield Forestry Ltd	www.highfieldforestry.com	Scotland	info@highfieldforestry.com	01738 442 903	Agent
Irish Forestry	www.irish-forestry.ie	Ireland	info@irish-forestry.ie	353 1 284 1777	Advisor
John Clegg	www.johnclegg.co.uk	Oxford	thame@johnclegg.co.uk	01844 215 800	Agent
New Zealand Overseas Investment Offices	www.linz.govt.nz	NZ	info@linz.govt.nz	64 4 460 0110	Advisor
UPM Tilhill	www.upm-tilhill.com	Stirling	info@upm-tilhill.com	01786 435 000	Agent

Highfield Forestry (www.highfieldforestry.com) based in Perth, Scotland provides advice, management and acquisition services throughout the UK.

Irish Forestry Service (IFS) Asset Management (www.ifsam.ie), established in 1997, launches two forestry funds each year, details of which can be found on the site.

John Clegg (www.johnclegg.co.uk) is a firm of chartered surveyors specialising in the forestry market. It does not undertake forestry management but does offer independent investment advice by way of investment analysis and cash flow appraisals. The firm has offices in Thame, Edinburgh and Monmouth.

Oxigen Investments (www.oxigen-investments.com) specialises in ethical and sustainable forestry investments. It offers various investment options including direct purchase, agro-forestry, open-ended investment funds and pension-related investments. Oxigen currently has forests in Sri Lanka, Costa Rica, Paraguay and Argentina.

Phaunos Timber Fund (www.phaunostimber.com) is a closed-ended investment fund based in Guernsey and is the first UK-quoted timber fund.

Savills (www.savills.co.uk) has specialist consultants to advise on all commercial forestry investment and management, including purchase and sale, valuation, taxation and planting and maintenance. All of its experts can be contacted by email from the site.

UPM Tilhill (www.upm-tilhill.com) has a wealth of information on forestry as an investment, including the tax advantages, market reports and a list of forests for sale. UPM Tilhill can supply site assessment reports, valuations, investment appraisals, surveys, negotiate the purchase, and then provide full ongoing management support.

Forestry REITs

A number of real estate investment trusts (REITs) in the USA invest exclusively in forestry. A selection of these are shown in the following table. As in the UK, REITs distribute most of their income in the form of dividends to shareholders. Most of those listed below have yields in the 5%-7% region. Weyerhaeuser – the largest US forest products company – announced in December 2009 that it will convert to a REIT in the course of 2010.

Funds and REITs

Entity	Web address	Main location	Email address	Telephone	Category
Forestry Investment Management	www.fimltd.co.uk	Burford, Oxon	fim@fimltd.co.uk	01451 844 655	Investment funds
Phaunos Timber Fund	www.phaunostimber.com	Guernsey	On site	01481 722 260	Listed investment fund
Plum Creek Timber	www.plumcreek.com	USA	info@plumcreek.com	206 467 3600	Listed investment fund (REIT)
Potlatch	www.potlatchcorp.com	USA	On site	509 835 1500	Listed investment fund (REIT)
Rayonier	www.rayonier.com	USA	info@rayonier.com	904 357 9100	Listed investment fund (REIT)

Plum Creek Timber Company (www.plumcreek.com) is based in Seattle and owns approximately 7.4 million acres of timberland in the US.

Potlatch Corporation (www.potlatchcorp.com) owns and manages timberland located in Arkansas, Idaho, Minnesota and Oregon.

Rayonier (www.rayonier.com) owns, leases or manages timberland in the USA, and in Australia and New Zealand through a joint venture.

Information and data

The Confederation of Forest Industries (www.confor.org.uk) has information on the timber markets, timber products and forest services, together with information on topics such as climate change and the timber supply market.

The Forestry Commission (www.forestry.gov.uk) is the UK government department responsible for the production and expansion of British forests and woodlands, and supervises grant schemes and felling licences.

The Forest Industry Network (www.forestindustry.com) has links to companies offering forest investment in Canada and the USA.

The Forest Research Group (www.forestresearchgroup.com) is a US company that provides services such as timber price forecasting, portfolio analysis and forest economics and policy studies. It also publishes a quarterly newsletter dealing with topics in forest economics and timberland investment.

The Forestry Stewardship Council (www.fsc.org) is an internationally-recognised standard-setting organisation whose purpose is to improve forest management worldwide. The site has a resource centre which may be of interest.

The Institute of Chartered Foresters (www.charteredforesters.org) is a UK organisation that sets standards for professional foresters. The site has a list of members in consultancy practice that can offer services such as valuing forestry properties, negotiating sales and purchases, management of forests, and litigation and arbitration. Chartered foresters are the only professionally qualified foresters and arborists in the UK and must have a minimum of five years study and experience to qualify. Many have degrees in forestry.

Information and data

Entity	Web address	Main location	Email address	Telephone	Category
Confederation of Forest Industries	www.confor.org.uk	Edinburgh	Through site	0131 240 1410	Information
Forestry Commission	www.forestry.gov.uk	UK	On site	Many on site	Information
Forest Industry Network	www.forestindustry.com	Canada	Through site	1 877 755 2762	Information
Forestry Journal	www.forestryjournal.co.uk	Dumfries	Through site	01387 702 272	Information
Forest Research Group	www.forestresearchgroup.com	Massachusetts	jlutz@forestresearchgroup.com	978 432 1794	Information
Forestry Stewardship Council (The)	www.fsc.org	Germany	fsc@fsc.org	49 228 367 660	Information
Investment Property Databank (IPD)	www.ipdindex.co.uk	London	enquiries@ipd.com	020 7336 200	Data
Malaysian Timber Council	www.mtc.com.my	Malaysia	Through site	603 9281 1999	Information
New Zealand Ministry of Agriculture and Forestry	www.maf.govt.nz	NZ	info@maf.govt.nz	64 4 894 0100	Information
Smallwoods	www.smallwoods.org.uk	Telford	Through site	01952 432 769	Information
Timber Trades Journal	www.ttjonline.com	Sidcup	On site	020 8269 7844	Publication
Food and Agriculture Organization of the United Nations	www.fao.org/forestry	New York	On site	n/a	Information

The International Tropical Timber Organization site (www.itto.int) has extensive information and publishes international statistics on global production and trade of timber with an emphasis on the tropics.

The Ministry of Agriculture and Forestry (New Zealand) (www.maf.govt.nz) publishes production and trade statistics together with various regularly updated reports on the New Zealand forestry industry.

The New Zealand Forest Owners' Association (www.nzfoa.org.nz) publishes an online forestry bulletin, together with facts and figures on the forestry industry in New Zealand and many useful links.

The New Zealand Overseas Investment Office (www.linz.govt.nz) assesses applications from overseas investors who intend to make investments in New Zealand.

The Small Woods Association (www.smallwoods.org.uk) has a guide to planning legislation and small woodlands, together with other articles which may be useful.

The following miscellaneous information sites may also be of interest

Forestry Journal (www.forestryjournal.co.uk) covers all aspects of the forestry industry.

Investment Property Databank (www.ipd.com) releases annual performance figures for UK forestry calculated from a sample of private sector coniferous plantations, and charts long-term financial returns. The data, which is contributed by a dozen firms in the industry, is available on subscription. Savills and Tilhill also issue annual reports on the forestry market and timber price trends (see www.upm-tilhill.com for more information).

The Malaysian Timber Council (www.mtc.com.my) promotes the development and growth of the Malaysian timber industry. The site has statistics which may be of interest.

The Royal Forestry Society (www.rfs.org.uk) is a charitable institution with extensive information on woodland management, trees and timber.

Timber Trades Journal (www.ttjonline.com) is an industry publication.

The Food and Agriculture Organization of the United Nations (www.fao.org/forestry) is a good source of information on the world's forests.

The Timber Trade Federation (www.ttf.co.uk) is the leading trade association for the UK timber industry.

Forestry

Associations

Entity	Web address	Main location	Email address	Telephone	Category
Institute of Chartered Foresters	www.charteredforesters.org	Edinburgh	Through site	0131 240 1425	Association
International Tropical Timber Organization	www.itto.int	Japan	itto@itto.or.jp	45 223 1110	Association
New Zealand Forest Owners' Association	www.nzfoa.org.nz	NZ	nzfoa@nzfoa.org.nz	64 4 473 4769	Association
Royal Forestry Society	www.rfs.org.uk	Tring	frshq@rfs.org.uk	01422 822 028	Association
UK Timber Trade Federation	www.ttf.co.uk	London	ttf@ttf.co.uk	020 3205 0067	Association

7.
Gold

Of all tangible investments, gold is often seen as the ultimate. It has been recognised for centuries that its indestructibility and scarcity make it an ideal store of wealth. Currencies may come and go and stock markets may rise and fall. But gold, so the theory goes, is a permanent asset that will hold its value come what may. This is not quite the whole truth. Those who bought gold at the last peak in its price in the late 1970s would have not only seen its value decline in real terms but missed out on the bull market in stocks in the 1980s and 1990s and the subsequent attractive returns seen in bonds. Conversely, those who bought when the UK and other governments were selling gold reserves at an average $270 an ounce between 1999 and 2002 have seen the price quadruple in the space of less than a decade. In a way, though, this illustrates the point. Gold's lack of price performance in a raging equity bull market and its resilience in bear markets is its attraction. It is one of the few assets that moves counter to the stock market. Nor does it depend for its value on the spending power of collectors, in the way that coins, stamps or rare books do.

It is, as one expert noted, "the only truly divisible asset that is not someone else's liability". It also appeals to those with a jaundiced view of the political process and the ability of governments to manage economies. As Herbert Hoover said: "We have gold, because we cannot trust governments." Others have described it as a "small, globally accepted currency, but one that cannot be printed". Because of these characteristics, gold is much loved by the more apocalyptic commentators – particularly those who see geopolitical uncertainty continuing indefinitely, a wholesale loss of confidence in fiat currencies and a return to much higher levels of inflation. Remember that gold last hit its zenith in the late 1970s, when inflation was rising and the world had suffered two major oil price shocks.

This time around the gold price surged as a result of the crisis of confidence in banking in 2008, and because of concerns that the vast sums being spent on propping up banks and other institutions, and in administering fiscal stimulus to the economy, would lead to much higher than normal levels of inflation in a few years time. The effects of monetary policy and fiscal stimulus are, after all, hard to reverse rapidly, and in any event the reversal is likely to prove unpopular with voters. Conspiracy theorists may also suspect that a period of inflation may be one way – perhaps the only way – that the US and UK economies can escape from the crushing burden of household and public sector debt that has built up in recent years.

There are those that argue that, spectacular though its performance has been of late, the rise in the gold price has much further to go. For gold to return to the equivalent of the peak price seen in the late 1970s would, in inflation-adjusted terms, require its price to rise to more than $2000 an ounce, roughly double the current level. More sober analysts suggest, however, that since the price only attained this level on a single day, it is better to take a moving average price of gold around that period, which leads to a conclusion, according to data from the World Gold Council, that the true and sustainable inflation-adjusted price is around $1200 an ounce.

This chapter looks at the background to investing in gold and other precious metals, and at how to acquire and hold the metal. For investors of modest means this will almost certainly be in the form of bullion coins, but there are other ways too. Note that collectable coins are a quite different market. These were covered in a separate chapter.

Basics

Price movements

The value of gold waxes and wanes over time but ultimately it holds its value in real terms. The chart shows the real value of gold in the US since 1900. This shows it maintaining its real value over this 100-year-plus period. The same is also true over 200 years.

Gold price since 1900 © World Gold Council

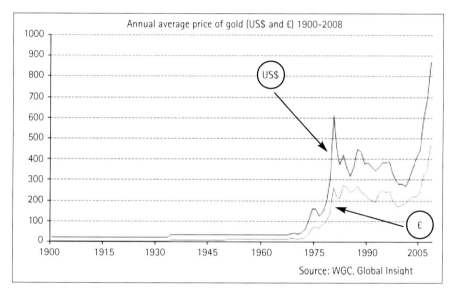

The particularly sharp rise and subsequent fall in the price of gold between 1970 and 2002, and its more recent appreciation, is untypical. There have been many periods when gold has exhibited only limited amounts of volatility. Back in 2003, just prior to the first version of this book being published, I recorded that "gold's value is currently close to the lowest point it has reached in real terms during the last century, and in terms of the price of stocks, bonds and property it is widely acknowledged to be almost as cheap as it has ever been. This argues strongly for investment in gold as a portfolio-diversification right now." This statement has been proved correct by subsequent events. And the potential for further price rises to return to a more normal inflation-adjusted price for gold, argues that even now it may not be too late to invest – despite the fact that the potential for really spectacular gains has probably passed.

Scarcity and sources

The strength of gold as a store of value lies in its physical characteristics, and its scarcity, which in turn is linked to the difficulties involved in extracting it. Gold can be melted down to change its form and shape, but once extracted and refined is virtually indestructible. Because of its density, all of the gold ever mined in the world – about 150,000 tonnes – would fit into a cube with sides of 20 metres, if refined to 24-carat purity, or in an easier-to-visualise double Olympic-size swimming pool. Virtually all of the gold ever mined is still in existence in some form, whether in the form of bullion bars, bullion coins, jewellery, or as an industrial component.

Mining gold is difficult. It often takes place in politically unstable countries. Even South Africa, for many years the world's largest producer, extracts less than 300 tonnes of the metal a year. World production is currently around 2,300 tonnes a year, with scrap gold adding a further 1000 tonnes a year to total gold supply. Even the more productive mines in South Africa produce only 8-10 grammes per tonne of ore, meaning that it takes three tonnes of ore to produce one ounce of gold. Production costs vary from mine to mine and from country to country, but are generally reckoned to be around $300 per ounce before taking exploration and production costs into account. For this reason, mining for gold becomes uneconomic below a certain price level, generally reckoned to be in the region of $400 per ounce after exploration and development costs have been added in. This puts a floor under the spot price of gold, which is set in the free market and underpinned by an active market in gold futures.

From wedding rings to futures markets

Annual demand for gold for jewellery and industrial use is roughly 3000 tonnes but has been even higher than this in relatively recent times. In normal times it is appreciably more than is currently produced each year, although the recent high price has stunted demand from jewellers. The other major influences on the market are:

- The position of central banks' gold holdings
- The degree to which gold mining companies are using the futures market to lock in prices they receive for future production

- The scale of gold flowing into financial institutions to back up investor demand for exchange-traded funds that track the gold price, a very big factor in recent years
- The views of traders expressed through futures markets and the 'souk'

Total annual demand for gold in 2008 was in the region of 3800 tonnes. Central banks have been large holders of gold since the 19th century, and currently account for a fifth of existing stocks. Central bank independence and a more commercial approach to managing gold and convertible currency reserves has meant that some central banks have been reducing the size of their official stockholdings. This is principally because the gold they hold in reserve yields no return, although you could criticise this as being short-sighted and argue that gold should be a strategic reserve for any central bank. That said, the process of reserve adjustment now appears mostly complete and the banks concerned have reaffirmed that they continue to see gold as a major reserve asset for the foreseeable future, more particularly since they have seen that earlier sales of gold at the 'wrong' price have been a source of embarrassment and provided ammunition for political opponents. Some government sales are likely in the future, but they should take place in a predictable and strictly controlled way. Less than 300 tonnes of gold was sold in 2008 by central banks. It is also possible that official buying of gold by the Chinese central bank may neutralise the effect of any sales from Western governments or supranational entities. At the time major sales were undertaken, the fact that central banks telegraphed their intention to sell gold in the open market meant that the price moved against them in advance – hardly the shrewdest of moves. Central bank selling was arguably responsible for the lows in the gold price around the $250 mark seen in the early years of this decade.

Forward selling of mining output also had a significant effect on the gold price in times past. It generally placed a ceiling on the price, above which additional supply came on to the market, driven by unwinding forward sales. The general consensus is that sales from these sources have now largely worked through the system and the surge in prices has generally led to companies preferring, on the whole to take their chances in the spot market rather than sell forward. Mining companies remain more optimistic than most about the outlook for the gold price, as you might expect. Net producer hedging has subtracted around 300-400 tonnes of gold a year from supply in recent years.

Purchases of bullion by exchange-traded funds (ETFs) that track the gold price have emerged in the last couple of years as a major 'swing' factor in the market, and the trend in the holdings of funds like this, of which there are now several (see the later section in this chapter), is closely watched by traders. Hedge fund positions in gold have also been an important factor in the market in recent years. ETF demand was identified in 2008 by World Gold Council statistics at some 321 tonnes, approximately 15% of demand from all sources.

Demand from Middle Eastern and Far Eastern gold souks, in turn reflecting demand from the man in the street in these countries, is often underestimated as an influence on the price. Demand channelled through the souks has over the last ten years taken an estimated 77% of world gold jewellery output (about 45% of the total physical off-take of gold). Despite being what are sometimes inaccurately viewed as primitive street markets, the gold dealers in the souks are plugged into the international market just as closely as if they operated in London or New York.

Golden dollar

Finally, by convention, gold is always priced in US$. Since gold holds its value come what may, weakness in the dollar by definition is likely to lead to an increase in the US dollar gold price. For those investing in other countries, both the exchange rate of the home currency versus the dollar and the gold price itself needs to be monitored. At times of extreme uncertainty both gold and the dollar are viewed as safe havens, which tends to produce a particularly benign price performance for any investors who have bought gold in a currency viewed as less strong. The gold price is strong and the dollar is strong, giving a highly positive 'double whammy'.

The Right Alternative Asset for You?

Most investors with a substantial portfolio of assets invested in the stock market should view gold as a sensible diversification into an asset that should move in a way largely uncorrelated with movements in equity and bond prices, and that will hold its value in periods of inflation and crisis. There is no getting away from the fact that gold is 'real money'. But investing in gold requires investors to answer 'yes' to a number of crucial questions.

A long-term investment?

It's hard to say whether or not the gold price will appreciate further this year, next year or the one after that. The price has been strong in recent years, and some investors may consider that future price action may be more muted, even negative. All one can say is that gold has a permanence that can be a source of considerable comfort to investors buffeted by the ups and downs of the stock market. As investment newsletter publisher Bill Bonner observes, "while we cannot predict the future, eventually and always paper currencies disappear and gold remains". Alan Greenspan, in testimony to the US Congress in 2001, said: "In extremis paper money is accepted by nobody and gold is always accepted as the ultimate means of payment."

Capital requirements?

Gold can be bought in amounts as little as $1100 (about £720) for a single one ounce coin, to around $35,000 for a one kilo bar of bullion, and in larger multiples of this. Ten kilos of gold, heavy but easily portable and compact, are worth around $350,000 at current prices and exchange rates. How much you invest in gold depends on how worried you are about the current international situation and the proportion of your overall wealth you want to protect in this way. Buying physical gold usually entails paying a small (non-refundable) premium over the spot price.

Storage and insurance costs?

If an investor wants to hold the gold physically on their own property, then both insurance and security measures, such as installing a safe in which to keep it, are necessary. Alternatively it could be entrusted to a bank safety deposit box or an entitlement to gold purchased in the form of an exchange-traded fund or a certificate from a mint. These, however, are indirect means of ownership that rely on the integrity and permanence of the issuing institution, which in a cataclysm cannot be guaranteed. To be totally safe, investors may feel they need to own gold physically in a place where they can look at it and access to which they can control. Most serious gold investors would say it is worth paying for this privilege.

Portfolio diversification potential?

Gold has a negative correlation with most other financial assets, and particularly with stock and bond markets. So it brings with it specific risk reduction characteristics that are independent of where its price might stand at any one time. It is an insurance policy against seemingly improbable but, if they occur, highly damaging events. Investors can generally take one of two opposing views. One is that gold's price is too high, that its cost of ownership and lack of income is a negative factor, and that financial crises will blow over, and therefore that a recovery in stocks and a diminution in the gold price are the most likely events. The contrary view is that any crisis is far worse even than it appears now, that any stimulus measures will have little effect other than producing inflation, and therefore that gold will come to be increasingly prized by investors.

An apocalyptic view of the future?

Gold is undeniably the right investment for those with an apocalyptic view. If an investor believes the world could collapse into chaos, that paper money will be debased and that even more banks will fail, then gold is the right asset to hold. If an investor believes that there will be lawlessness, anarchy, imposition of exchange controls, and capital flight, then gold is the one sure anchor. This is always provided the investor is confident about being able to keep it safe and secure. It is salutary to remember that in the Middle and Far East gold has been prized as a portable liquid asset for centuries, and that the Chinese and Asian communities have been big buyers of gold in recent years. So for those concerned about currency stability, and willing to bear the charges that are entailed in holding it, gold may well be the right way to diversify.

Returns

Calculating returns from investing in gold is easy. Unlike investing in art, stamps or fine wine, gold is homogeneous, with a single price quoted on an international market every business day. Unlike the market in some other forms of tangible assets, the gold market offers instant liquidity. If investors want to buy or sell they can do so quickly and easily.

The following table shows returns from investing in gold over differing time periods in the past up to 1996.

Returns from investing in gold over various time periods (US$)

Period	Average annual return (%)	Maximum annual return (%)	Minimum annual return (%)	Standard deviation (%)
1968-1996	4.21	77.6	-28.8	10.5
1896-1996	0.60	77.6	-28.7	4.5
1796-1996	0.31	77.6	-28.7	2.5
1596-1996	0.04	72.2	-29.7	1.4

The table shows that gold has always exhibited a positive return over whatever timescale you might choose, suggesting that there is a strong tendency for it to revert to the long-term mean value. Its price has, however, been getting steadily more volatile over the years, as indicated by the standard deviation. Recent years have seen the sharpest extremes of year on year price movements.

The simplest example of the durability and power of gold as an investment comes if you calculate the return from the day in 1971 when President Nixon was forced to cut the link between gold and the dollar. This removed the shackles that had held the gold price artificially low, or the dollar artificially high. The day before Nixon's decision an investor could have bought an ounce of gold for $35. Today, 38 years later, it sells for 26 times that amount. That is an annual rate of return of exactly 9% compound.

The problem with this calculation is its starting point. Gold increased sharply in value during the 1970s precisely because its price had been held down artificially before then. The price of gold had not changed in relation to the dollar prior to that since FDR raised the dollar price of gold from $20.67 an ounce to $35.00 in 1934, 37 years previously. Even so, gold's strongly positive price action in recent years can scarcely be denied. In the last decade, returns from gold have averaged an annual 12% compound.

Academic research commissioned by the World Gold Council some years ago showed a somewhat different picture when the returns from gold are compared with those of other types of asset. The results are shown in the next table. The data also goes up to 1996.

Risk and return of trading gold versus other investments (in US$)

Category	Year	Average annual return (%)	Maximum annual return (%)	Minimum annual return (%)	Standard deviation (%)
Stocks	1896-1968	6.05	55.8	-37.8	4.8
	1968-1996	6.29	34.2	-34.4	7.2
LT bonds	1896-1968	0.12	52.3	-36	3
	1968-1996	3.70	45.6	-16.1	8.3
T-Bills	1896-1968	0.02	42.6	-32.7	2.9
	1968-1996	2.43	9.9	-10.9	2.7
Gold	1896-1968	0.33	58.1	-27.2	3.6
	1968-1996	4.21	77.6	-28.7	10.5

The results undermine gold's image as a stable store of value. In fact, though stocks and shares have better returns over almost all time periods, and though gold beats holding bonds and cash, the returns seen from gold have been more volatile than most other categories. But this is not strictly a weakness; it has its basis in what in fact makes gold a good counter-cyclical asset. This data excludes the later stages of the bull market, the following bust, and subsequent recovery. It nonetheless highlights the big plus point for investment in gold – that its returns come when stock markets are doing badly, and that this is precisely when investors do need something different in their portfolios. In other words, gold's returns may not be intrinsically stable in themselves, but they tend to occur in such a way that they offset the damage done to an investor's wealth when stocks and bonds are in bear market conditions.

How to Invest

There are several different ways of getting exposure to gold. We need, however, to distinguish between holding physical gold on the one hand, and a right to a specific amount of gold or an economic exposure to its price on the other. Those with an apocalyptic view of life will insist on holding gold in physical form in a place where they can get easy access to it. If what an investor wants is simply a convenient, hassle-free way of holding it, and the right to claim a specific physical amount of gold stored at a trusted institution, then there are other alternatives. And if all the investor wants is an economic exposure with no physical complications, then there are yet more alternatives that can be pursued.

Physical bullion and coins

Assuming an investor has either a safety deposit box or a heavy-duty safe in which to store a physical investment in gold, what's the best way of buying the physical metal?

It depends in large measure on how much is to be invested. Gold bulls will generally say that it is advisable to have around 10% of a portfolio represented by the gold 'anchor'. Bearing in mind that many investors considering a move of this sort may have substantial equity in the house they live in, and other savings and investments as well, a gold investment in the kilos rather than ounces might well be contemplated. At 32.15 troy ounces to the kilo, at the current price (Q2 2010) a kilo of gold costs approximately $35,000, making $1 million equate to 28 kilos of bullion.

There is a small premium payable over the cost of the gold by weight in a bar, to cover the cost of manufacture. Larger bars carry a smaller premium than smaller ones. Bullion coins carry a higher premium than bars. A rough guide to the premium on Krugerrands, the most commonly used bullion coin, is that for most dealers in normal times it will be in the region of around 7%, perhaps slightly less if a significant quantity of coins is being purchased. At the time when, at the height of the credit crunch, retail investors were clamouring for gold coins, outstripping the ability of mints to produce them, premiums for gold bullion coins rose sharply.

Most dealers consider gold coins such as Krugerrands as equivalent to circular one-ounce bullion bars. Coins like this (and American Eagles, Canadian Maple Leafs, Chinese Pandas and other variations on the theme) are sometimes available in a range of weights including one ounce, half ounce, quarter ounce and so on. As noted earlier, premiums on coins are generally higher than on bars, but, if bought in significant quantities, the premium on coins can fall to levels comparable to small bars. Premiums on commonly traded coins like Krugerrands are almost always smaller than on the more esoteric ones, which may be harder for a dealer to source. Coins and small bars do, however, have the distinct advantage of divisibility.

Premiums (%) over spot price on gold bullion coins

Type of bullion coin	Premium over spot price (%)
Manx Angels	11
American Eagles	10
Austrian Philharmonics	10
Chinese Pandas	10
Canadian Maple Leafs	9
Krugerrands	8.25

Divisibility is important. It may be at some stage an investor wishes to sell gold to take advantage of a rise in price, or for other reasons. Holding it in the form of coins or small 100 gram bars allows relatively small amounts to be removed and sold as required, without having to sell more than is strictly necessary.

Premiums paid do, however, depend on supply and demand at the time and can fluctuate. Large bars are usually the most efficient way to buy gold, but in certain circumstances coins can be a better investment. The Krugerrand is usually the cheapest to buy of all the one ounce gold coins.

Investors should beware of buying through dealers who send unsolicited mail. These often sell gold at inflated prices designed to catch the unwary. In one instance, gold coins were priced in pounds sterling at the same level as the dollar price, which would result in investors paying roughly 40% more than the correct price. The World Gold Council website (www.gold.org) has a list of bona fide dealers, including large UK players such as Baird & Co and Chard.

Buying sovereigns

Sovereigns are venerable British gold coins and among the most widely collected UK coins worldwide. The first was issued in the reign of Henry VII in 1489, but the modern gold sovereign dates from the reign of George III in 1817 and has remained largely unchanged since then. Sovereigns circulated as currency until 1914, but after that gold coins ceased to circulate in most countries and production was stopped in the 1930s. Production of gold sovereigns as bullion coins restarted in the UK in 1957, although there have been a number of breaks in production since then.

From 1817 onwards all sovereigns have had the same physical characteristics – a diameter of 22.05mm, a weight of 7.98 grams and 91.66% fineness. This equates to an actual gold content of 0.2354 troy ounces. In other words, four sovereigns roughly equate to one Krugerrand. However, many earlier sovereigns had a reverse side with a shield coat of arms, as opposed to the later St George and the Dragon motif. The so-called 'shield-back' sovereigns tend, other things being equal, to sell at a premium to the rest. Early shield-back sovereigns date from the reign of George IV (the first was issued in 1825) up to the 'young head' ones issued in the early years of the reign of Queen Victoria. The St George and the Dragon motif was reintroduced in 1871.

Many sovereigns, especially those issued from the 1930s onwards, are treated as bullion coins, although there are some exceptions. Most sovereigns were produced in the millions and consequently sell at a standard price that reflects their bullion content. Some adjustment is occasionally made for condition. But some sovereigns fetch higher prices. Shield-back sovereigns of most types fetch a significant premium over bullion content, implying some numismatic value. Later St George and the Dragon sovereigns typically sell at or around bullion content with the exception of young head Queen Victoria ones, which fetch a modest premium. Some sovereigns were produced in very small quantities and there were a number of proof issues produced in very small quantities. Coins like this also fetch an appreciable premium over bullion content. There are good quality forgeries of such sovereigns from the George V era (1911 to 1936), so extreme care needs to be taken when buying these. The George VI proof sovereign from 1937 is also considered a particular rarity.

Spink's annual publication *Coins of England & the United Kingdom* contains extensive details of sovereigns, scarce dates and designs for all periods during which they were produced, and all mints at which they were struck. While most sovereigns were struck at the Tower Mint in London, some were produced in Canada, India and Australia from dies delivered from the mint in London. These coins can be identified by a small letter (generally under the design on the reverse of the coins signifying the origin: S for Sydney, M for Melbourne, O for Ottawa and so on).

Rare dates for gold sovereigns

Monarch	Date	Other features
George III	1819	Only 3,574 minted
George IV	1823	Rare in excellent condition
George IV	1825	Rare in excellent condition
George IV	1828	Rare in excellent condition
William IV	1831	Some with die error
William IV	1836	Some with die error
Victoria	1841	Some with die error
Victoria	1848	With 'first head' in year of change to 'second head'
Victoria	1860	Some with die error
Victoria	1862	Some with die error
Victoria	1863	Unusual die number
Victoria	1879	Regarded as very rare
Victoria	1880	Sydney mint with die error
Victoria	1880	Melbourne mint (rare with shield-reverse, ditto 1886 and 1887)
Edward VII	1908	Ottawa mint satin proof (633 minted)
Edward VII	1902	Sydney mint proof
George V	1916	Ottawa mint (6,111 minted)
George V	1917	Considered rare, but often faked
George V	1920	Sydney mint
George V	1922	Sydney mint
George V	1923	Sydney mint
George V	1926	Sydney mint
George V	1923	Pretoria mint proof (655 minted)
George V	1924	Pretoria mint
Edward VIII	1936	Proof (only five proof sets produced)
George VI	1937	Proof (only 5,501 minted)
Elizabeth II	1953	From coronation set (regarded as of highest rarity)
Elizabeth II	1989	500th anniversary of gold sovereign (10,535 minted with special design)

Source: AH Baldwin; Coin News; Spink

There are many instances of rarities being thrown up in the history of sovereigns, and it is these coins which attract collectors and investors, and lead to the coins in question being bought and sold for many times their underlying bullion value. The additional and sometimes substantial numismatic value arises for a number of reasons:

- Restricted minting and consequent rarity (only an estimated nine specimens of the London Mint 1819 sovereigns, for example, and the 1828 date is also scarce).

- Errors in setting dies for coin production. These include full points being omitted, letters printed upside down or in some other incorrect form (inverting a V for an A or vice versa is a frequent example), or in the wrong place, a capital 'I' substituted for a figure 1.

- Changes to die design and different die numbers, some of which are recorded on the coins, but where mintage in certain cases may have been restricted.

- Monarchs with short reigns, where very limited numbers of coins were produced, Edward VIII being the obvious example.

The attraction of sovereigns is that many local coin auctions will throw up examples for sale, and these will typically be bid for up to an amount that, with the buyer's premium factored in, equates to the price of the bullion content. This is something of an advantage in that dealers will typically charge a significant premium (15% or more in some cases) over bullion value for sovereigns bought 'retail'. Condition matters slightly more for sovereigns than for other bullion coins. 'Extremely fine' and 'uncirculated' examples will fetch a larger premium. This is because there is a collectors' market for sovereigns and condition matters more to those forming a collection.

One attraction of sovereigns for UK investors is that, as sterling currency, sovereigns issued from 1837 onwards are not subject to capital gains tax if their value increases and a profit is made on their sale. This also applies to other UK-issued gold coins, the main ones being gold Britannias.

Buying onshore

Since 2000, gold bought for investment purposes has not attracted VAT in the UK or the rest of the EU, but there are a number of terms and conditions that UK bullion dealers (and those in other countries) apply to purchasers – mainly for anti-money laundering and tax purposes. In the UK, for example, purchasers must provide proof of identity. In addition, the first purchase of gold by any individual of more than £5000, or an aggregate purchase of more than £10,000 of gold in one 12-month period, will be reported to the tax authorities (HM Revenue & Customs in the UK).

Buying offshore

Is this worth thinking about? It depends whether or not you already have an existing offshore bank account. Some investors look to Switzerland for the purchase and storage of precious metals, and specifically to private banks. The private banks are chosen because they provide safety and confidentiality. Many private banks deal in precious metals in addition to their other activities. Investment advisors and accountants will be able to determine whether an investor will gain a significant, or indeed any, advantage from doing this, bearing in mind that the activities of tax havens are increasingly coming under much greater scrutiny than in the past.

Types of account

It is possible an investor may not want physically to hold a purchase of gold on his or her own premises. It may be better kept in a bank vault. Whether an investor chooses to have an offshore or onshore bank account, there are three types of physical ownership (apart from holding it oneself) to bear in mind.

These are: a claims account, a custodial account or a safety deposit box arrangement. Clearly a safety deposit box needs no further explanation. They are anonymous but not 100% secure, since robberies do occasionally take place. The claims account is basically an account where the amount owned by an investor is identified, but in physical terms may be part of a large bar stored in a bank's vaults. The only downside to this method of purchase and storage is that the bank client has a claim on the books of the bank and does not own the metal outright. Should the bank have financial problems, the bank account owner could become a creditor of the bank. Some commercial and private banks offer a custodial account, allowing investors to buy and store a 'specific and divided' amount of gold. The purchase could be of coins or bars. This arrangement is 'off the books' of the bank, and thus not at risk in the event of a bank default and not therefore subject to creditor claims. Clearly this way of buying and storing in a segregated manner is safer in the event of an apocalypse, but more expensive. Annual custody fees can be as much 3-4% of the value of the gold held.

Bullion certificates

Many investment advisors regard bullion certificates as a hassle-free way of owning gold (and indeed other precious metals). Those of an apocalyptic view might prefer outright physical ownership, but the best certificate programme is backed by a government guarantee and therefore about as secure as investments like this can get.

The safest precious metals investment programme in the world today appears to be the Perth Mint Certificate (PMC). The PMC is a document that gives the holder legal title to precious metals stored on either an allocated (segregated) or an unallocated (unsegregated) basis with the Perth Mint in Western Australia. The important thing is that the PMC is safe and secure. A PMC holding is a conservative investment managed by the Perth Mint – a venerable, century-old institution. The government of Western Australia guarantees Perth Mint obligations; Western Australia is one of Australia's wealthiest states; the government of Western Australia is rated AAA; and the PMC programme is the only one with a government guarantee.

There are minimum investment levels involved in owning a certificate, but they aren't that onerous. You don't have to be a millionaire to afford an initial coin investment of $10,000 (£6,500), with subsequent purchases of $5000 (£3,250) or more. The low certificate fee (£40), coupled with no storage fee on unallocated accounts, makes this investment very attractive.

The certificate is non-negotiable but transferable, and exchangeable into physical gold on demand. There are approved dealers in key markets in the world. Delivery of the underlying gold or other precious metal can be made in

Perth, Western Australia or in primary precious metals centres elsewhere in the world at any time. Investors have the option of holding any or all the precious metals – gold, silver, platinum and palladium – in either bullion, coin or bar form.

Gold bullion shares

These are a well-established means of owning gold. They amount to buying shares in a mutual fund backed by a reserve of gold, where each share normally represents one-tenth of an ounce of the metal held in a bank vault. The shares owned by investors are in each case traceable back to a specific numbered bar and are traded on a recognised stock exchange. The system, initiated by the World Gold Council, has been operating successfully in many countries for some time. Gold bullion shares trade in London, New York, Australia, on European stock markets and in South Africa and elsewhere. There is a gold bullion security issued in Dubai that is considered acceptable for strict Islamic investors.

The popularity of funds like this, and their trading volume, has risen in leaps and bounds since their introduction a few years ago. The inflow of gold bullion into funds like this, in order to back the issuing of shares to satisfy demand from investors, has been a major factor in demand for gold in recent years and is likely to stay important in the future. The management cost of the typical fund is 0.24% per annum, and even if you add in dealing costs the total cost of owning gold in this way compares very favourably indeed with the custody costs of holding the physical metal in a segregated account, although less well with a gold certificate programme. Since gold is priced in US$, non-US investors also avoid the transaction fees involved in acquiring the necessary foreign exchange to buy gold, although movements in the dollar exchange will affect the value of their investment in their home currency.

This table shows the different gold bullion securities available, together with their size, management company and ticker symbols.

Gold ETFs (exchange-traded funds)

Name	Exchange	Ticker	Website
Gold Bullion Securities	ASX	GOLD	www.etfsecurities.com
Gold Bullion Securities	LSE	GBS	www.etfsecurities.com
Gold Bullion Securities	Euronext	GBS	www.etfsecurities.com
SPDR Gold Trust	NYSE	GLD	www.spdrgoldshares.com
SPDR Gold Trust	SGX	GLD	www.spdrgoldshares.com
NewGold	JSE	GLD	www.absa.co.za
iShares COMEX Gold	NYSE	IAU	us.ishares.com
iShares COMEX Gold	TSE	IGT	us.ishares.com
ZKB Gold ETF	SWX	ZGLD	www.zkb.ch
ETFS Gold	LSE	BULL	www.etfsecurities.com
ETFS Physical Gold	LSE	PHAU	www.etfsecurities.com
Gold BeES	NSE (India)	GOLDBEES	n/a
UTI Gold ETF	NSE (India)	GOLDSHARE	www.utvi.com
GoldLinked ETF	OSE (Japan)	1328	n/a
DB Gold Long	NYSE	DGL	www.dbfunds.db.com
DB Gold Double Long	NYSE	DGP	www.dbfunds.db.com
DB Gold Short	NYSE	DGZ	www.dbfunds.db.com
DB Gold Double Short	NYSE	DZZ	www.dbfunds.db.com
Julius Baer Gold ETF	SWX	BAER	www.juliusbaer.com

Buying gold through derivatives

Another way of achieving economic exposure to the gold price (and prices of other precious metals) is via derivatives: spread betting, futures, CFDs (contracts for difference) and covered warrants and certificates. Buying through derivative instruments has plus and minus points. More often than not it simply represents a geared investment on the direction of the price rather than, as is the case with a gold ETF, a specific claim on a specific bar of gold.

Spread betting, CFDs and futures are, in most respects, interchangeable. But there are big differences between them that need taking into account. Chief among these is that while spread betting is usually based around prices generated by an underlying futures market, it allows trading to be undertaken in smaller quantities than a 'lumpy' futures contract. Spread betting profits are also free of any form of capital gains tax in the UK. CFDs work on essentially the same principle, except that they are (like futures trades) subject to UK capital gains tax. The main other difference is that CFDs, which are effectively a form of trading on margin, break out the cost of assuming, say, a long position, and charge interest on the margin loan on a daily basis (usually at a fixed premium over LIBOR). Dealing spreads are narrower than in the case of spread betting, but the extra costs are charged on top. Commission is also charged on the full value of the contract, not simply the relatively modest amount of margin deposit that has to be put up at the outset. All of these methods of trading allow for going short as well as long. All allow (for the payment of a small extra amount) the ability to place stop-loss orders. By way of illustration, the following looks very briefly at how the spread betting scenario works. Investors first need an account at a financial bookmaker to operate a spread betting account. Firms like this operate by making a two-way price in a range of shares, stock market indices and commodities, usually where there is an active futures market that allows them to offset any net exposure they might incur. In spread betting, investors can bet on either a fall or rise in the price of the item in question, and dictate the size of their financial commitment by nominating the size of stake they wish to bet.

In the case of gold, prices are quoted in 10-cent 'ticks'. If an investor places an 'up bet' (buy) gold at 1100 ($1100) at £1 a point and the price rises by $10 an ounce, he or she makes a profit of £100 or $153 at current exchange rates – roughly equivalent to holding 15 ounces of the metal. At £2 a point, the exposure is roughly equivalent to holding 30 ounces of the metal at current exchange rates. One important plus point is that by denominating the bet in sterling the investor is getting exposure to the movement in the price of gold, but not to the underlying dollar exchange rate. In other words, a £1 a point bet on the gold price pays out based on the movement in the dollar price, but the winnings are in sterling. There is no translating of the dollar value into and out of sterling to work out the profit.

The drawback to spread betting in this way is that it is not designed to be a long-term investment medium. Most spread bets are based around futures prices. Futures have expiry dates and although bets can be rolled forward from one expiry date to the next, this does entail a cost. Spread betting on gold is best confined to situations where an investor believes that the price is temporarily and significantly out of line with events and may quickly correct itself.

Spread bets are based on margin requirements. Bets that lose money consistently may require more funds to be added to the account. A £1 per point bet on the price of gold would normally require an investor to have a minimum of £150 in his or her account, and in practice significantly more than this to cover day-to-day fluctuations in the price.

The spread in the gold price is currently around 10 points, in other words roughly a dollar. Investors buy at the equivalent of $1101 and sell at $1100. This is small beer compared with the costs of buying and holding physical gold and compared with the price movements that can occur. As mentioned earlier, spread betting on gold also falls outside the capital gains tax regime.

Covered warrants, certificates and structured products are also available based around spot gold. Covered warrants are dealt in through normal stock exchanges but are in essence option-like products issued by investment banks. Certificates are covered call warrants with a zero strike price and indefinite expiry and hence track the underlying price almost exactly. These can be dealt in relatively easily. SG, for example, has an open expiry gold bullion tracking certificate priced in sterling and dealt through the London Stock Exchange with the code S940, with 100 units being equivalent to an ounce of gold at the spot price in sterling.

Some investment banks also issue structured products based around gold. These are over the counter instruments. They generally involve using options to achieve some form of income, whole or partial capital protection and some form of participation in the price upside in the metal itself. They inevitably represent a compromise and in my view are best avoided.

The basic problem with derivatives and other such devices is that they are essentially dependent on the financial soundness or otherwise of the company promoting them. All of them also require investors to keep unused cash balances in their accounts to meet potential margin calls. Spread betting, CFDs and futures are, furthermore, all instruments designed for geared-up relatively short-term trading, whereas most alternative investors who have got this far in this book will have done so because they recognise the importance of having some physical gold in their position to offset the vagaries and fluctuating values of paper assets like shares and bonds. In short, though they are a means of gaining exposure to the gold price, they don't satisfy the requirement that what investors own is theirs, and not simply someone else's liability, on which the institution in question can potentially default.

Other Precious Metals

Gold isn't the only option when it comes to investing in precious metals. But it is the most widely known, and does have a cachet that some of the others do not possess, at least in the imagination if nowhere else. Investors can buy gold tax-free in the UK, in Switzerland and throughout the EU countries. However, silver, platinum and palladium (normally known as 'white' metals) are subject to VAT. Having to pay VAT is clearly prohibitive for investment purchases. The result is that for the most part the 'white' metals are bought and stored in a VAT-free zone. Silver, platinum and palladium are also predominantly industrial metals, with industrial demand predominant in their price action. They do not therefore possess quite the same long-term investment potential as gold, which remains, above all, the classic store of value for investors.

Nonetheless, silver, platinum and palladium coins and bars of various weights are available through the normal dealer network. Exchange-traded funds are available in platinum and silver, and bullion certificates in silver and platinum are also available through the Perth Mint programme.

Where to Go for More Information

More information on gold and how to invest in it may be found at the following sites.

Dealers

Allgold Coins (www.allgoldcoins.co.uk) specialise in the supply of high-quality sovereigns and modern proof sets. The site contains useful information, plus a link to the live gold price with charts.

ATS Bullion (www.atsbullion.com) was set up to take over a bullion and modern coins business previously run by Spink. The site has information on buying and selling gold, live charts and facts concerning bullion coins and bars.

Baird & Co (www.goldline.co.uk) is a bullion merchant based in East London. It supplies precious metal and investment products. Bullion coins and investment bars can be bought online and price information is updated twice daily on the website. Investors are offered either trading in gold or silver, where the metal may be held in an unallocated account and dealt in the spot market or on the twice daily London fixing, or in an allocated account for specific numbered bars. Baird also has an over the counter cash trade branch in Hatton Garden, where a range of gold coins and small bars can be purchased.

Chard (www.taxfreegold.co.uk), based in Blackpool, buys and sells high-quality gold jewellery, gold sovereigns, Krugerrands and other coins as well as gold bars. The live gold price and an extensive online catalogue can also be accessed through their site GoldCore (www.goldcore.com) is a financial services company specialising in 'wealth preservation strategies'. It buys and sells gold, silver and platinum coins and bars. The site has a wealth of useful information, including a year-end review and outlook, a beginner's guide to gold investing and live charts.

The London Coin Company (www.thelondoncoincompany.com) specialises in buying and selling gold, silver and platinum modern coins from around the world.

Dealers, mints, etc.

Entity	Web address	Main location	Email address	Telephone	Category
Allgold, Coins	www.allgoldcoins.co.uk	Surrey	sales@allgoldcoins.co.uk	0844 544 7952	Dealer
ATS Bullion	www.atsbullion.com	London	sales@atsbillion.com	0207 240 4041	Dealer
Baird & Co.	www.goldline.co.uk	London	sales@godline.co.uk	0207 474 1000	Dealer
Chard	www.24carat.co.uk	Blackpool	enquiries@chards.co.uk	01253 343 081	Dealer
Goldcore	www.goldcore.com	London	Through site	020 3086 9200	Dealer
London Coin Company, The	www.thelondoncoincompany.com	London	info@thelondoncoincompany.com	020 8343 2231	Dealer
Perth Mint, The	www.perthmint.com.au	Perth	info@perthmint.com.au	61 8 9421 222	Mint
Pobjoy Mint	www.pobjoy.com	Surrey	sales@pobjoy.com	01737 818 181	Mint
South African Gold Coin Exchange	www.sagoldcoin.com	South Africa	info@sagoldcoin.com	27 11 784 8551	Dealer
Tanaka	gold.tanaka.co.jp/english	Tokyo	soba1s@ml.tanaka.co.jp	81 3 6311 5551	Dealer
Tax Free Gold	www.taxfreegold.co.uk	Blackpool	enquiries@chards.co.uk	01253 343081	Dealer
United States Mint, The	www.usmint.gov	USA	On site	202 898 6468	Mint

The South African Gold Coin Exchange (www.sagoldcoin.com) has been trading since 1972. It is the largest distributor of gold investment, bullion and collectable coins in South Africa, especially Krugerrands. There is an online shop which sells worldwide.

Tanaka (gold.tanaka.co.jp/english) operates one of the largest gold refineries in the world and is Japan's largest bullion house. Apart from gold coins it sells a range of goods made from gold, including an 18-carat bathtub made for a Japanese hotel.

The United States Mint (www.usmint.gov) sells US gold coins online.

Information

The Bullion Desk (www.thebulliondesk.com) was formed in 1999 by three former members of the London Bullion Market. It provides comprehensive online precious metal information. Included on the site are live prices, charts, financial data, numerous links and daily and periodic reports from sources such as HSBC, Mitsubishi, Reuters and Investec.

Coin Link (www.coinlinkbullion.com) has spot price charts and daily news on the precious metals market.

The Free Gold Money Report (www.fgmr.com) is an investment newsletter available on subscription which analyses the precious metals and financial markets. It is published 20 times per year and delivered by email in pdf format.

Gold Price (www.goldprice.org) has charts of the current gold price per ounce, gram or kilogram in 27 major currencies (as well as the prices for silver and platinum). The site also has historical charts, commentary on the market, future quotes and prices, together with many useful links including dealers worldwide. A new service is now available by subscription whereby alerts can be received via email when the spot gold price moves outside user-defined limits.

The London Bullion Market Association (www.lbma.org.uk) has prices and statistics plus a quarterly journal, the *Alchemist*, which can be downloaded from the site. This covers topics relating to every sector of the international precious metals market.

Gold

Information

Entity	Web address	Main location	Email address	Telephone	Category
Bullion Desk (The)	www.thebulliondesk.com	London	On site	020 7929 2231	Information
Coinlink	www.coinlinkbullicn.com	Florida	news@coinlink.com	407 786 5555	Information
Freemarket Gold Money Report	www.fgmr.com	USA	contact@fgmr.com	603 323 8182	Information
Gold Price	www.goldprice.org	Sydney	Through site	61 2 800 508 86	Information
London Bullion Market Association	www.lbma.org.uk	London	mail@lbma.org.uk	020 7796 3067	Information
World Gold Council	www.gold.org	Worldwide	info@gold.org	n/a	Information

189

The Perth Mint (www.perthmint.com.au) is an informative site, providing comprehensive information on gold and precious metal investment. Areas covered include purchasing gold and precious metals, live spot prices and statistical data. The certificate programme and depository services are also covered in detail. The online shop is extensive, with worldwide delivery.

The World Gold Council (www.gold.org) is an international, non-profit organisation founded in 1987 by the world's leading gold mining companies and has offices around the world. The site has everything you need to know about gold, silver, platinum and palladium. A wide range of research reports is available, looking at gold's investment characteristics. The statistics section has a rolling programme of data collection and analysis covering prices, investment information, supply and demand statistics and gold reserve numbers. The quarterly report *Gold Investment Digest* offers concise analysis of recent gold market trends.

Spread betting/ETFs in gold

Cantor Index (www.cantorindex.co.uk) has an online brochure covering all aspects of spread betting and live prices for gold, silver and platinum.

City Index (www.cityindex.co.uk) has an introduction to spread betting plus a downloadable brochure. Account holders have access to live prices, market reports, charting and market and investment research.

IG Index (www.igindex.co.uk) has a downloadable dealing guide. As with all spread betting firms, IG is not allowed to give trading advice.

All the spread betting firms offer 24-hour online trading and will quote a price and deal immediately.

As the earlier text indicated there are a large number of ways of investing in gold through exchange-traded funds, as an alternative to holding physical bullion. Their web addresses and other relevant information is shown in the table on page 180.

APEX
The Name for Philatelics

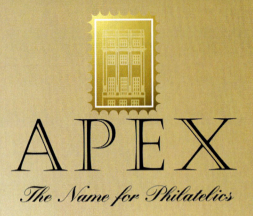

Consistent Returns in Uncertain Times

Stamps offer an affordable diversification away from mainstream investments with proven mid-long term returns. We offer an honest and transparent advisory service to collectors and investors based both on the long-term nature of the business and the short-term day-to-day international pricing levels.

This approach gives our clients the flexibility to compile a portfolio through auction at levels consistently below typical retail prices.

Apex has been one of the UK's leading dealers and auctioneers of world stamps since 1994 and hold eight public and postal auctions each year.

As a Noble Investments (UK) PLC company we pride ourselves on the amiable and professional service we provide and our world-class specialists have over 100 years combined experience in all areas of Philatelics.

For more information
contact Tim Francis or Rick Warren
admin@apexstamps.com
or call our London showroom on
+44 (0)207 930 6879
to make an appointment with our specialists.

For a free auction catalogue email admin@apexstamps.com and quote the reference AIGS

11 Adelphi Terrace, London, WC2N 6BJ
tel: +44 (0)20 7930 6879 fax: +44 (0)20 7930 9450
www.apexstamps.com
A Noble Investments (UK) PLC Company

8.
Stamps

Weight for weight, stamps are probably the most valuable tangible asset an investor can buy. A single stamp in mint condition weighs about a tenth of a gram but can be worth thousands of pounds. In fact, Stanley Gibbons, the leading stamp dealer, recently sold an exceptionally high-quality Great Britain Penny Black for £250,000. But many high-quality stamps are available for lower prices than this.

Stamp collecting is arguably the largest hobby there is, with an estimated 30 million enthusiasts worldwide, or perhaps as many as 80 million if the uncertain number of collectors in mainland China is included. Collectors are diverse. The British Royal Family has one of the world's great collections, much of it originally assembled by HM King George V, who was a noted philatelist. And, at odds with stamp collecting's traditional image, the Inter Milan footballer Luis Figo is also an award-winning collector. Many astute philatelists have put together a collection over their lifetime that has proved to be worth a small fortune when it eventually came to be sold.

Tangible asset investors are, however, pursuing a somewhat different approach to collectors. They are motivated mainly by the returns that can be made over a period of years by putting together a portfolio of stamps that are scarce objects in their own right. It may be that eventually they come to be interested in the history of the stamps that form part of their portfolio, but that is not a necessary part of capturing the returns that stamps can bring them.

Like many areas of tangible asset investing, stamp investment is in some ways analogous to investing in the stock market. Certain stamps and genres of stamps move in and out of favour; and demand for some types of stamps is broadly linked to the economy, and to the spending power of the underlying collector base. Investors pick a portfolio of ten or 20 items to avoid undue dependence on any particular one. They can buy additional items if they wish as they go along, adding to their portfolio over time. The stamp dealer can play the role of an advisory broker, drawing attention to possible new portfolio additions, and perhaps highlighting the potential to take a profit in an item that has risen too far in value relative to the rest of the market. Most stock market investors are inherently comfortable with this approach. They need not (and perhaps even should not) keep the stamps at home. Because condition is such an important component of an individual stamp's value, dealers often keep investors' portfolios stored under ideal conditions on their premises rather than risk storage in conditions that may detract from their value. Thus, like shares, stamps become an investment that, in effect, becomes a paper transaction rather than a physical one (although the portfolio can be viewed at the dealer's premises from time to time).

Basics

Since the postage stamp was born in Britain in 1840, the idea has been imitated and developed across the world. Once stamp issuing became widespread, collectors began to take an active interest. A number of basic elements tend to contribute to a stamp's attractiveness for these collectors and, hence, their investment value.

Politics

In those countries with a monarchy, stamp issues generally change when monarchs change, providing a punctuation mark for the collector. When a monarch changes, it means that the supply of stamps issued with that monarch's image stops, and the items thus attain some kind of scarcity value. Generally speaking, the further back in time it was issued the more valuable the stamp will be. The same is true of when countries have taken new names as a result of political change, such as gaining independence from colonial rule. When this has happened, the stamps have changed, and those previously issued have acquired a scarcity value. Stamps issued by Rhodesia or Nyasaland, for instance, have greater cachet than those issued by their present-day successor countries of Zimbabwe and Malawi.

War plays its part too. The Japanese occupation of Malaya led to special issues of stamps, as did the German occupation of the Channel Islands. Any event of this nature, particularly of relatively short duration, leads to the creation of stamps that potentially in the future will have serious scarcity value.

Creation and cancellation

The ways in which stamps are printed also contribute to scarcity and collectability. Stamps that originate from specific printers or from numbered printer's plates can become rare items. Those that are at the edge of a sheet, and which therefore contain a blank paper margin next to the usual perforations, also have scarcity value.

The way in which a used stamp has been cancelled by the application of a postmark may contribute to its value. But a smudged or poorly applied cancellation can significantly reduce a stamp's value. Being fragile paper items, wear and tear over the years also erodes the supply of older stamps. This enhances the value of those that remain, provided that their condition is maintained. Condition is vital, and a separate section is devoted to it later in this chapter.

Modern market flood

One important reason for not collecting contemporary stamps for investment purposes has been the fact that, in recent years, some postal authorities have been far too profligate at issuing so-called 'collectors sets' of stamps. Gambia and Liberia, for example, each issued more than 500 different stamps in one recent year (in the same year the UK's Royal Mail only issued 75). The abundant supply of material like this makes newly issued sets worthless for investment purposes, although it does not detract from the value of early issues. Gambia's early issues are, for example, highly sought-after. Only those taking an exceptionally long-term view or those collecting contemporary stamps for thematic reasons (say, for example, any stamps featuring birds), can expect to profit significantly from assembling collections featuring stamps like this.

An example of the scale of this problem is that, in the Stanley Gibbons checklist *Collect British Stamps*, the period from 1840 to 1952 occupies pages 1-13, while the present Queen's reign occupies pages 14 to 163. Stamps issued in this latter era are unlikely to make good investments unless there are significant varieties or errors in them. Serious collectors have tended to bypass modern stamps of countries that currently operate profligate issuing policies – that is to say, most countries.

Popularity

One important parameter for investors is the number of collectors. Collectors provide a ready market for investment-quality stamps held in portfolios, assuring investors of a fair price should they choose to sell. The number of collectors far exceeds the numbers of investors in rare stamps. Latest estimates suggest that there are around 30 million stamp collectors worldwide, or, as noted earlier, perhaps 80 million if the uncertain number of Chinese collectors is included. The number of non-collector investors, if one can specify such a category, is probably in the low thousands in the UK, compared with collectors numbering in the hundreds of thousands. The amount of collectors in any geographical area is less relevant than you might suppose since, for example, there are collectors of rare British stamps all over the world, and not just in the UK. Many British collectors do, however, simply collect stamps from Great Britain, and present or former British colonies and Commonwealth countries.

This brings us onto the subject of collecting themes.

Collectable themes

Geography

Since it is the postal authorities of particular countries that issue stamps, collecting the stamps of a particular country or group of countries is a natural and probably the primary collecting theme. Those that are popular include British stamps, perhaps because the concept of the postage stamp originated in Britain. Stamps from Commonwealth countries, particularly those that have historical significance in some way – Cyprus, Canada, the Falklands and Hong Kong – are also popular with collectors. The stamps of the USA, France, China, Russia and parts of the Middle East all have large collector bases as well.

Other

Collectors pursue many different themes, but popular ones include stamps and postal material connected with transmission by air; postal material related to space travel; and items related to key events in postal history. There are many others besides: pictorial postage stamps related to ornithology or animals, only unused stamps, or only used ones. Some collectors collect stamps used for revenue and excise tax purposes, rather than for postage.

From an investment standpoint, however, investors need to stick to those areas and themes where there is a substantial body of active collectors, preferably international ones. This will provide liquidity in the market should the investor choose to sell, and prices will be sufficiently well bid for dealers' spreads to be narrow. For the most part this means classic British stamps from the Victorian era to the start of World War II, and those of selected foreign and Commonwealth countries over a similar period. Whatever the chosen theme, though, errors are an important extra component in creating value (and can be a theme in their own right, too). Stamps with incorrect or missing colours, pictures printed upside down, a misspelt legend, incorrect or missing perforations and a range of other variants can combine to create a unique object or set of objects. It has to be the right kind of error, however, and not something which merely falls under our next section – condition.

Condition

The condition of a stamp has a dramatic affect on its price. Prices for stamps in a dealer's catalogue will typically be listed for examples in 'fine' condition; that is, for a stamp without creases and tears and, if used, with a clear cancellation mark. The issue of condition is more complex than this explanation might suggest, however. While today stamps are generally kept in albums under clear plastic strips that retain the stamps without affecting their quality in any way, earlier generations of stamp collectors used hinges or mounts to keep their stamps in their album. Successive applications of hinges or mounts in earlier years detract from the quality of a stamp and therefore will affect its price, although more allowance is made in this respect for stamps from early years – issued, say, before 1900.

For unused stamps, of paramount importance is that the gum on the back of the stamp should be intact and original. Stamps where the gum has been disturbed by the application of mounts or hinges generally fetch lower prices, especially in the case of stamps issued during the 20th century. Discoloration or cracking of the gum on stamps also affects their price.

Perforations and margins are another key aspect of the condition of stamps. Early stamps like the Penny Black did not have perforations, but were cut from a sheet. It is important in examples like this that the margins should be as large and even as possible on all four sides of the stamp. A set of intact perforations on a stamp is the ideal. More common is that one or two perforations will have been damaged but the remainder left intact. There is a whole specialised vocabulary dealing with the degree of damage to perforations, from 'nibbed' through 'short' to 'pulled' and 'missing'. More than one or two missing perforations on a classic stamp from the early 20th century will likely reduce its value drastically.

Where used stamps are concerned these considerations also apply, but an additional variable is introduced – the quality of the cancellation mark. In the case of early stamps, symbols like a Maltese cross were often used, in a colour such as red. Subsequently the norm became a black circular cancellation date stamp (often abbreviated to CDS). Clear and lightly applied postmarks are the things to look for; heavy, smudged ones to be avoided. Some stamps were cancelled by hand in manuscript. Cancellations that are exactly centred in the stamp may also be worth a premium.

Because condition is so vital when it comes to determining the value of a stamp, this area has been fertile ground for forgers, sometimes called by the euphemistic term of 'stamp improvers'. Various tricks are used, for example, to redistribute the gum on a stamp where heavy hinging has damaged it. Another instance might occur with an unused stamp where the gum has been removed. This could be turned into a more attractive proposition by the addition of a forged cancellation mark, turning it from a poor quality unused example to a fine quality used one. Then again, stamps displaying forged cancellations can be collectors' items in their own right.

There is a clear trade-off between condition and price, and a buyer needs to be satisfied that the stamp meets their criteria in both respects before agreeing to a purchase. This is particularly true when considering stamps as an investment.

Investment-quality stamps

Investors demand stamps that hold their value. Typically these will be stamps that the dealer can guarantee to be in superior condition with, if used, a desirable single circular date stamp cancellation mark. Unused stamps will normally be in pristine unmounted condition, but this may be unrealistic for older issues. Used stamps will be classed as fine or very fine examples. All such stamps will have a minimal amount of damage to perforations, or in the case of older examples, have a full set of margins. A certificate of authenticity from one of the major 'expertising' bodies is desirable and may add to the resale value of the item.

The following table shows some statistics on prices of sample portfolios of British and British Commonwealth stamps of pre-World War 2 and earlier. These are either pre-built portfolios supplied by Stanley Gibbons, or, in the case of the Commonwealth portfolio, one generated automatically from the firm's portfolio generator system.

Stamp investing – sample portfolios

Great Britain Portfolio – Example 1				£50,000
Country	SG Code	Stamp	Type	Value
GB	SG441var	1934 1 1/2d Bradbury trial (24)	Trial	18,000
GB	SG2	1840 Spooner No 10 comic envelope	Postal history	11,500
GB	SG417var	1929 10s 'Seahorse'	Experimental plate proof	8000
GB	SG147var	1873 6d proof on card	Die proof	6,500
GB	SG212	1890 £1 green	Unmounted original gum	6000
Great Britain Portfolio – Example 2				**£51,450**
Country	SG Code	Stamp	Type	Value
GB	SG112var	1867 10s die proofs (3)	Die proofs	18,000
GB	SG455var	1934 1 1.2d Silver Jubilee	Colour trial	10,000
GB	SG435var	1929 1d and 1 1/2d Postal Union	Die proof	8,500
GB	SG O109	1904 1 1/2d Dull purple/green (4)	Unused	7,500
GB	SG404	1913 £1 Dull blue-green	Unmounted original gum	4,500
GB	SG134	1882 5s Rose (plate 4)	Used	2,950
Commonwealth Portfolio – Example				**£50,975**
Country	SG Code	Stamp	Type	Value
Hong Kong	MY28	1882 10c Green used on envelope	Postal history	325
Gibraltar	SG108	1925 £5 violet and black (4)	Unmounted original gum	8,500
Labuan	SG139	1904 $1 blue type 21 (4)	Used	3,250
Cape of Good Hope	SG14a	1861 4d milky blue type II	Used	2,750
ICS Chamba	SG14a	1887 8a dull mauve error	Used	3,500
ICS Chamba	SG2/b	1887 1a brown/purple error(2)	Unused	1,300
Cape of Good Hope	SG20	1863 6d bright mauve (4)	Unmounted original gum	1,950
Long Island	SG21	1916 1s blue	Unused	1,600
Canada	SG341/51	1935 $11 to $1 (4)	Unmounted original gum	4,950
Madagascar	SG45b	1886 1s rose (consular mail)	Unused	1,200
Ireland	SG46	1922 10s dull grey-blue	Used	1,200
Ireland	SG83/5	1925 2s 6d, 5s, 10s type 11 (3x4)	Unmounted original gum	1250
Australia	SGD43	1902 10s dull green 'postage due'	Original gum	1,800
Hong Kong	SGF5	1874 $3 dull mauve	Original gum	600
Tanganyika	SGM21/6	1915 GEA fiscal stamps (6)	Used	4000
Cayman Islands	SGMP1b	1908 stampless cover	Postal history	6000
ICS Chamba	SG o15a	1887 1r slate error	Unused	5000
ICS Chamba	SG o2/c	1887 brown purple error (3)	Unmounted original gum	1,800

Source: Stanley Gibbons (These figures are based on Stanley Gibbons' catalogue prices and are for illustrative purposes.)

These portfolios show the variety of postal items that are available for investment purposes and in particular the role that multiple blocks of stamps, items of postal history, and errors, often play in collection. They also demonstrate the important point that, to perform well, stamps must combine scarcity and good condition. Many of the stamps shown in the table are intrinsically very scarce, have certificates of authenticity, and also well-documented provenance. It shows, further, the key fact that stamps in isolation are not the only philatelic investment medium. Items of rare postal history, that is to say examples of the use of stamps on their original envelopes, and letters sent prior to the issue of stamps in 1840, have shown some of the greatest rises in value over the past few years. They are highly sought after by leading collectors. The selection of items like this, however, needs to be made by dealers who are experts in this area, since the value depends on a number of different factors, including the rarity of the cancellation, the number of stamps used, the scarcity and destination of the letter, or the routing of the letter.

Multiples (blocks of more than one stamp of the same type) are inherently rarer than the individuals of which they are comprised, but the same standards related to condition, gum, perforations, clarity of cancellation mark and so on, also apply with equal force.

The Right Alternative Asset for You?

Like gold, most investors with a substantial portfolio of assets invested in the stock market can use stamps as a sensible diversification move. Like gold, stamps can act as a hedge against inflation. Moreover, they are a discreet and portable form of wealth. Stamp prices also tend to rise with the general level of prices. Unlike gold, however, stamps will not protect an investor from a truly apocalyptic investment fallout, since their value is largely determined by the spending power of the collector base.

There are several questions that require an answer in order to determine whether stamps should take a place in a wider portfolio of investments.

A medium to long-term investment?

The typical timescale for stamp investment to pay off is said by dealers to be in the region of five to ten years. Holding a portfolio of stamps for this length of time or longer should produce the optimum level of returns. While stamps are a relatively liquid market and a portfolio could be sold sooner than this, an investor may not get the full benefit of owning them if they choose, or are forced, to sell too early.

Capital requirements?

In theory there is no maximum or minimum amount to be invested, although a dealer such as Stanley Gibbons will probably stipulate that to be cost-effective an investment in the region of a minimum £5000 or £10,000 is probably the right size for a long-term portfolio. The portfolio examples given in the earlier table show portfolios valued in the region of £50,000, which is perhaps a more appropriate minimum level to consider in order to access some of the choicest items available. Generally speaking, it is the items of proven rarity that have shown the best rises in the past. Whether or not an investor feels able to afford this depends on the scale of their other assets and investments, and what, if any, other tangible asset investments have been made or are being contemplated.

Storage and insurance costs?

Investors can hold the stamps they own physically on their own property. In this case, however, it will be necessary to invest in both insurance and security measures, such as installing a safe in which to keep them. Security measures are arguably less necessary for stamps than for items like antiques or bullion, since they are easily concealed and their value is not readily apparent to the untutored eye. However, a more serious objection is the requirement to maintain the stamps in the best condition possible – stamps being fragile and susceptible to damage from the damp. Careless handling could also severely affect their resale value. Many stamp investors opt to have a dealer store and insure the stamps for them. The normal cost of this service, at a well-known dealer like Stanley Gibbons, is 1% of the value of the portfolio per annum.

Portfolio diversification?

Stamp prices rise in line with economic growth and inflation. They are a diversification in that sense, but unlike gold, for example, will not protect an investor's wealth particularly well in the case of a severe economic downturn. They should therefore rise in line with the overall trend in the stock market, but not exhibit the same degree of volatility as stocks and shares. In that sense investors might consider them to be a more liquid and portable form of property than, for example, real estate. The supply of classic stamps is restricted in the same way that land is, and therefore the value of items like this tends to rise steadily in value. Unlike property and the stock market, however, the element of volatility added by purchases being made with borrowed money is by and large not present in the stamp market, although some dealers do offer favourable payment terms.

Other considerations?

Philately is an interest that combines history from the mid-19th century onwards, with the endless twists and turns of geopolitics since then. A particularly rich vein for stamp collectors over the years has been the changes that have taken place in the Commonwealth as increasing numbers of countries have gained independence. Countries like Hong Kong, the Falkland Islands, Cyprus and Malaysia all have a rich philatelic heritage. The stamps issued by many former British and European colonies in Africa and the Middle and Far East that have since gained independence are interesting historical curios in their own right.

To have at least a passing interest in the political and historical development of these territories is, if not a pre-requisite, then something of an asset when it comes to making a judgement about the worth of a portfolio a dealer may have put together, and of any acquisitions or disposals that the dealer may subsequently suggest.

Stamp Prices

Stamps vary considerably and those items considered rare by the general public may not be the most valuable in a collection. Most people consider Penny Blacks to be the scarcest, but in fact a decent example of a used 1840 Penny Black, for example, may be had for around £200 at the time of writing (five years before this it was probably £150), whereas a Tuppence Blue of the same vintage may fetch considerably more. A used £5 Orange from 1883 may fetch over £4,500 (£3000 five years ago) in perfect condition.

A Penny Black – the stamp world's 'icon'

At the other end of the scale, Victorian stamps issued between 1858 and 1870 had a variety of plate numbers. The rarest of these plates on a penny rose-red stamp was plate 77. Find a used example of this stamp and it is worth a sum in six figures. A Penny Black from the rarest plate, plate 11, has a catalogue value of £4000 used (£2,500 five years ago) but may be picked up for considerably less depending on condition, perhaps around £2,400.

This brings up a major issue when it comes to buying stamps. The price in a dealer's catalogue is the price at which a dealer will sell an example in 'fine' condition. A flawless example will often command a premium over the catalogue price. It is rare for stamps to have no flaws and the price also reflects a dealer's margin, which in some cases can be substantial. Stamps are routinely available at less than the dealer's catalogue prices at auction and elsewhere.

Commonwealth stamps can also have expensive price tags. Latest catalogue prices show that a Kenya & Uganda mint black and brown £50 from the reign of George V as catalogued by Stanley Gibbons would be priced at £30,000 (£25,000 five years ago), a pair of 6d imperforate mint British Solomon Islands

Protectorate at £6000 (£3750 five years ago), and a marginal £10 purple and ultramarine mint Nyasaland Protectorate Edward VII at £9000 (£7000 five years ago).

Often it is the most unprepossessing items that will have the greatest value, since the scarcity of an individual stamp is not readily apparent to the untutored eye. This is part of the attraction of the hobby to collectors – the fact that one day they may happen across a rare stamp and be able to acquire it for a fraction of its true value. In reality this hope is probably a vain one. The fact remains that, more than antiques and art, stamps are arguably the best documented and most intensively researched of all collectables. There is extensive data on the price history of particular items, and a large body of collectors. London is also the recognised international centre for stamp dealing, and hence there is every chance that British investors will get the best prices, both buying and selling, for their stamp portfolios – provided they shop around. Many collectables do not possess this characteristic – namely a reasonably predictable price when an item is resold.

It is perhaps worth touching at this point on the role of Stanley Gibbons, which is the largest stamp dealer in the world by some margin. Gibbons has the largest stock of stamps and also publishes the definitive price catalogues. This gives it a powerful position in the market. Although rival dealers often complain about Stanley Gibbons' influence in the market, the fact remains there are many other stamp dealers (many of whom trained at SG), and many auctions at which stamps are sold in a free market in which buyers from Stanley Gibbons will be only one of several bidders for sought-after items. All stamp dealers in collectables operate on the basis of a wide bid-offer spread, and stamps are no exception. In the author's own experience, with two stamp portfolios purchased from Stanley Gibbons and sold in April and October 2008, the price received was in the region of 80% of catalogue value, the stamps having been purchased at the catalogue price four years previously. Fortunately the gain in prices over that period was sufficient to ensure a substantial profit. But this experience goes to show that timing a purchase correctly, above all not getting drawn into the market when it is experiencing bubble conditions, and holding for a reasonable length of time, are the key factors to bear in mind when buying stamps. Most of the gain in the portfolio came from one or two rare items, suggesting that the best strategy is to buy relatively few stamps of very high quality.

Returns

Although it has always been possible to trace the returns from stamps from successive annual catalogues produced by dealers, little formal work was done on this for many years, chiefly because stamps had been largely a collectors' market rather than an investors' one ever since philately began as a hobby in the 19th century. That said, it should be remembered that enthusiasm for stamps as a store of value has come in waves that coincide with fears of rising inflation. There was a speculative bubble in stamp prices in the late 1970s and early 1980s, just as there was in wine and whisky for much the same reason, a bubble which, when it subsided, left some investors nursing losses.

It is only relatively recently, however, that Stanley Gibbons has compiled several indices of the most actively traded stamps, which allow the general level of prices to be compared from one year to the next and for returns to be worked out from them. The following table shows some of the underlying data and how returns have panned out over different time periods for these indices, together with charts of their performance, followed by some notes on the method by which the indices are compiled.

Stanley Gibbons – Selected Stamp Price Index Data

SG100

Year-end	1998	1999	2000	2001	2002	2003	2004	2005	2006	2007	2008
Index number	246.8	271	291.5	299	326.8	364.0	389.5	409.8	428.5	450	465.1
Annual Change (%)	n/a	9.8	7.3	2.6	9.3	11.3	7	5.2	4.6	5	3.4
Cumulative Change (%)	n/a	9.8	18.1	21.1	32.4	47.5	57.8	66	73.6	82.3	88.5

Stamps

Performance over period	(%)
1 year	3.4
3 years	13.4
5 years	27.8
10 years	88.5

10-year CAGR (%pa): 65
CAGR on FTSE over period (%pa): -2.8
Number of constituents: 100
Weighting: by value and trading volume

GB Rarities

Catalogue	1998	1999	2000	2001	2002	2003	2004	2005	2006	2007	2008	2009
Total value (£000s)	423.5	447	505.3	526	561	639.5	777.5	861	959.5	1055	1462	1484
Annual Change (%)	n/a	5.5	13	4.1	6.7	14	21.6	10.7	11.4	10	38.6	1.5
Cumulative Change (%)	n/a	5.5	19.3	24.2	32.5	51	83.6	103.3	126.6	149.1	245.2	250.4

Performance over period	(%)
1 year	1.5
3 years	54.6
5 years	90.9
10 years	232

11-year CAGR (%pa): 12.1
CAGR adj. for dealing spread (%pa): 9.8
CAGR on FTSE over period (%pa): -2.6
Catalogue published: April
Number of constituents: 30
Weighting: none

The Handbook of Alternative Assets

Commonwealth Rarities

Catalogue	1998	1999	2000	2001	2002	2003	2004	2005	2006	2007	2008
Total value (£000s)	391.8	421	447.5	472	495	583.0	621	762	830	897	951
Annual Change (%)	n/a	7.5	6.3	5.5	4.9	17.8	6.5	22.7	8.9	8.1	6
Cumulative Change (%)	n/a	7.5	14.2	20.5	26.4	48.8	58.5	94.5	111.9	129	142.8

Performance over period	(%)
1 year	6
3 years	24.8
5 years	63.1
10 years	142.7

10-year CAGR (%pa): 93
CAGR adj. for dealing spread (%pa): 6.9
CAGR on FTSE over period (%pa): -0.7
Catalogue published: August
Number of constituents: 30
Weighting: none

The SG100 Stamp Price Index is based on actual prices, either retail or at auction, for 100 of the world's most frequently traded stamps. It includes selected items from all major collecting areas. It is weighted towards the most frequently traded and higher value stamps and its components are carefully reassessed on a continuous basis to ensure that it continues to reflect the total market accurately.

www.stanleygibbons.com

The items which make up the SG100 are those "most frequently traded" and the index therefore gives an accurate picture of the state of the market for the more popular stamps. The index provides a monthly barometer of the health of the stamp market as a whole but not necessarily of the market in rare investment-grade stamps. It is, however, a useful benchmark for investors, providing evidence of the overall health of the collectors' market.

The GB30 Rarities Index lists Great Britain rarities available on the open market, and gives an accurate picture of the market for scarce items. Stamps included in the index are examples of classic investment-grade stamps, considered most likely to show consistent returns over the medium to long term, as demand from collectors and investors exceeds what in many cases is a very restricted supply. In the case of this index, and the Commonwealth Rarities Index described below, the prices quoted are from Stanley Gibbons published catalogues which represent the estimated selling prices at the time of publication. They are for examples in fine condition for the issue concerned. Higher quality examples would sell for more; those of a lower quality considerably less.

The Commonwealth Rarities 30 Index lists rarities and stamp errors available on the open market, and gives an accurate picture of the market for scarce items. Stamps included in the index are again examples of investment-grade material and considered the most likely to show consistent returns over the medium to long term. In this case as well, supply of stamps of such quality is restricted.

The tables demonstrate the underlying growth in the stamp market over the periods in question, and also the fact that over the 10 or 11 year periods covered, the performance of stamps traded by Stanley Gibbons, particularly rarer investment-grade ones, has beaten the FTSE 100 index (and other leading world stock market indices) by some considerable margin. While the indices of investment-grade stamps (GB rarities and Commonwealth rarities) are based on catalogue prices, even assuming that a portfolio of stamps bought at catalogue prices might only be able to be sold at 80% of subsequent catalogue prices, the performance over the long term is still significantly positive and bears favourable comparison with equities. Trade outside of Stanley Gibbons may of course be different.

How to Invest

Unless an investor is already an expert philatelist, help is needed in the process of selecting a portfolio of investment-quality stamps to buy. Stanley Gibbons and other similar firms like Scotia Philately (set up by former Stanley Gibbons alumni) operate discretionary and advisory services for investment-grade stamps and will usually commit to buying back stamps in a portfolio at a later date, should the investor wish to sell one or all of them. The minimum level of investment to start a portfolio of this sort is in the region of £2000, although the optimum size is probably £5000 or more. Stanley Gibbons, for example, offer a number of pre-built investment-grade portfolios of established rarity, as shown in the tables earlier.

It is a wise precaution to have investment-grade stamps stored by a dealer because of the potential for damaging stamps by careless handling. In this case the dealer will provide the investor with a detailed scanned record of the items in your portfolio and proof of ownership. Investors can withdraw the items from storage at 48 hours' notice. As mentioned earlier, there may be modest charges for the service, although sometimes these are offered free of charge.

Good dealers will be aware of their clients' portfolio and from time to time be able to suggest stamps that will complement those existing holdings. The same principles of good diversification probably apply to stamps as much as they do to stock market investing. Other than perhaps focusing a portfolio around early British stamps, it is probably not wise to have too many stamps of the same type, in case an external event affects their value.

Since condition is all-important, viewing stamps is essential to appraise them correctly for investment purposes. Buying investment-grade stamps over the internet is unwise, unless the dealer is prepared to guarantee that they are of a specific minimum quality. Stamp fairs are a possibility, at least for making new acquisitions. These allow an investor to compare the prices offered by different dealers, and buy a particular stamp there and then, having satisfied themselves as to its quality. Large dealers with retail outlets are also likely to have better quality stock available from which to select. Unless it is narrowly focused on a 'hot' area, it is unlikely that a collection will be valued at more than the sum of its parts, simply because, unlike a work of art, there are usually many virtually identical stamps available of similar quality.

When it comes to disposing of a portfolio, a dealer from whom an investor bought may offer to buy back the stamps. If the price offered is not deemed to be providing satisfactory fair value, then it is possible to sell a significant portfolio through an auction house, where it may fetch more than the dealer's price. For those who pursue this avenue it is imperative to set a reserve that allows the investor to be guaranteed that the portfolio will fetch more than the dealer is offering, taking into account the commission taken by the saleroom. Once the bidding surpasses this figure, it becomes clear that choosing this route to market has been validated and that a better return has been achieved as a result.

A few years ago, stamp auctions generally saw prices of investment-quality stamps regularly fetching more than expected and significantly in excess of dealer's prices. This was part of the process by which the market for investment-quality stamps was opening up to a larger number of new and wealthy investors, thanks in part to Stanley Gibbons devoting particular attention to this aspect of the market. More recently, price trends have been more variable, with continental European stamps seeing prices under some pressure and year-on-year gains in general somewhat lower.

Stanley Gibbons has been particularly innovative in expanding the range of products on offer to investors. Mention should be made in particular of the guaranteed return contracts. These offer a guaranteed minimum return based on simple rather than compound interest for a fixed contract term from five years up to ten years. Five and six-year contracts pay a 3% annual return, seven, eight and nine-year terms pay 4% and the ten-year contact pays 5% a year. The contracts are backed by stamp portfolios. At the end of the term, the holder of the contract has six different (and mutually exclusive) options. He or she can either: take the guaranteed minimum return; sell the stamps independently and pocket any profits; sell at auction through Stanley Gibbon's own auction house at zero commission; sell the items back to Stanley Gibbons at 75% of catalogue value; keep the items; or roll the contract over for another term. Assume a contract ran for five years with a 4% a year guaranteed minimum return, that the amount invested was £10,000 and that the catalogue price doubled to £20,000 over that period. The options at the end of the period would be to: take the guaranteed return of £12,000; sell back the portfolio to SG for £15,000; auction them through SG, commission-free, for an uncertain return; roll the contract over; keep the items; or try to sell them privately for more than the £15,000 offered by SG.

The contracts are flexible in the sense that they offer a range of options at the end of the period, but cash has to be locked up for the period of the contract. It is of course also worth bearing in mind that SG has control over prices published in the catalogues and might make charges for placing a reserve on the items in question if the auction option were chosen. In addition, the interest rate in the contract is low relative to compound rates on offer on financial products, for example through fixed-term bonds offered by financial institutions, which also have the benefit of protection through the normal compensation schemes. Having said that, the various options allowed for in the contract terms have a value, which should be allowed for when calculating the true value of the contracts. In effect, buyers are getting a free call option over the stamps that comprise the portfolio. It is worth remembering at this point that, according to Stanley Gibbons, there has been no five-year period in the last 50 years during which stamp prices have declined. Others may disagree, particularly as there was a sharp decline in values in the aftermath of the peak in prices in 1979.

In its other investment dealings, Stanley Gibbons also offers financing, if required, for purchases of stamp portfolios on the basis of a 10% non-refundable deposit and the balance payable after a year. It also provides a discretionary rare stamp trading facility, based on offering investors the chance to buy stamps at a discount to the normal retail price, and splitting profits 50/50 when the stamps are subsequently sold.

Where to Go for More Information

Stanley Gibbons has extensive philatelic literature available at its Strand showroom and publishes a monthly magazine – *Gibbons Stamp Monthly* – devoted to the subject. *Gibbons Stamp Monthly*, *Stamp Magazine* and *Stamp & Coin Mart* are all available from newsagents each month. *The British Philatelic Bulletin* is published monthly by the Royal Mail. An annual subscription currently costs £12.95 in the UK, and £17.95 for the rest of the world. This publication is, however, mainly concerned with current British issues, which are unlikely to be of interest to would-be stamp investors. There is an increasing amount of information available on the web from dealers, philatelic societies and other information providers. What follows is a small selection of those available, presented in broad categories. Many of the sites are aimed at collectors. At the end of the chapter we look in brief at some books that would-be stamp investors will find useful.

Dealers

There are a large number of stamp dealers worldwide and the following are only a small selection. See the later section for details of sites that have links to a much larger number of dealers worldwide.

Arthur Ryan & Co (www.gbstamps.co.uk) specialises in stamps of Great Britain and is the largest mail-order stamp dealer in the country. The site has a stamp price list, all items of which can be purchased online. A free copy of the monthly price list, or the private treaty list, is available by completing the online enquiry form.

Brandon Galleries (www.brandonstamps.com) is a major dealer trading in classic British and Commonwealth stamps and modern major errors. The site also has a short guide to philatelic investment.

Dealers and auction houses

Entity	Web address	Main location	Email address	Telephone	Category
Apex	www.apexstamps.com	Lingfield, Surrey	admin@apexstamps.com	01342 833 413	Dealer/auction house
Arthur Ryan & Co	www.gbstamps.co.uk	Richmond, Surrey	netenquiry@gbstamps.co.uk	020 8940 7777	Dealer
Bonhams	www.bonhams.com	London	info@bonhams.com	020 7393 9789	Auction house
Brandon Galleries	www.brandonstamps.com	Guildford	peter@brandonstamps.com	01483 503 335	Dealer
Bridger and Kay	www.bridgerkay.com	Bristol	sales@bridgerkay.com	01934 863 656	Dealer
Cherrystone Philatelic Auctions	www.cherrystoneauctions.com	New York	info@cherrystoneauctions.com	212 977 7734	Auction house
Dorotheum	www.dorotheum.com	Vienna	stamps@dorotheum.com	43 1 515 60298	Auction house
Grosvenor Philatelic Auctions	www.grosvenorauctions.com	London	info@grosvenor-auctions.co.uk	020 7379 8789	Auction house
Harmers	www.harmers.com	London	info@harmers.com	020 8747 6100	Auction house
John Bull Stamp Auctions	www.jbull.com	Hong Kong	info@jbull.com	852 2890 5767	Auction house
Nalbandian (Jack)	www.nalbandstamp.com	USA	nalbandianj@earthlink.net	401 885 5020	Dealer
Sandafayre	www.sandafayre.com	Cheshire	stamps@sandafayre.com	01565 653 214	Dealer
Schlegel	www.auktionshaus-schlegel.de	Berlin	mail@auktionshaus-schlegel.de	030 8870 9962	Auction house
Scotia Philately	www.scotiaphilately.com	Hampton Court	info@scotiaphilately.com	0208 873 2854	Dealer
Sotheby's	www.sothebys.com/stamps	London	richard.ashton@sothebys.com	020 7293 5224	Auction house
Spink	www.spink.com	London	info@spink.com	0207 563 4000	Auction house
Stanley Gibbons	www.stanleygibbons.com	London	investments@stanleygibbons.co.uk	0207 836 8444	Dealer
Warwick and Warwick	www.warwickandwarwick.com	Warwick	info@warwickandwarwick.co.uk	01926 499 031	Auction house
Western Auctions	www.westernauctions.co.uk	Cardiff	info@westernauctions.co.uk	029 204 84934	Auction house
Whytes	www.whytes.ie	Dublin	info@whytes.ie	353 01676 2888	Auction house

Bristol-based Bridger & Kay (www.bridgerkay.com) was established in 1897 and specialises in British Commonwealth stamps pre-1952.

Jack Nalbandian (www.nalbandstamp.com) specialises in mint and used United States classics and major and minor stamp errors.

Sandafayre (www.sandafayre.com) is one of the biggest stamp mail order companies. It has been trading for over 30 years from its base in Knutsford, Cheshire. A non-commercial feature of the site is an extensive stamp catalogue with images and descriptions. It also holds regular online auctions.

Scotia Philately (www.scotiaphilately.com) was established in 1984 by two ex-Stanley Gibbons employees. In their words, their "[i]nvestment portfolios are carefully assembled from selected auctions and private collections". A specialist register is available to enable buyers to be informed when items come up that are of interest.

Stanley Gibbons (www.stanleygibbons.com) was established in 1856 and specialises in classic Great Britain and Commonwealth stamps. This site has everything you need to know about stamp collecting, whether as a hobby, an investment, or both. The site has a section for investors, which includes comments on the current state of the market based on the SG100 Stamp Index and details of the other stamp indices compiled by the firm (see the previous section for more details). Apart from stamps for sale, the site includes a newsletter, catalogues, philatelic terms and FAQ section.

- All World Stamps (www.allworldstamps.com) is the online version of the Stanley Gibbons series of stamp catalogues. Subscriptions are no longer possible, as SG are rolling out a new My Collection service alongside it: mycollection.stanleygibbons.com.

- Gibbons Stamp Monthly site (www.gibbonsstampmonthly.com) is a digital copy of the magazine, with the main features and articles from each month's issue available, plus an archive. Some articles are free to non-members.

- The company also sponsors Collector C@fe (www.collectorcafe.com), an online global collecting community with a section devoted to philately, including articles and links to dealers.

Auctions

Apex (www.apexstamps.com), owned by Noble Investments (UK) plc, offers online auctions, sales and other services.

Bonhams' (www.bonhams.com) stamp department based in Knightsbridge deals with every level of the stamp market, from private collections to rarities.

Cavendish Auctions (www.cavendish-auctions.com) is based in Derby and has been in business since 1952. The site has a historic auction search facility with over 100,000 lots and over 25,000 images.

Cherrystone Philatelic Auctions (www.cherrystoneauctions.com) holds a sale every two months in New York. The sales can be accessed online via CherrystoneLIVE, the company's online bidding system.

The Viennese auction house Dorotheum (www.dorotheum.com) holds regular stamp auctions covering classical and modern issues of stamps from Europe and abroad. Stamps may also be purchased for fixed prices.

Grosvenor Auctions (www.grosvenorauctions.com) holds regular auctions at its premises in London. Home visits can be arranged without obligation, for clients considering selling.

Harmers (www.harmers.com), founded in London in 1894, holds around ten auctions a year. Its all colour catalogue is available free to clients. Real-time internet bidding is available with a simulator for practice purposes. Other services include insurance valuations, private treaty sales and estate planning. The site also has a list of philatelic books for sale.

John Bull Stamp Auctions (www.jbull.com), located in Hong Kong, holds regular auctions.

Schlegel (www.auktionshaus-schlegel.de) is a leading German philatelic auctioneer based in Berlin.

Sotheby's (www.sothebys.com) stamp department specialises in selling high value, single-owner collections.

Spink (www.spink.com) offers a wide range of auctions throughout the year including general sales, single-owner sales and specialist one-country sales.

Other services include valuations both in person and online, estate planning and insurance advice. Spink also has branches in Singapore, New York and Dallas.

Warwick & Warwick (www.warwickandwarwick.com) holds stamp auctions each month in Warwick, with special auctions of named collections held periodically.

Information

The Bath Postal Museum (www.bathpostalmuseum.org) shows how 18th century Bath influenced and developed the postal system, which was later introduced throughout Europe and the British Empire. The site has a history of the UK postal system and the key people involved.

The British Library (www.bl.uk) houses the National Philatelic Collection of the UK. The site includes numerous articles and information on its collections, and various links. The library's philatelic collections are estimated to comprise over eight million items from around the world, including stamps, artwork, postal stationery, airmails, etc. The Library also houses a major collection of philatelic literature, which is available to researchers in the Reading Room with a pass (which can be applied for online).

La Philatelie Française sur Internet (www.philatelie.fr) has links to dealers, auctions worldwide, magazines, organisations and accessories.

Joseph Luft's Philatelic Resources (www.josephluft.com) had 4,214 links at the time of writing, covering general resources, shows and societies, postal authorities, collector's pages, downloadable images and auctions.

Information and publications

Entity	Web address	Main location	Email address	Telephone	Category
Bath Postal Museum	www.bathpostalmuseum.org	Bath	info@bathpostalmuseum.org	01225 460 333	Information
British Library Philatelic Collection	www.bl.co.uk	London	philatelic@bl.co.uk	020 7412 5120	Information
French Stamp Directory	www.philatelie.fr	France	info@philatelie.fr	n/a	Information
James Bendon	www.jamesbendon.com	Cyprus	info@jamesbendon.com	n/a	Publisher
Joseph Luft's Philatelic Resources	www.josephluft.com	USA	joeluft@execpc.com	1 262 242 5120	Information
Philaguide	www.philaguide.com	Netherlands	On site	n/a	Information
Philatelic Exporter (The)	www.philatelicexporter.com	Hampshire	On site	01425 472 363	Publication
Museum Post Archive	www.postalheritage.org.uk	London	info@postalheritage.co.uk	020 7239 2570	Information
Prinz	www.prinz.co.uk	UK	info@prinz.co.uk	01736 751 910	Accessories
Royal Philatelic Collection	www.royal.gov.uk	London	n/a	n/a	Information
Stamp Auction Network	www.stampauctionnetwork.com	USA	tldroege@mindspring.com	919 403 9459	Information
Stamp2.com	www.stamp2.com	Singapore	info@stamp2.com	65 629 523 42	Information
Stamp Circuit Club	www.stampcircuit.com	Israel	On site	972 4 837 2831	Information
Stamp Magazine	www.stampmagazine.co.uk	Croydon	On site	020 8726 8243	Publication
Stampshows.com	www.stampshows.com	USA	On site	n/a	Information
US National Postal Museum	www.postalmuseum.si.edu	Washington	Through site	202 633 5555	Information
Wardrop & Co	www.wardrop.co.uk	Colchester	Through site	01376 563 764	Miscellaneous

PhilaGuide (www.philaguide.com) is a directory of philatelic websites compiled by a Dutch enthusiast, including dealers, stamp museums, online auctions and online publications.

The Philatelic Exporter (www.philatelicexporter.com) is an independent magazine for the international postal stamp trade. It can be subscribed to online.

Philately and Postal History (www.philatelyandpostalhistory.com) has links to clubs and societies, dealers, auction houses, philatelists and events.

The British Postal Museum & Archive holds records of the British Post Office from the 17th century to the present-day (www.postalheritage.org.uk and www.royalmail.com/heritage). The archives include a background on stamp production as well as proof impressions of date and cancellation stamps.

The Royal Philatelic Collection (www.royal.gov.uk) is housed at St James's Palace and is the most comprehensive collection of UK and Commonwealth stamps in the world. Items from the collection are occasionally on display and each season the opening display of the Royal Philatelic Society traditionally consists of items from the collection. An overview of the collection is available on the site.

Stamps (www.stamps.net) is a US online philately magazine with numerous articles and a basic resource centre for beginner collectors, including coverage of topics such as buying stamps, philatelic terms and stamps on covers.

Current market values can be found at Stamp Finder (www.stampfinder.com). A searchable database provides the names of dealers with a particular stamp for sale, together with the price. Other features include a 'want list', where it is possible to register for special items required, and a calendar of events and auctions worldwide. The site includes an overview of stamps as an investment since 1992. It publishes individual country guides on the price histories and investment potential of individual stamps. Following from this analysis there is a list issued of 'best buys', which are considered likely to perform well above average. Also on offer are accessories, publications and software for sale.

Stamp2.com (www.stamp2.com) is a comprehensive resource site with numerous links and content, including books, auctions, a stamp terms translator and video interviews.

Stamp Auction Network (www.stampauctionnetwork.com) has links to auctions worldwide.

Stamp Circuit Club (www.stampcircuit.com) is an online forum for collectors and dealers. The site has numerous links to auction houses, dealers, and associations.

Stamp Magazine (www.stampmagazine.co.uk) has been in existence for 75 years. The magazine has an online as well as a print version. Free content includes information on rarities, famous collectors and stamp designers as well as links to fairs, auctions and exhibitions.

Stamp Shows (www.stampshows.com) is an online directory with links to thousands of sites in 62 categories.

UK250 (www.stampwebsites.co.uk) has a list of UK sites devoted to stamps.

The United States National Postal Museum (www.postalmuseum.si.edu) has an online database of its extensive collection as well as a history of the collection, and information on stamp collecting.

Associations and societies

The Philatelic Traders' Society (www.philatelic-traders-society.co.uk) organises the Stampex exhibitions and has links to dealers worldwide, along with their particular speciality.

The American Stamp Dealers Association (www.asdaonline.com) has an international membership with links online.

The American Philatelic Society (www.stamps.org) is the largest, non-profit society for stamp collectors, with 50,000 members in more than 110 countries. Members can buy and sell online and receive the 100-page monthly journal. Online learning is provided by Virtual Stamp Campus (www.stampcampus.org), with a demo lesson available on the site.

The Great Britain Philatelic Society (www.gbps.org.uk) aims to "promote, encourage, and contribute to the advancement of the philately of Great Britain". The society meets eight times a year in central London, but also has provincial meetings. The site includes a glossary of terms, a style guide and many useful links, including dealers who are GBPS members.

Stamps

Associations

Entity	Web address	Main location	Email address	Telephone	Category
American Philatelic Society	www.stamps.org	USA	doris@stamps.org	814 933 3803	Association
American Stamp Dealers Association	www.asdaonline.com	New York	asda@asdaonline.com	516 759 7000	Association
Association of British Philatelic Societies	www.ukphilately.org.uk,ABPS	UK	feedback@ukphilately.org.uk	n/a	Association
Great Britain Philatelic Society	www.gbps.org.uk	UK	gbps@mjpublications.com	n/a	Association
National Philatelic Society	www.ukphilately.org.uknps	London	nps@ukphilately.org.uk	020 7239 2571	Association
Philatelic Traders' Society	www.philatelic-traders-society.co.uk	Fleet, Hampshire	office.pts@btinternet.com	01252 628 006	Association
Royal Philatelic Society London	www.rpsl.org.uk	London	n/a	020 7486 1044	Association

223

The Royal Philatelic Society London (www.rpsl.org.uk) is the oldest philatelic society in the world and is strictly limited to amateur collectors. Members receive *The London Philatelist* ten times a year. This is the society's journal, which has been published since 1892. The site includes handouts from society meetings and links to other societies worldwide. The society's London premises include a philatelic museum and library.

UK Philately (www.ukphilately.org.uk) is the home of three organisations:

- The Association of British Philatelic Societies (ABPS) is the national association catering for the needs of local and specialist societies, philatelic federations, individual collectors and anyone interested in philately. It organises various events and exhibitions throughout the country, a calendar of which appears on the site. The association publishes a journal four times a year as well as various leaflets concerning the hobby. Membership details are available on the site.

- The National Philatelic Society (NPS) is one of the largest general philatelic societies in Great Britain, with members worldwide. Members receive *Stamp Lover* magazine six times a year, and can buy and sell online, as well as taking part in auctions. The society has an extensive library (by post if outside London) with a searchable online database. Members who live near the capital can attend monthly meetings at the headquarters in Charterhouse Street.

- The British Philatelic Trust (BPT) is an educational charity established by the Post Office in 1981, from which it is independent. Its objective is the promotion of the "study, research and dissemination of knowledge of philately".

Miscellaneous

James Bendon (www.jamesbendon.com) is a philatelic publisher based in Cyprus, who also sells philatelic miscellanea such as forgeries and specimen stamps.

Prinz (www.prinz.co.uk) sells stamp and coin collecting accessories.

Wardrop & Co (www.wardrop.co.uk) are insurance intermediaries specialising in philatelic insurance. Apart from insurance information the site has numerous links including auctions, dealers and philatelic software.

Books

Stanley Gibbons publishes the world's most comprehensive range of price catalogues, the listings and prices of which are the basis of the philatelic market. They include the following:

Commonwealth and British Empire Stamps 1840-1970

Great Britain Concise Stamp Catalogue

Specialised Great Britain Stamp Catalogue (five volumes)

Stamps of the World (this includes every stamp ever issued)

Stamp Collecting: How to Start

Enjoy Stamp Collecting

Stanley Gibbons' Guide to Stamp Collecting

Philatelic Terms Illustrated

Also worth looking at is:

Top Dollar Paid!: The Complete Guide to Selling Your Stamps, by Stephen R. Datz (General Philatelic Corporation, 1997). The book explores the pitfalls to avoid when selling stamps, and includes information on methods of sale, valuing stamps and stamps as investments. The main messages are reinforced by numerous anecdotal stories delivered in an entertaining and informative style. Two other books by the same author are *Stamp Collecting* and *Stamp Investing*.

9.
Wine

Investing in wine has always had attractions for a certain type of investor. They reason that, if the worst comes to the worst, they can always enjoy their investment by drinking it. Yet the pleasure of owning fine investment-quality wine can often of necessity be a remote one. Most wine merchants will advise clients to store their investments at their own, or an independent, temperature-controlled bonded warehouse. This chapter looks at investing in wine using the headings we have established for other chapters – the basics; whether or not it has the appropriate characteristics for portfolio-style investment; the tax implications, if any; and the returns that investors can derive from investing in this way.

Basics

Bordeaux blue-chips

Wine is produced in many parts of the world. But from an investment standpoint, investing in wine should mean investing in the blue-chips. This means primarily the best Bordeaux wines, including Saint-Émilion and Pomerol, the best Burgundy (such as Romanée-Conti), and a few of the best wines from Italy (say Sassicaia or Solaia) and Australia (Penfolds Grange, for example). In practice there are few reasons for ever straying beyond top-rated claret.

The history of wine making in Bordeaux dates back to Roman times. It took off when Henry II married Eleanor of Aquitaine in 1152 and received as a dowry a large part of south-west France. Thereafter the English took to the wines of Bordeaux in a big way. In 1855 Napoleon III laid the foundations for wine investment by classifying all of the vineyards in Bordeaux on a scale of 1-5. As a result we have the terms first growth (premier cru), second growth and so on. The laws enacted then have held good with almost no change to this day. They are vigorously upheld, and category changes are almost unheard of. As one wine merchant put it, "everyone in the know, knows what should be where". Wines from St Emilion and Pomerol, to the east of Bordeaux (on the so-called 'right bank' of the Gironde), were not included in this original classification and have only become more appreciated from the 20th century onwards. This does not detract from their potential as investments, particularly because they tend to be produced in somewhat smaller quantities.

Because of this history and quasi-regulated structure, Bordeaux has a pre-eminent place among the world's wine regions. The geographical and climatic conditions in the area mean that it can produce more fine wine with greater regularity than any other part of France or any other country. There are many thousands of vineyards in Bordeaux but only the top-flight ones are worthy of investment money. In virtually no other places are the greatest wines made in such limited quantity. The top 30 chateaux in Bordeaux can produce no more than 500,000 cases of wine in any one vintage, of which a third goes immediately to satisfy demand from the hotel and restaurant trade. Only the output of the best chateaux in Burgundy is smaller. This creates conditions of scarcity that should, in theory, make wine ideal for investment purposes. This is reinforced by the fact that there is a long back-history of wine prices and the quality of particular vintages, and that there is an active auction market in which wine is bought and sold. There is another advantage of focusing on Bordeaux, and particularly red Bordeaux of the highest quality. It is that doing so limits to a manageable size what would otherwise be a bewildering range of investment choices.

What should investors seek in a wine for it to be viewed as a serious investment-grade product? The best chateaux of Bordeaux are well known to wine experts. But if an investor is contemplating serious investment, guidance is needed from reference books. Even one as simple as *Hugh Johnson's Pocket Wine Book* (Octopus Publishing Group, published annually) is an excellent aide-memoire, with authoritative thumbnail assessments of individual chateaux and observations on vintage quality.

The best-known names are ones like Lafite-Rothschild, Latour, Haut-Brion, Mouton-Rothschild, and Margaux, but there are many others. Some of the best produce wine in very small quantities. It is a moot point whether to differentiate between first and second growth. The classification of 1855 was based on more than a century of trading practice, so second growths have been up there among the best for 250 years. Some second growth chateaux have been termed 'super-seconds'. This is because in recent years the experts feel they have produced wine of more or less the same standard as the first growths.

All can make good investments if the right vintage is bought at the right time, or bad ones if bought at the wrong time or the wrong price. This table shows some of the best-known names in Bordeaux.

Key Bordeaux chateaux

Name	Area
Angelus	Saint-Émilion
Ausone	Saint-Émilion
Cheval Blanc	Saint-Émilion
Climens	Sauternes
Clinet	Pomerol
La Conseillante	Pomerol
Cos d'Estournel	Saint Estephe
Ducru-Beaucaillou	Saint-Julien
L'Eglise-Clinet	Pomerol
L'Evangile	Pomerol
Figeac	Saint-Émilion
La Fleur Petrus	Pomerol
Haut-Brion	Pessac (Graves)
Lafite-Rothschild	Pauillac
Lafleur	Pomerol
Latour	Pauillac
Laville-Haut Brion	Pessac
Léoville-Las Cases	Saint-Julien
Margaux	Margaux
La Mission Haut Brion	Pessac
Mouton Rothschild	Pauillac
Palmer	Cantenac
Pétrus	Pomerol
Pichon Longueville	Pauillac
Le Pin	Pomerol
Rauzan-Ségla	Margaux
Rieussec	Sauternes
Suduiraut	Sauternes
Tertre-Roteboeuf	Saint-Émilion
Trotanoy	Pomerol
De Valandraud	Saint-Émilion
Vieux Chateau Certan	Pomerol
D'Yquem	Sauternes

Note: This list is based on chateaux rated 4∗ quality by wine expert Hugh Johnson. No comment is made as to their value for money or status as investments. See *Hugh Johnson's Pocket Wine Book* for more detailed comments.

Selected recent prices

Chateaux	Vintage	Price per case £
Margaux	1996	4000
Lafite Rothschild	2006	3150
Lafite Rothschild	2008	3100
Latour	2008	2995
Lafite Rothschild	2001	2800
Margaux	2008	1940
Lafite Rothschild	1982	1820
Pichon Lalande	2003	640
Léoville Poyferré	1996	540
Pichon Baron	1999	485
Lynch Bages	2008	375
Talbot	2005	340

This table demonstrates that there are substantial differences in price between vintages and between different chateaux for the same vintage. Hugh Johnson's excellent book contains comments on which vintages are regarded as the best for each particular chateau and general comments on which vintage years are the best for laying down. This raises the obvious point that the wine produced each year differs from chateau to chateau, and of course each vintage year is different for the Bordeaux region as a whole. Some vintages, such as 2000, have been deemed excellent across the board, and prices already reflect this. The best chateaux can produce decent wines even in a difficult vintage year. Above all, they produce wine of consistently top quality.

Vintage advice

The quality or otherwise of a vintage is a product of the climatic conditions during the growing season and harvesting period, and can therefore be determined with a broad degree of accuracy once the wine has been produced and tasted. Much depends on the quality-control policies operated by the chateaux. Typically between 10% and 30% of the wine made from any one harvest may be rejected as unsuitable to be classed as vintage. The best wine takes time to mature. It will, at some stage, reach a peak and thereafter begin to deteriorate. From an investment standpoint it follows that the best policy can be to buy wine of a quality that will last in what is known, or strongly suspected to be, a good vintage, and to buy it as early as possible in its life. While some wines produced in, say, 1945 or 1961 are still superb, they are unlikely to improve further and in investment terms have little appreciation potential. Most wine experts would advise against buying anything produced before 1980 unless it can be guaranteed to have been stored in ideal conditions.

En primeur

There are several ways of buying wine. From an investment standpoint, the best method to capture returns may be by buying *en primeur*. This is buying after the wine has been produced and after an initial tasting, but prior to its being bottled for the mass market. Wine can also be bought in bottle through a wine merchant in the normal way, usually around two years later. The timescale is roughly as follows: the grapes are harvested between the end of August and the beginning of October; the wine is then made and stored in barrels, and the following April/May it is available to be tasted and rated by wine experts in this *en primeur* form. The wine is then made available in bottled form roughly two years later. So the *en primeur* 2009 vintage will be available in April 2010, but not available in bottle until early 2012. Buying at the *en primeur* stage, in effect using what is to all intents and purposes a futures market for bottled wine, allows investors to get in at the earliest possible point in a wine's lifecycle. But there are risks. There have been scams in the past involving *en primeur* wine, so watertight documentation is essential. In addition, with *en primeur* there is always the chance that, despite what the experts may say, what is thought to be an outstanding vintage at the earliest stage may turn out to be pedestrian when it finally reaches the bottle.

Bottle bank

Storing bottled wine is best left to the experts. Investment-quality wines may take years to reach their peak and can be ruined if not stored correctly in the appropriate temperature and humidity. The ideal is for wine to be stored in a temperature that fluctuates little and which is between 10 degrees and 13 degrees Celsius, with humidity of around 60%, in a dark and vibration-free environment. Since few individual investors have the benefit of sufficient space of the right sort to store wine properly, it makes sense to leave the storage of investment-grade wines to an expert. The additional advantage of having a wine portfolio stored by an expert is that it can be kept under bond, in a customs-controlled warehouse. This means it is not treated as having entered the UK market and there is therefore no duty or VAT to pay on it, as there would be if it were cleared for use in the UK. If the sole objective is that the wine be treated as an investment, and subsequently sold, then this system is ideal. Wine is kept securely, registered in the client's name, and stored properly, free of tax. Clearly this is not possible if investors buy *en primeur*, and in such a case there is no alternative but to trust the chateau and the wine merchant to deliver the goods when the wine is eventually bottled. Only then can it be shipped to the bonded warehouse chosen by the investor, and stored to his or her requirements. For this reason it is best to use the services of an established and highly reputable wine merchant if an investor is planning such a course of action. In any event, the best strategy is to deal with someone well known, someone the investor knows well and trusts on a personal basis, or someone with good credentials (a Master of Wine, for example) – qualifications that can be checked out and are, to all intents and purposes, a guarantee of probity.

These quirks in the system mean that there are various styles of wine investment possible, with various risk levels attached, and various time horizons involved. Buying *en primeur* is riskier, but may offer much better returns.

The Right Alternative Asset for You?

As in previous chapters, this section looks at the questions that need to be answered in order to determine whether wine could form a part of a wider portfolio of investments for you.

A medium to long-term investment?

Wine investment is not necessarily an ultra long-term business, but some of the best wines do take a number of years to reach their full potential. In some cases, by buying *en primeur* (before the wine is bottled) the investor is likely to benefit from what has traditionally been the steepest increase in price, in the early years of a classic vintage's life. However, buying *en primeur* is not necessary in all cases to capture the best returns from a particular vintage. In some instances the best returns come five or more years into a wine's life, or from a sea change in the appreciation of the quality of a particular chateau. Investors need to buy wine with a five to ten-year time horizon in mind. Remember too that buying *en primeur* does not guarantee a steady or immediate increase in value. The wine may drift for a while, before possibly increasing sharply in price two or three years into its life.

Capital required?

In theory there is no maximum or minimum amount to be invested, but wine merchants will typically recommend a minimum investment of at least £3000, and ideally perhaps rather more than this in order to create a balanced, long-term investment portfolio.

Many leading wine merchants, such as Berry Bros. & Rudd, operate 'cellar plans', by which an individual invests a fixed amount per month and accumulates a portfolio of wine for investment or drinking purposes over a period of years. Minimum amounts invested under plans like this are typically in the region of £100-£250 per month, payable via direct debit, with the higher figure being the minimum if the wines are being held for investment purposes. Lump sum additions can also be made into the plan. Cellar plans operate on a basis rather like that of an advisory broker/client relationship. The would-be investor, through a plan like this, has a designated advisor who will be aware of the client's objectives and will be able to advise what type of wine should go into the plan, although the client has the ultimate control over what is bought. In the case of investment-grade wine cellar plans, wine merchants suggest that their advisors are given discretion over which wines to buy, drawing on their extensive knowledge of the liquidity or otherwise of the secondary market for particular wines when the time comes to sell. Wines held under a cellar plan are invariably stored in the wine merchant's own facility, for which a charge will be made. In the case of Berry Bros., for example, the charge is in the region of £9 per case per annum, plus VAT.

In fairness to those offering plans like this, it should be stressed that the firms in question are primarily orientated towards wines for future drinking, rather than looking at them with a view to capital appreciation. Prices reflect this. They may also charge commission if investors subsequently wish to sell the wine rather than drink it. However, there has, in recent years, been increasing emphasis on operating cellar plans for investors as well.

Storage and insurance costs?

It is a false economy for investors to store wine themselves in the hope of making savings on storage and insurance costs. Wine merchants are able to store wine under bond in tightly controlled conditions, which preserve the investment in optimum condition and saves paying VAT and duty. Charges are either a flat rate per case (typically around £7.50 to £9.50 per case per year) or about 1% of the underlying value of the wine. Investors need to choose a wine merchant very much with an eye to the firm's expertise, but also bear in mind the cellar charges. If these are felt to be excessive, it may be possible to negotiate an alternative arrangement so that the wines can be stored in a third-party warehouse.

Some merchants specialising in wines for investment will charge for their services, either an upfront figure of, say, 5% or perhaps an annual 1% fee, or hidden charges like consultation fees or commission charges when wines are sold. The extent to which charges of this nature apply needs to be investigated at the outset, before signing up. In the case of Berry Bros., currently no charges are made other than for storage. In the case of all wine merchants there will be a normal bid-offer spread (that's to say the merchant will typically re-sell the wine at a higher price than the seller receives).

Portfolio diversification?

Some wine investment firms would have investors believe that wine prices outperform both the stock market and some other classes of alternative investment over the longer term. In selected instances this has been true, but there are many mundane wines that do not behave in this way. Stamps, coins and art are dependent on the relative prosperity of the collector market. Wine prices reflect demand from drinkers as well as investors. This has pluses and minuses. Those who invest are doing so in conditions where not only is supply restricted, but also where supply will contract as consumers (as opposed to investors) drink it. As this happens, the wine becomes increasingly scarce.

On the other hand, investment-grade wine is something of an affluent person's hobby, and wine in general is subject to extreme fashion swings. A considerable amount of investment bankers' bonus money went into wine in the good times, which meant that prices of fine wine were severely affected at the time of the extreme financial crisis in late 2008, and for several months thereafter, when money was withdrawn from these investments. Because of this phenomenon, which has been quite a long-standing feature of the market (in a similar way to high-end art), prices of fine wines have proven rather more susceptible to conditions in the financial markets than some other areas. Coins and stamps, for instance, are more the preserve of long-term collectors, and have better though by no means absolute immunity.

Tax considerations?

One of the big plus points for investing in wine in the UK is that the tax authorities sometimes consider wine to be a wasting asset. Therefore, provided an investor does not buy and sell wine often enough to be regarded as a dealer and thus make themselves subject to income tax on their profits, there may be no capital gains tax (CGT) levied on the gains made on sales of any wine bought as an investment. Those banking on a tax-free return, however, should bear in mind that this is not guaranteed. Fortified wine, which has a much longer drinkable shelf life, is certainly not exempt from CGT when an investment is finally sold. In the case of fine wine, however, HMRC guidance is ambiguous, since it tends to regard fine wine as 'maturing' rather than 'wasting', unless there is evidence to the contrary to suggest that its theoretical shelf life is less than 50 years. The appropriate HMRC document says that "where the facts justify it, we would normally contend that wine is not a wasting asset if it appears to be fine wine which not unusually is kept (or some samples of which are kept) for substantial periods sometimes well in excess of 50 years". This seem to suggest that capital gains made on investment-grade wines from outstanding vintage years are likely not to be considered as deriving from wasting assets and would therefore be subject to CGT.

If considerations such as these are important to an investor, the likely tax treatment of investments like this should be checked with an accountant before investing. Tax treatment of issues like this is also likely to differ substantially from country to country.

Prices and Returns

This is an area that is hotly disputed. Let's begin with the basics. The starting point for a fine wine portfolio is probably a lump sum investment of ideally around £10,000, plus an ongoing investment of £250 a month. Investing this amount allows a wine merchant to assemble a balanced portfolio over a period of time. Prices of individual wines on a per-case basis vary, but first growth Bordeaux from classic chateaux are typically in the region of £700-800 per case and upwards.

Data on returns is difficult to evaluate, but there is a general belief that in the long term (25 years or more) fine wine can outperform most other tangible investments. According to Decanter Fine Wine Tracker, fine wine prices rose more than eightfold since 1978, a compound return of over 8% a year. This ties in closely with research conducted by Emotional Assets Management & Research, which cites annual returns in the region of 8.6% a year over 20 years, with volatility of less than 5%.

Before we take that too literally, many performance calculations do depend on the starting point you choose and the vintage you select, and arriving at any generalised measurement can be fraught with difficulty. As an example, research available at journalist Jim Budd's 'Investdrinks' website (www.investdrinks.org) has shown that increases in value of fine wine can be patchy. In summary, the research attempted to find those chateaux that showed the most consistent performance, and then the scale of the gains in good years, and of the declines in bad years. The conclusion was that wines from average or poor years made poor investments, but over a span of 22 vintage years only a third of vintages showed gains over a three-year period in excess of 20% and then only at the top performing chateaux. Fewer than half of them showed gains of 10% or more over three years. This argues for being *highly* selective and for taking advice from highly qualified wine merchants with detailed knowledge of different vintages and the secondary market for them. This conclusion is confirmed by Liv-ex (www.liv-ex.com), the London International Vintners Exchange. This is an independent trading and settlement organisation serving the fine wine trade. Among other data, Liv-ex produces an index of prices of the top 500 wines from what it describes as "the most celebrated regions and vintages". This index, with a base date of May 2001, currently stands at exactly 200, little changed by late 2009.

Since the first edition of this book was published, the Liv-ex indices have built up additional price history, and the range of indices calculated has been expanded, allowing would-be investors to get a much more accurate picture of long-term returns. These are examined in more detail in the next few paragraphs and the related charts and tables.

Liv-ex 100 Index

This index measures the price movements of 100 of the most sought-after fine wines for which there is an active secondary market. The overwhelming majority (over 90%) of the index is represented by Bordeaux wines, with some wines from Burgundy, the Rhône, Champagne and Italy also forming part of it. Wines that are included are weighted for relative scarcity and for the original production level in order to reflect their relative importance in the market. To be included the wines must have attracted a score of 95 points or greater from wine guru Robert Parker, be physically available in the UK market, and be regularly traded. Recent vintages trading *en primeur* are not included.

Data for the index goes back to July 2001, although the base for the index is January 2004. The index traded narrowly around 100 until mid 2005 and then rose steadily to reach an initial peak in August 2007. After a slight setback it advanced further and peaked at 264 in June 2008 and then fell back sharply to around the 205 mark in the second half of the year, since when it has seen some modest recovery.

Liv-ex 100 returns

As at July	2001	2002	2003	2004	2005	2006	2007	2008	2009
Index number	93.1	102	98	97.2	101.8	161	247.8	262.6	215.6
Annual Change (%)	n/a	9.6	-4	-0.8	4.7	58.1	53.9	6	-17.9
Cumulative Change (%)	n/a	9.6	5.3	4.4	9.3	72.9	166.2	182.1	131.6

Performance over period	(%)
1 year	-17.9
3 years	34
5 years	121.8
8 years	131.6

8-year CAGR (%opa): 11.1
CAGR on FTSE over period (%opa): -2.3
Number of constituents: 100
Weighting: by original production levels and relative scarcity

By contrast the Liv-Ex 500, a broader based index designed to reflect more broadly based movements in the wine market, and not specifically those that might be bought by investors, has shown a much smoother upward trend. From its base level of 100 in January 2004, the index currently stands at 203.

Liv-ex Fine Wine Investables Index

This is a relatively recently created index, albeit one with data that stretches back to January 1988. It is designed to track the wine commonly found in investment portfolios. The constituents are exclusively red Bordeaux wines from 24 leading chateaux from vintages within the last fifteen years or particularly strong ones prior to that. The oldest wines in the index date back to 1982. Wines must have a Parker rating of 95 or more. The prices are weighted in much the same way as for the Liv-Ex 100 index for price and, for vintages over 15 years, for scarcity.

The weightings in the index are shown in the table by both chateau and vintage.

By vintage

Year	Number	Weighting (%)
2005	19	16
2004	10	3.7
2003	15	8.6
2002	8	3.1
2001	8	3.4
2000	20	18.3
1999	10	4.4
1998	9	5.2
1997	4	1.5
1996	11	7.3
1995	13	6.1
1994	6	3.1
1990	15	7.2
1989	11	4.9
1986	9	4
1983	6	0.4
1982	14	2.8

By chateau

Chateau	Number	Weighting (%)
Lafite Rothschild	17	17.9
Latour	14	13.3
Margaux	16	12.4
Cheval Blanc	13	9.3
Haut Brion	14	9.2
Mouton Rothschild	14	8
Petrus	15	5.5
Mission Haut Brion	4	3.5
Pavie	7	2.8
Léovillé les Cases	8	2.7
Angelus	6	2.2
Ausone	14	1.8
Palmer	5	1.6
Montrose	5	1.6
Conseillante	5	1.5
Pichon Lalande	6	1.5
Cos d'Estournel	6	1.4
Ducru Beaucaillou	3	0.8
Pichon Baron	4	1.7
Léovillé Poyferré	3	0.6
Lynch Bages	2	0.6
Grand Puy Lacoste	3	0.5
Léoville Barton	2	0.4
Pontet Canet	2	0.3

The long price history of the index, which has been compiled through exhaustive research with a range of wine merchants within the industry, makes it particularly suitable for calculating long-term returns from investment-grade wines. Over the 20 years to May 2009, the index has shown a compound annual percentage growth of 13.5%, and 9.5% per annum over the last ten years. This is consistent with the magnitude of returns found by other studies into the subject. Performance of the indices over various time periods is shown in the table.

Liv-ex Investables returns

As at May	1999	2000	2001	2002	2003	2004	2005	2006	2007	2008	2009
Index number	84.7	89.3	96.1	102.1	96.5	99.1	102.9	133.7	211.7	243.1	209.1
Annual Change (%)	n/a	5.4	7.6	6.2	-4.5	2.7	3.8	29.9	58.3	14.8	-14
Cumulative Change (%)	n/a	5.4	13.5	20.5	13.9	17	21.5	57.8	149.9	187	146.8

Performance over period	(%)
1 year	-14
3 years	56.4
5 years	111
10 years	146.8

10-year CAGP (%pa): 9.5
CAGR on FTSE over period (%pa): -3.4
Number of constituents: 188
Weighting: price-weighted and by scarcity

In recent years, the Liv-ex Investables index has risen sharply. After a strong rise from 1994 to 1998, it fluctuated around the 100 mark for some years, before beginning a sharp rise from 2006 onwards, reaching a peak of 248 in August 2008 before falling back sharply to around the 200 mark by the end of 2008. Since then, there has been modest recovery in prices. This confirms what anecdotal evidence has suggested, namely that fine wines were used as a home for investment banking bonus cash, which was withdrawn rapidly, and possibly not entirely voluntarily, at the time the financial crisis reached its height in 2008.

Liv-ex Claret Chip Index

Similar remarks can perhaps be made about the Claret-Chip Index, which is exclusively composed of first growth clarets, many of which will also be the type of wine sought after by investors. This index also increased sharply between 2005 and its peak in September 2008, almost tripling over this period before dropping back somewhat in the final quarter of 2008, from which point a modest recovery in prices has been seen. The index is compiled in a very similar way to the investables index.

Liv-ex Claret Chip Index returns

As at July	2004	2005	2006	2007	2008	2009
Index number	98.2	103.1	173.6	286.1	298.3	242.1
Annual Change (%)	n/a	5	68.3	64.8	4.3	-18.8
Cumulative Change (%)	n/a	5	76.8	191.3	203.8	146.5

Performance over period	(%)
1 year	-18.8
3 years	39.5
5 years	146.5
10 years	n/a

5-year CAGR (%pa): 19.8
CAGR on FTSE over period (%pa): 0.9
Number of constituents: 35
Weighting: price

What the indices in general show is the degree to which the presence of investor money flowing into fine wine has led to something of a two-tier market, with the highest quality wines increasing sharply and, on the evidence of price movements as a result of the impact of the financial crisis, becoming somewhat more volatile than the more broadly based indices that track prices of less exclusive wines. It can, however, be argued that the financial crisis of late 2008 was an extreme event and should not be used as an indicator of future performance. Nonetheless it seems likely that price movements for the next few years may be more modest (although probably still upwards).

Investors do need to remember that there is no sure route to making money, either in the stock market or in tangible assets. While wine prices have in the main been less volatile than the stock market, wine is in the same category as art in investment terms; that is to say, an alternative to the stock market but not necessarily an investment that offers diversification away from it, given the degree to which it is favoured as diversification by those who work in investment banking! There is also the pitfall of fashion: in the case of wine, what is in vogue one year may not be so favoured a year or two later.

Despite all this, there is something to be said in favour of wine investment, and some advantages that it possesses. The appreciation in prices over the long term, especially for top-quality wine, does seem to bear out the claims made by some wine merchants in the past that *long-term* returns from wine can more than keep pace with the stock market. While Bordeaux has occasional bad years, some winemakers can make acceptable wines even in these years, and it may become evident from the outset whether or not the wines from any year are suitable for investment. A poor year or two only serves to enhance the scarcity value of good vintages. And as noted previously, one reason for the potentially useful returns from wine investment is the fact that investors can retain their wine for a reasonably long period, during which a sizeable quantity of a particular vintage will have been bought and drunk by non-investors, thereby increasing the scarcity value of the remainder. There is also the possibility that an influential wine writer will give a particular chateau the seal of approval and revolutionise its pricing almost overnight. The well-known wine writer Robert Parker famously achieved this with Château Pétrus, whose cause he championed. While other wine writers may or may not share his opinions, there is no doubt that he wields considerable influence, particularly among American buyers.

So good returns can be captured but the qualifications I have mentioned earlier about performance of different categories of wine should be borne in mind. Just as some investors in the stock market are highly successful and others do less well, with wine investment it is as well to remember that there are no guarantees that past performance can be repeated, no repealing of the law that states that high returns usually come with high risks attached, and that wine investment is unregulated.

How to Invest

It takes some educated guesswork to spot those wines that will produce the best returns from an investment standpoint. Rather like picking shares, it is a matter of spotting which ones offer the right combination of quality and value. It is also the case that investors need to be careful about the way they approach investment in wine. There have been a number of scams that have trapped investors in the past, and examples of ostensibly bona fide wine investment operations where, after a company has gone into liquidation, investors have found it difficult to establish title to the wine they thought they owned. So there are a number of ground rules to observe to make sure the investment is a safe one.

The first is to run an independent check on the price of the wine being offered by anyone who is suggesting it as an investment. Websites of leading wine merchants generally allow investors to do this, as does www.wine-searcher.com. A good source is Fine+Rare (www.frw.co.uk), which has updated prices on a wide range of chateaux and vintage years. Liv-ex, referred to earlier, also gives a regular update in the public part of its website on recent prices for the most popular chateaux, covering the better vintages from 1982 onwards. Many scams don't involve fake wine but registered wines – selling them, however, at prices in excess (sometimes well in excess) of their current market value. So would-be investors can detect frauds as well as simple overpricing in this way, too.

Second, investors should check that the firm with which they are dealing has not been involved in suspect dealing before. The website www.investdrinks.org carries the names of companies whose dealings are suspect. If in any doubt, investors in the UK should run a Companies House search (www.companieshouse.gov.uk) on the company and its directors to see whether or not they have a bona fide business. Investors in other countries can use their local company registry in the same way. On balance it is best to deal only with an established and well-known wine merchant, many of which have recently begun to cater to the investment market.

Third, it is important to make sure that the portfolio of wines being purchased is appropriate in terms of its risk profile and in terms of the time the wine is likely to take to achieve its peak value. High-quality is also the watchword.

To be suitable for investment, the wine must be recognised as a high-quality product (i.e. from one of the key Bordeaux chateaux listed earlier), and of a proven high-quality vintage, and not simply an 'undiscovered gem' that is likely to remain undiscovered for some time. As a rule of thumb, for example, if a particular chateau does not merit at least a four-star rating in the Bordeaux section of Hugh Johnson's book, referred to earlier, then chances are it does not merit inclusion in an investment portfolio.

Fourth and extremely importantly, it is crucial to establish exactly how and where the wine bought as an investment is to be delivered and stored. Investors should only deal with firms that will confirm that wine is specifically identified with their name on the case and stored in an independent warehouse like Octavian Vaults, which operates a large specialist facility in Wiltshire. Storage in a public bond means that the wines in question are specifically identified as your property and cannot be removed from the warehouse without your specific written consent. If dealing with an established wine merchant who may wish to store the wine on their own premises, it is important for investors to verify that they have title to the products being stored and that they do not become available to creditors should the firm cease trading.

Fifth, it is important that investors pay only against invoice and confirmation that the wine is delivered either direct to the investor or into storage under their name at the warehouse.

Finally, investors should, as a matter of prudence, establish at the outset what charges they will bear. Firms differ in the charges they make. Some charge only for storage at the market rate or less. Some charge an upfront fee of perhaps 5% of the total value of the wine, others an annual 1% management charge. Storage costs are typically levied on a per-case per year basis. Some firms pass these on straight to the client; others add a mark-up of their own on top.

Where to Go for More Information

For the consumer there is generally no shortage of information about wine. Magazines like *Decanter*, *Harpers Wine & Spirit*, and all the national daily and especially Sunday newspapers have regular columns about wine written by acknowledged experts. For investors, a little further digging is of course also required. Prominent wine merchants are a good starting point and many have sophisticated websites aimed primarily at selling wine to would-be drinkers, but recently have also begun catering to investors. These can prove useful sources of information for investors and an all-important check on prices quoted by those promoting investment schemes.

Dealers

Acker Merrall & Condit (www.ackerwines.com), founded in 1892 in New York, is America's oldest wine shop. The auction side of the business started in 1998 and offers live auctions in New York and San Francisco, with internet participation.

Berry Bros. & Rudd (www.bbr.com), established in 1698 in St James', is Britain's oldest wine and spirits merchant. Apart from London, Berry Bros. have retail premises in Hong Kong, Japan and Dublin. The award-winning website is entertaining and informative, with coverage of everything investors could ever wish to know about wine, including its investment potential. The company also runs a series of wine tasting events, including courses and tastings.

Bloomsbury Auctions' New York operation (www.ny.bloomsburyauctions.com) has recently entered the wine auction arena in collaboration with Sokolin (www.sokolin.com), a leading American fine and rare wine merchant.

Dealers, auction houses and services

Entity	Web address	Main location	Email address	Telephone	Category
Acker, Merrall and Condit	www.ackerwines.com	New York	ackerstore@aol.com	212 787 1700	Dealer/auction house
Berry Bros. & Rudd	www.bbr.com	London	Through site	0800 280 2440	Dealer
Bloomsbury Auctions	www.ny.bloomsburyauctions.com	New York	wine@bloomsburyauctions.com	1 212 719 1000	Auction house
Bonhams	www.bonhams.com	London	wine@bonhams.com	0207 947 7447	Auction house
Chicago Wine Company, The	www.tcwc.com	Illinois	info@tcwc.com	630 594 2972	Auction house
Christie's	www.christies.com	London	On site	020 7752 3366	Auction house
Edward Roberts International	www.eriwine.com	Illinois	info@eriwine.com	847 295 8696	Auction house
Fine + Rare	www.frw.co.uk	London	wine@frw.co.uk	020 8960 1995	Dealer
James Nicholson	www.jnwine.com	Northern Ireland	shop@jnwine.com	028 4483 0091	Dealer
London City Bond	www.lcb.co.uk	Tilbury	info@lcb.co.uk	01375 853 700	Cellar
Magnum Fine Wine	www.magnum.co.uk	London	wine@magnum.co.uk	0207 629 5607	Dealer
Millesima	www.millesima.co.uk	London	On site	0800 917 0352	Dealer
Octavian	www.octavianvaults.co.uk	Wiltshire	care@octavianvaults.co.uk	01225 818 714	Cellar
Premier Cru	www.premiercru.com	London	sales@premiercru.com	020 8905 4495	Dealer
Richard Kihl	www.richardkihl.ltd.uk	Suffolk	sales@richardkihl.ltd.uk	01728 454 455	Dealer
Sokolin	www.sokolin.com	New York	Through site	631 537 4434	Dealer
Sotheby's	www.sothebys.com	London	Through site	020 7293 50 50	Auction house
Vinotheque	www.vinotheque.co.uk	Burton-on-Trent	sales@vinotheque.co.uk	01375 853 777	Cellar
Wineandco	www.wineandco.com	Bordeaux	Through site	33 5 56 49 81 81	Dealer
WineBid	www.winebid.com	Napa, California	info@winebid.com	888 638 8968	Online auction
Zachys	www.zachys.com	New York	On site	1 866 922 4971	Dealer/auction house

Bonhams (www.bonhams.com) hold seven fine wine auctions per year in London, specialising in the classic regions of Europe.

The Chicago Wine Company (www.tcwc.com), founded in 1974, holds 20 auctions a year and is the only wine auction company in the USA that has no buyer's premium. Wine can also be bought outright.

The wine department at Christie's (www.christies.com) has international sales centres across three continents. *The Fine Wine Report*, which is available by email, provides information on forthcoming sales, events such as wine tastings, and features from Christie's wine specialists.

Edward Roberts International (www.eriwine.com) holds live auctions in Chicago and San Francisco, with absentee and real-time internet participation.

Fine+Rare (www.frw.co.uk) are wine brokers based in London. Their wine sourcing technology called 'Wine Desk' has up-to-date prices and availability from a network of sources across Europe, ranging from growers to auction houses. Over 30,000 wines are listed from 170 vintages, and over 2,500 suppliers.

James Nicholson Wine Merchant (www.jnwine.com) of Crossgar, County Down, is Northern Ireland's leading fine wine dealer with a thriving mail-order business. The site has links to wine producers worldwide, particularly those in France.

Magnum Fine Wines (www.magnum.co.uk) specialises in wine investment and the website has a comprehensive section devoted to the process, including sections on storage, how to buy and sell, and investment news. A performance graph compares wine prices since 1975 with other forms of investment over the same period. Wine can also be bought online, and tasting notes are included.

Millésima (www.millesima.co.uk) is a leading European fine wine merchant based in Bordeaux.

Premier Cru (www.premiercru.com) offers a full investment service, including purchase, storage management and eventual sale. The site has detailed information on wine investment and market information.

Richard Kihl Ltd (www.richardkihl.ltd.uk), a fine wine merchant in Aldeburgh, Suffolk, offers advice on wine investment and storage facilities.

Sotheby's (www.sothebys.com) hold sales of fine wine in London, New York and Hong Kong.

WineBid.com (www.winebid.com) of Napa, California, is the largest internet auction for fine and rare wines.

Wineandco (www.wineandco.com) is a Bordeaux-based trader that will deliver to the UK.

Zachys (www.zachys.com), based in Scarsdale, New York, is one of the USA's leading dealers in Bordeaux wines. Their site boasts a video library with videos by buyers, connoisseurs and professionals on various aspects of the wine trade. It is also possible to email the site's experts with specific queries.

The company's auction department, which was formerly run in conjunction with Christie's, holds regular auctions in New York, as well as occasional auctions in Hong Kong and Los Angeles.

Information

Bordeaux (www.bordeaux.com) is the website of the Conseil Interprofessionnel du Vin de Bordeaux (CIVB) a private association which operates under the aegis of the French Ministry of Agriculture. The site contains everything an investor could wish to know about wines of Bordeaux including varieties and blends, classifications, the winemaking process and purchase tips. The CIVB also run numerous courses throughout the year.

Decanter (www.decanter.com) is the UK's oldest consumer wine magazine. The online version has news, a wine tracker, information on courses, wine education and much more besides.

Harpers Wine & Spirit (www.harpers.co.uk) is a weekly subscription-only magazine for the British wine and spirit trade, providing comment, reviews, analysis, etc. It provides considerable free information online.

Investdrinks (www.investdrinks.org) is a site dedicated to the dangers of drinks investment. Jim Budd, who set up and runs the site, specialises in tracking down the perpetrators of drinks frauds. He lists the companies to avoid, as well as those he considers reputable and those who may have committed unknowingly to supply firms offering dubious investment schemes or perpetrating scams. The directory of fraudulent companies makes interesting reading. It is accompanied by information taken from their Companies House returns. The site is full of advice and help for would-be investors, together with advice for investors who have been the victims of fraud.

Information and publications

Entity	Web address	Main location	Email address	Telephone	Category
Bordeaux	www.bordeaux.com	Bordeaux	Through site	33 05 56 00 2266	Information
Decanter	www.decanter.com	London	On site	020 3148 5000	Publication
Harpers Wine and Spirit	www.harpers.co.uk	West Sussex	On site	01293 613 400	Publication
Jancis Robinson	www.jancisrobinson.com	London	Through site	0845 056 4117	Information
Investdrinks	www.investdrinks.org	n/a	jim@investdrinks.org	n/a	Information
Liv-ex	www.liv-ex.com	London	exchange@liv-ex.co.uk	020 7228 2233	Information
RobertParker	www.erobertparker.com	USA	info@erobertparker.com	617 938 3984	Information
Wine and Spirit Education Trust	www.wset.co.uk	London	wset@wset.co.uk	020 7089 3800	Information
Wine Doctor (The)	www.thewinedoctor.com	N/A	chris@thewinedoctor.com	n/a	Information
Wine Gang (The)	www.thewinegang.com	Glasgow	Through site	0141 416 4958	Information
Winemega	www.winemega.com	n/a	Through site	n/a	Information
Wine Spectator	www.winespectator.com	New York	Through site	212 684 4224	Magazine
Wine-Searcher	www.wine-searcher.com	New Zealand	Through site	64 9 825 0102	Information

Jancis Robinson (www.jancisrobinson.com) is a Master of Wine (the most prestigious and sparingly awarded qualification in the industry) and well-known broadcaster and writer. She has an informative site boasting wine news, a list of books on wine, and a directory of merchants, auction houses, publications and trade associations. Further information is available to subscribers.

Liv-ex (www.liv-ex.com) is the London International Vintners Exchange, an independent trading and settlement organisation serving the fine wine trade. Subscribers to the site have access to a price database of over three million wines. Other services include tracking cellar values, comparison with other asset classes, price histories, indices, etc. The Liv-ex 100 Fine Wine Index, which is the industry's leading benchmark, as well as other indices, are available free on the site in both chart form along with the underlying data.

eRobertParker.com (www.erobertparker.com) is an independent consumer's guide to fine wine, providing articles by the world's most famous wine critic as well as other leading experts from around the world. The site has a database of over 130,000 wines, with tasting notes, plus extensive information on fine wines and numerous links.

The Wine & Spirit Education Trust (www.wset.co.uk) organises wine education courses and wine tastings for professionals and enthusiasts in 47 countries worldwide. The '3 Minute Wine School' section of the site is a collection of 12 short films exploring different wine styles and regions. This is available for free once registered.

Wine doctor (www.thewinedoctor.com) provides an independent opinion on wine, as well as useful information, including producer profiles, trading tastings, information on vintages and regions, and numerous links.

The Wine Gang (www.thewinegang.com) is a collaboration between five of the UK's most influential wine critics, providing a "comprehensive assessment" of wines for sale in the UK. The site includes a searchable database. At the time of writing, membership is £19.99 per year.

Winemega.com (www.winemega.com) is a guide to purchasing Bordeaux wines. Since 1997 Winemega has been collecting and classifying the tasting scores and notes from international wine critics. The site also includes

StatWine (www.statwine.com), which publishes in-depth studies on Bordeaux growths.

Wine-Searcher (www.wine-searcher.com), originally started by an employee of Berry Bros., provides an impartial service for wine availability and pricing. The free part of the site is useful for locating hard-to-find wine and is searchable by country. The subscription service locates the best prices and stockists of your chosen wine, with worldwide price comparisons.

Wine Spectator (www.winespectator.com) is an American magazine providing up-to-date news and information on the wine trade worldwide. Online subscribers have access to a database containing information on more than 213,000 wines.

Storage

London City Bond (www.lcb.co.uk), based in Tilbury, is a privately-owned warehousing company for the wine and spirit trade The company also owns Vinotheque in Burton-on-Trent, which offers the same service.

Octavian Vaults (www.octavian.co.uk) is an independent specialist, offering a full cellarage service at premises in Corsham, Wiltshire.

How do you select the right manager for investment success?

At St. James's Place Wealth Management we have an effective solution to this problem.

St. James's Place Wealth Management is a FTSE 250 company, we build long-term, trusted relationships with our clients and manage over £21 billion funds under management. At St. James's Place, we have a distinctive approach to investment management, recognising that no single investment house has a monopoly of investment expertise.

We provide our clients with a carefully selected group of external managers of outstanding ability, to manage our range of funds. The managers are closely monitored by our Investment Committee, chaired by Sir Mark Weinberg and advised by the City's highly respected investment consultants, Stamford Associates.

We provide clients' with a wide range of funds. By giving our clients exclusive access to this distinctive approach to investment management, we can provide them with peace of mind that their money is being well looked after and the opportunity to obtain consistent performance over the long term.

Introducing Richard Broughton...

As a highly experienced financial professional and a member of the elite St. James's Place Partnership. I work with a range of high net worth clients, including many professionals. To find out more about our range of exclusive funds and how I can help you successfully preserve and build capital for the future, contact:

Richard Broughton
St. James's Place Partnership

Tel: 07976 764129

Hammond House, 117 Piccadilly, Mayfair, London, W1J 7JU

A view from a clients perspective...

"I have known Richard Broughton for five years and been involved with him in business for most of that time. He is a rare commodity himself, being a straight down the line, no grey areas man. His judgement is sound and his word is everything to him, to his clients and to his colleagues.

On a personal note he has a sharp sense of humour and a certain charisma, both of which make him enviable company.

On a professional note Richard Broughton is a dedicated professional — and a credit to his profession."

John Bly
Antiques Specialist & Consultant

Winner
WEALTH MANAGER OF THE YEAR 2008 & 2009
ST. JAMES'S PLACE WEALTH MANAGEMENT
INVESTORS CHRONICLE FT
Wealth Management AWARDS

Winner
The Daily Telegraph
Wealth Manager of the Year 2007 & 2008

Winner
The Daily Telegraph
Best Performing Fund 2009

10.
Auctions and Dealers

One of the most important decisions to be made with many alternative investments is whether it is best to buy and sell through a dealer or via an auction. Each method has its pluses and minuses, so there is no one correct answer to this question. In some areas we have covered in this book – forestry, for example – auction markets do not exist. But in most others, investors have a choice of buying and selling either at auction or through a dealer. In some categories auction markets are the most efficient; in others, dealers are a better bet.

Auctions Versus Dealers

One common answer to the dilemma of which to use is to *buy* through a dealer and *sell* at auction. This is sweepingly general advice, though, and not necessarily correct. Two main reasons are usually given for it. One is that, by selling at auction, investors can benefit from aggressive competition between buyers, which can drive the price to unexpectedly high levels. The second is that many individuals avoid buying at auction because of the hefty charges that auction houses impose, in the form of the so-called buyer's premium. This is generally a percentage added to the hammer price (the price at which the bidding stops and the lot is sold to the highest bidder). On lower-priced items at large salerooms it may be as much as 20% plus VAT of the hammer price. Even on high-priced items it may be as much as 12% plus VAT.

In reality there is a trade-off between the two. While an investor may incur hefty charges buying at auction, paying the dealers' mark-up, which can be a hefty amount, is avoided. With auctions, the charges are a known quantity at the outset. Some dealers will add a margin, depending on the alternative investment category involved and the degree to which there is competition for investors' and collectors' business – anything from 40% to 100%. And while regular customers may often get a discount (typically 10% or so off the posted price) this only makes up a small amount of the difference. A dealer is a one-stop shop, and can sometimes source sought-after items that even the most dedicated collector or investor would struggle to locate on his own, but investors pay heavily for this service.

When it comes to selling, too, dealers may be the more expensive route. Dealers will typically buy in a collection or portfolio of investment-grade items – even one formed with their help – at appreciably less than the 'retail' value. In my own case, I recently sold a portfolio of investment-grade Victorian stamps through Stanley Gibbons (purchased from them some years previously) and received a price that equated to around 80% of the 'catalogue' value. Although the stamps had risen in price substantially while I owned them, there is no denying that this is a hefty discount. The plus point of selling through a dealer, however, is that sellers receive the value instantly. In the case of an auction, the outcome is less certain, even with a reserve price on the items in question; and sellers pay commission.

The following table shows contact details for major auction houses in different alternative investment categories.

Auctions and Dealers

Alternative investment auction houses

Entity	Web address	Main location	Email address	Telephone	Category
Artcurial	www.artcurial.com	Paris	On site	33 42 99 20 20	Auction house
Artfact Live!	www.artfact.com	USA	support@artfact.com	(617) 219 1090	On line auction database
Bonhams	www.bonhams.com	London	info@bonhams.com	020 7447 7447	Auction house
Bruun Rasmussen	www.bruun-rasmussen.dk	Denmark	info@bruun-rasmussen.dk	445 8818 1111	Auction house
Bukowskis	www.bukowskis.se	Stockholm	On site	46 (0) 8 614 08 00	Auction house
Christie's	www.christies.com	Worldwide	info@christies.com	n/a	Auction house
Dorotheum	www.dorotheum.com	Vienna	On site	43 515 600	Auction house
Doyles	www.doylenewyork.com	New York	info@doylenewyork.com	212 427 2730	Auction house
Freemans	www.freemansauction.com	Philadelphia	info@freemansauction.com	215 563 9275	Auction house
International Auctioneers Group	www.internationalauctioneers.com	Geneva		41 (22) 310 21 80	Auction house alliance
Koller	www.kollerauktionen.ch	Zurich	office@kollerauctions.com	41 44 445 63 63	Auction house
Lempertz	www.lempertz.eu	Cologne	On site	49 221 925 729 0	Auction house
Lyon and Turnbull	www.lyonandturnbull.com	Scotland	info@lyonandturnbull.com	0131 557 8844	Auction house
Philips de Pury	www.phillipsdepury.com	New York	On site	1212 940 1200	Auction house
Pierre Berge	www.pba-auctions.com	Paris	contact@pba-auctions.com	33 01 49 49 90 00	Auction house
Porro	www.porroartconsulting.it	Milan	On site	02 72 094 708	Auction house
Society of Fine Art Auctioneers and Valuers	www.sofaa.org	Surrey	secretary@sofaa.org	0207 0968 417	Association
Swann Galleries	www.swanngalleries.com	New York	swann@swanngalleries.com	212 254 4710	Auction house
Tajan	www.tajan.com	Paris	On site	Many on site	Auction house
Tennants	www.tennants.co.uk	Yorkshire	enquiries@tennants-ltd.co.uk	01969 623 780	Auction house
the-saleroom.com	www.the-saleroom.com	Online	On site	On site	Online link to auctions
Venator and Hanstein	www.venator-hanstein.de	Cologne	On site	49 221 257 54 19	Auction house
Weschler's	www.weschlers.com	Washington	info@weschlers.com	202 628 1281	Auction house
Whytes	www.whytes.ie	Dublin	info@whytes.ie	353 01676 2888	Auction house

Why dealers use auctions

The choice between dealers and auctions is not, therefore, quite as clear-cut as it might seem – as the presence of many dealers at auctions will testify. Indeed many dealers source their stock from auctions; some who attend auctions are bidding on behalf of clients, but many are buying for their own stock. They will bid for lots up to a level at which they calculate that, even including the buyer's premium, they can add their own margin to a particular lot and still find ready buyers.

There are other reasons, too, why dealers frequent salerooms. Salerooms may be the only source of scarce items for which they know they will have buyers. Some collectors know they have items that the market wants, and will calculate that a sufficiently scarce item will attract a lot of interest. It is not necessarily in their interest to sell it to a dealer, because a dealer's bid is likely to be on the low side. A rational dealer's motivation on the other hand is to make as much profit from a scarce item as possible, perhaps exploiting the seller's ignorance about how much the piece might really be worth. The auction is the only true arbiter of value for that item on that day. Even then, it is an imperfect one.

Dealers also bid at auctions – and collectors and alternative investors should consider doing so for the same reason – because there are often opportunities to snap up worthwhile items at advantageous prices. This particularly applies to less well-publicised auctions, especially those taking place outside of major capital cities. Out in the provinces, auctions may be less well attended yet still have worthwhile items for sale. Buying at a sparsely attended small regional auction can yield bargains that can sometimes be sold at a substantial profit through a larger auction in a major capital city. A few years ago, on a dark day in February, I bought a small Victorian watercolour with an attractively carved mahogany frame at a provincial auction for a very modest price. I was subsequently told by a dealer that the frame alone would probably fetch double the amount I paid for the lot, if it were sold at auction in London.

There is one proviso about attending local auctions. Generally speaking, the broad mass of lots available may not be of the same quality as those that might be assembled by a major auction house in London, Paris, New York or Berlin. Alternative investors also need to satisfy themselves as to the provenance of the item in which they are interested, and that the grading placed on it is accurate. In my experience, whereas in a major capital city auction most lots will be attractive and often of investment grade, in a regional or provincial auction fewer than 10% of the items (and sometimes a lot fewer than that) will be of interest. Those bidding for investment purposes need to be very choosy indeed.

The Essence of Auctions

Auctions rely on assembling a crowd of interested buyers and, on occasion, for reasons beyond their control, only a few turn up. The buyers that do turn up may not be interested in all the lots, and in this eventuality, low bids on particular lots may be successful – provided they reach the reserve price, if there is one. If so, this means that even allowing for the buyer's premium, buying at auction will almost certainly be cheaper than buying from a dealer. By the same token, it also means that a collector can outbid a dealer and still get the item cheaper than he might pay by buying at the dealer's shop or from his catalogue. There is a proviso attached to this. The investor, or his or her advisors, needs to be sufficiently confident about investing in the chosen alternative investment field to know the true value of the item in question and that it is the genuine article. This can only be done by attending the auction in person and viewing the item before the sale.

Despite such possible bargains, in most instances bidders will not succeed in getting an item substantially below its estimate in the auction catalogue. Many (though by no means all) sellers set a reserve price on an item they sell through auction, below which the auctioneer will not sell. But there are of course exceptions now and then. This reserve price will not be more than the low end of the auctioneer's catalogue estimate, but could be significantly below it. Not all items have reserves on them. By bidding up to just below the bottom end of the estimated price, a bidder stands a chance of getting an item at a good price, and below what it might cost through a dealer. The auctioneer's language will normally give a clue as to whether the reserve has been met, a topic we'll go into in the next section.

Remember too that bidders make or withhold decisions for reasons other than price. I could have bought an attractive 46-volume first edition set of the works of Sir Walter Scott for £45 at a book auction but did not – simply because, though I like Walter Scott's books, I don't have the room to keep a set like this, such editions are common, and it was of such a size and weight that it would have been very inconvenient to take home. Large unwieldy items may sell for less than small compact ones.

How Auctions Work

Investors can buy most types of alternative investment categories at auction. The list of items auctioned includes stamps, books, coins and banknotes, art of various types, and wine. Most auctions have a number of characteristics in common.

Before the sale

The auction will be advertised well in advance so that would-be buyers will have plenty of time to make arrangements to be there in person. Except for particularly homogeneous items with precise grading and a known price history – like stamps, coins or wine – it makes sense to attend an auction in person and in particular to view the items to be bid for prior to the auction to satisfy oneself as to their condition and genuineness. Viewing items before bidding is generally a good idea if at all possible. Photographs in catalogues or on the internet often do not convey the grading of the item with sufficient accuracy for a confident bid to be made.

Even in situations where this is not strictly necessary, it makes sense to attend an auction in person, if humanly possible, in order to take advantage of opportunities that may occur where bidding in the room is slack, or to gauge the momentum of bidding for a particular item. Online bidding is now available for many auctions, complete with audio, so that a would-be bidder can easily gauge what is happening with a lot in which they are interested, and step in with a bid where necessary. Telephone bidding is also common, although arguably not quite as good as being in the room.

Commission bids, which set a maximum price beyond which a buyer will not go, can also be a useful way of avoiding being 'carried away' by the atmosphere in the room on the day and will sometimes carry the day. Placing a commission bid requires a degree of judgement to be shown, to balance the interest the auction is expected to generate, the degree to which the bidder wants to own the lot in question, and the guide price set in the catalogue.

If selling items at auction, it is also worth attending in person, although auctions are recorded and are open and transparent. If attending, investors can verify for themselves the progress of the bidding and the eventual price.

A catalogue will normally be published some time before the auction. This may range from a photocopied sheet, in the case of an auction at a small provincial saleroom, to a lavishly produced perfect-bound book in the case of a high-value auction at a leading London auction house. In the case of the latter, the items will be illustrated in colour. Some auction catalogues, particularly those from large salerooms, sometimes include a guide as to the source of the item, and, for important lots, its provenance. In many cases this can, however, be fairly sketchy, and may not be a foolproof guarantee of authenticity. Provenance may not be available for all items, although if an item is from a noted collection this is itself a reasonable guarantee.

Large auction houses employ experts on particular areas and the presence of these experts is in itself also a reasonable assurance that items offered for sale will be the genuine article, although attention needs to be paid to the precise description in the catalogue. Large auction houses offer what might best be described as conditional and time-limited guarantees that items sold are not counterfeit. Conditions include the buyer producing independent experts acceptable to both sides to check disputed authenticity. Buyers must also return the goods in the same condition as when they were sold. Subject to this, the auction house may return the full amount paid. This does not apply if the description of the item in the original catalogue accorded with the opinion of experts at the time and all reasonable steps available to verify authenticity at the time had been taken. Guarantees last for several years, but in view of the conditions set, it is best to assume that bidders make a purchase on the basis of the old maxim of caveat emptor (buyer beware).

There are unlikely to be such formal guarantees at small local salerooms.

On the day

What happens on the day of the sale? Auction rooms generally have a fixed cast of characters. There are bidders in the room, who may be dealers or private buyers. There are clerks manning telephones, each in contact with a telephone bidder (who normally remains anonymous), and the auctioneer, whose job it is to auction the lots and to bid on behalf of absentee or 'commission' bidders, who have set in advance a maximum price beyond which they will not go.

Lots are auctioned in the order they appear in the catalogue. An auctioneer will typically sell 50-100 lots an hour or more, depending on the type of item being sold. Bidding starts at some way below the minimum estimate value and progresses by predetermined amounts (normally a round figure around 10% of the previous bid – in £5 jumps up to £100, then in £10 jumps up to £200, then in £20 jumps and so on). Auctioneers may start and continue the bidding themselves if the price is below the reserve. If bidding on behalf of an absentee bidder the auctioneer will normally indicate this by pointing to himself (or herself).

Auctioneers will normally indicate when commission bids have been exceeded and bidding then continues in the room until all but one bidder drops out. The auctioneer will give fair warning that the lot is to be sold to that particular bidder, and then signal the end of the auction for that lot by a rap of the gavel. If the reserve has not been met, this is sometimes indicated by a simple and rather terse 'unsold'. If the auctioneer fails to note a successful bidder's number, this can also be an indication that the reserve price has not been met.

Astute observers of auctions can sometimes spot subtle changes in the auctioneer's language that indicate if a reserve has been met despite a lot being below the minimum estimate. If the auctioneer uses the phrase "selling then at …", this could be the time to jump in with a bid. The table below shows some of the phraseology used by auctioneers and what it means.

Auctioneer-speak

Says	Means
Against the room at [price]	Telephone bidder is bidding [price]
Against you all	Commission bid exceeds all other bids
Against you at [price]	Another bidder is bidding more, do you want to bid?
All done	Hammer about to go down
Bid is with me at [price]	Auctioneer is bidding [price] for a commission bidder
Commission bids all out	Commission bids have been exceeded
Fair warning	Hammer about to go down
Selling then at [price]	Price is above reserve and hammer about to go down
That clears me	Commission bids have been exceeded
Unsold [after hammer]	Reserve price has not been met
On the telephone at [price]	Telephone bidder has bid [price]

Those wishing to bid in an auction need to register prior to the sale and will be given a 'paddle' or a sheet of paper with a number on it, to indicate their identity to the auctioneer and that they are a bona fide registered bidder. After a sale, provided payment has been made in full in cleared funds, a successful buyer can take their purchase away there and then. Some auction houses will allow buyers to store their purchases for five days free of charge at their own risk. Shipping can also be arranged at the buyers' risk and expense.

If it turns out that a buyer can't pay, normally within five days, the auction house has the opportunity either to cancel the sale, or to re-auction the lot or sell it privately, with the defaulting buyer being responsible for any shortfall. An alternative may be for the auction house or the seller to pursue the defaulting buyer through the courts. The moral is: if you can't afford it, don't bid. Defaulting buyers will normally find it hard to show their face at another auction.

If investors wish to bid in absentia, via a commission bid, the procedure is to fill in a form and send it by post or email, or take it to the auction house. In the event of two or more identical absentee bids being the highest, the one received earliest carries the day.

Telephone bidding works the same way as if a bidder were in the room, with competing bids being relayed by an auctioneer's representative in the room via an open telephone line. In major auctions, telephone bidding is not normally offered for lots estimated at below £1000. Buyers can normally bid by telephone by simply registering with the bidding department at least 24 hours prior to the auction. Internet bidding is conducted through the auctioneer's own websites, or through third party sites such as the-saleroom.com, which obviously require proof of cleared funds (for example, payment via debit card) prior to accepting bids.

Charges

The charges levied by auction houses are a bone of contention with many dealers, collectors and alternative investors alike, but they are known in advance and bids can be tailored accordingly. The charges take two basic forms, with one or two extras on top. These charges are the buyer's premium, a levy added to the 'hammer' price and payable by the successful bidder. Seller's commission is deducted from the hammer price and paid to the buyer. The difference between these two prices represents the amount that the auction house takes for its services.

Buyer's premium varies from auction house to auction house. London salerooms take 20% plus VAT on the first £70,000. Sellers' commission is typically 15% for the first £1000-3000, and 10% thereafter. How this works out in practice can be seen in the following illustration. Let's look at an item that goes under the hammer at £10,000. The charges work out as follows:

Charges on an item with £10,000 hammer price

Buyer's premium (20% plus VAT)	£2350
Buyer pays	£12,350
Seller's commission (10% plus VAT)	£1175
Seller receives	£8825
HM Customs & Excise receives VAT of	£525
Saleroom receives	£3000

The bottom line here is that there is a 40% difference between what the seller receives and what the buyer pays. The saleroom receives three-quarters of this difference and VAT accounts for the remainder. While this seems a little unfair, let's not forget the dealers are in business to make money too, and there are differences between what dealers pay for items they want to sell, and the price they put on them when they sell them to customers. There is a sizeable mark-up applied by dealers, who have overheads to recoup just as auction houses do. The point with dealers, however, is that while a customer might not know what the mark-up is, there is some wiggle room. Most dealers will negotiate on price, especially if a collector or investor is a regular customer. As previously noted, discounts like this can often be as much as 10% of the retail price. Dealers do this because they believe offering a discount will attract customers back and ensure a regular flow of business from them.

Auctioneers

Entity	Web address	Main location	Email address	Telephone	Category
Artcurial	www.artcurial.com	Paris	On site	33 42 99 20 20	Auction house
Artfact Live!	www.artfact.com	USA	support@artfact.com	(617) 219 1090	On line auction database
Bonhams	www.bonhams.com	London	info@bonhams.com	020 7447 7447	Auction house
Bruun Rasmussen	www.bruun-rasmussen.dk	Denmark	info@bruun-rasmussen.dk	445 8818 1111	Auction house
Bukowskis	www.bukowskis.se	Stockholm	On site	46 (0) 8 614 08 00	Auction house
Christie's	www.christies.com	Worldwide	info@christies.com	n/a	Auction house
Dorotheum	www.dorotheum.com	Vienna	On site	43 515 600	Auction house
Doyles	www.doylenewyork.com	New York	info@doylenewyork.com	212 427 2730	Auction house
Freemans	www.freemansauction.com	Philadelphia	info@freemansauction.com	215 563 9275	Auction house
International Auctioneers Group	www.internationalauctioneers.com	Geneva		41 (22) 310 21 80	Auction house alliance
Koller	www.kollerauktionen.ch	Zurich	office@kollerauctions.com	41 44 445 63 63	Auction house
Lempertz	www.lempertz.eu	Cologne	On site	49 221 925 729 0	Auction house
Lyon and Turnbull	www.lyonandturnbull.com	Scotland	info@lyonandturnbull.com	0131 557 8844	Auction house
Phillips de Pury	www.phillipsdepury.com	New York	On site	1212 940 1200	Auction house
Pierre Berge	www.pba-auctions.com	Paris	contact@pba-auctions.com	33 01 49 49 90 00	Auction house
Porro	www.porroartconsulting.it	Milan	On site	02 72 094 708	Auction house
Society of Fine Art Auctioneers and Valuers	www.sofaa.org	Surrey	secretary@sofaa.org	0207 0968 417	Association
Swann Galleries	www.swanngalleries.com	New York	swann@swanngalleries.com	212 254 4710	Auction house
Tajan	www.tajan.com	Paris	On site	Many on site	Auction house
Tennants	www.tennants.co.uk	Yorkshire	enquiries@tennants-ltd.co.uk	01969 623 780	Auction house
the-saleroom.com	www.the-saleroom.com	Online	On site	On site	Online link to auctions
Venator and Hanstein	www.venator-hanstein.de	Cologne	On site	49 221 257 54 19	Auction house
Weschler's	www.weschlers.com	Washington	info@weschlers.com	202 628 1281	Auction house
Whytes	www.whytes.ie	Dublin	info@whytes.ie	353 01676 2888	Auction house

Auction house charges do not end with the buyer's premium and seller's commission. There are occasionally charges for placing a reserve on the item. It is also normal practice for sellers to pay a fixed amount for items illustrated in the catalogue. Buyers may also bear charges for credit card payment for lots acquired, and may also have to pay charges for shipping, packing and storage, if appropriate. Charges are made for insuring items while in the care of the auction, although sellers can opt out of this, or arrange their own.

When buying or selling through auction, or at least through large salerooms in major cities, any buyer, whether a serious collector or committed alternative investor, needs to take these charges into account. Successful bidders basically need to add 25% to the price of the lot they are bidding for, in order to work out what they will eventually pay.

Online Auctions

Online auctions like those on eBay have increased in importance dramatically in recent years. But are they the right place for an alternative investor to go prospecting for material? Before we look at the mechanics it is worth considering a couple of obvious pluses and minuses.

The big plus about online auctions is that they are continuous and they attract a very large number of buyers and sellers. Alternative investors and collectors alike need to devote time and money going to physical auctions and also have to wait until one of the auction houses, either a local or nationally known one, puts one on in their chosen area of interest. These may only happen a few times a year. On sites like eBay, items are being auctioned every day.

The large number of potential sellers means that there is a wide choice of items for would-be buyers. In some ways this is an advantage to the buyer, because the buying interest is diffused. If an item is of interest, there may only be a couple of other bidders involved, and a dedicated bidder may end up buying the lot cheaper than they would have done in a large, well-publicised auction in a noted saleroom.

The obvious minus from the standpoint of an online auction is that goods must be bought sight unseen. All that would-be buyers have to go on is a digital photograph of the item, which may not show the detail needed and is, in any case, no substitute for physically seeing and handling the item. Online auctions attempt to keep sellers from misdescribing and overgrading items, the condition of which is vital to their value, by operating a feedback system. This allows buyers who have had good service to register positive votes, and those who feel they have been let down to file negative feedback. Accumulated feedback ratings are displayed on the site, the aim being to drive traffic away from those with poor feedback and towards those with excellent customer ratings.

How they work

The usual auction rules apply, the only difference from a live auction being that the auctioneer's gavel is replaced by a strict time limit. The highest bid standing when the clock ticks down to zero wins the item, subject to a reserve. This has given rise to a certain amount of gamesmanship, with bids being submitted at the very last minute to beat the clock and yet not allow other bidders time to respond. eBay also operates other varieties of auction. Some items are offered as auction items but with a fixed 'buy it now' price that secures the item and stops the auction. Items can be offered with or without reserves.

Those wishing to buy in this way have to register to be able to bid. If they do bid successfully, the seller and buyer then continue the discussion regarding delivery options and payment via email. A note below the item generally contains details of acceptable forms of payment (some sellers will not accept credit card payment), delivery options, policy on returns and so on.

A useful adjunct to regular bidding on eBay is a PayPal account. This is a secure money transfer system operated by eBay and linked to a personal email address that allows the account holder to send cash to another PayPal account holder. Users can transfer money into and out of their PayPal account from their bank. Most sellers on eBay will accept payment via PayPal.

Experienced alternative investors will probably use eBay only sparingly, when particularly interesting items come up. Some professional dealers operate on eBay, and there are dealers on eBay who, though starting out as amateurs, have built a reasonable business buying and selling.

As regards the honesty of the items on offer, the author has checked this for two areas of personal interest in particular (books and watercolours). Sellers generally do appear to describe the items warts and all. Many items are, however, of a condition that would be unsuitable for alternative investing, but there are some that are experienced collectors could probably pick up the occasional bargain in this way. As an aside, some collector and trade publications now devote regular space to commenting on items that appear and are sold through internet auctions.

Dealing with the Dealers

One of the plus points of dealing with large salerooms is of course that they have a high public profile and they are sensitive to adverse publicity. This is particularly so among the top rank of auction houses. Local salerooms can, in my experience, be rather more variable in their standards, and it is vital here to attend the auction in person simply as a check that your instructions are being followed to the letter.

One problem auction rooms face in some areas is collusion among dealers before an auction, whereby groups of dealers will agree among themselves which lots are attractive and who wants what, and then agree not to bid against each other, and share out the ownership of the items after the event. 'Rings' like this are illegal and distort the market. But they do happen. It is said by some to be a particular problem in the antiques trade. But in some ways it doesn't matter. As a private individual, an experienced alternative investor will usually be able to outbid a dealer or a dealers' ring, because the dealers have to factor a potential future mark-up into their bid.

When it comes to buying through dealers and building relationships with them, there are a couple of golden rules. One is to make sure that the dealer understands your objectives as an alternative investor and only shows you top-quality items. A dealer needs to be chosen with this in mind. It is a very good idea to choose a specialist in the chosen investment area, and a dealer that deals in investment-quality material. A customer may pay slightly more in cases like this, but knows in the end that the dealer has a reputation to maintain, and wants to keep them as a customer because they represent a potentially reliable source of profitable future business.

It is usually the quality of dealer's stock that will mark him or her out as the sort of person worth dealing with. This is generally instantly apparent from the nature of the premises and the quality of the stock on offer.

The importance of building relationships with dealers varies from category to category. There is such stiff competition in the book trade that most rare book dealers will keep their prices competitive. Even so, book auctions are often cheaper than dealers, although quality can be more variable. For art, building a relationship with a dealer is vital, even though you may also from time to time buy at auction or elsewhere. For stamps, coins and banknotes, specialist dealers are an essential source of investment-grade material in prime condition.

There are, however, a number of other supplementary reasons why buying through a dealer may be worthwhile.

1. In the first place, would-be alternative investors will get the benefit of specialist knowledge and experience (although this can also be obtained from auction house specialists). While a dealer is trying to sell something and therefore to present it in the best possible light, a shrewd investor should be able to see through this and appreciate the underlying merits of the item being discussed.

2. Auctions are places for snap decisions. A dealer's premises, by contrast, are unhurried. Customers can view an item, talk about it, think about it, go away, come back, sometimes take it home on approval, get first refusal on it and a whole range of other options that are not available in the case of auctions which, by their nature, are 'sudden death' affairs.

3. Thirdly, dealers travel widely and generally buy stock shrewdly. While some try to pass off inferior items at excessive prices, well-informed buyers will be able to spot this. If they know their market and their own mind, and the dealer knows they know, customers will only get shown items that fit their criteria, and the temptation for a dealer to dissemble will be that much less.

Good dealers label items well so that investors should know pretty accurately what they are buying. In the event that an item has been misrepresented, the best dealers are generally part of trade associations that will have arbitration procedures for settling disputes of this nature. When buying through an auction, the guiding rule remains caveat emptor, but in both cases buyers ultimately have recourse to law if they feel an item was misrepresented.

Dealers like to both buy and sell. When a serious collector or alternative investor builds up a relationship with a dealer, the dealer may be prepared to buy back items for resale, accept them in part exchange for other items, or sell them on the client's behalf on commission. Provided an individual is satisfied that his bid is as good as the item would fetch at auction after allowing for charges, it can make sense to pursue this as an avenue for buying and selling.

Finally, in the event that a piece bought from a dealer is forged, stolen, or otherwise tampered with, and not as represented at the time of purchase, there is some comeback legally. The dealer is normally acting as a principal. He owns the goods he is selling. This contrasts with the position of an auctioneer, who is normally simply acting as an agent for the seller.

Other Sources of Investment-grade Material

Fairs

Fairs, which gather together dealers of one discipline in one place, are often good places to buy and sell, if a would-be buyer knows the market, and has a good appreciation of the price and value of particular items. Competition between dealers, particularly at larger fairs, tends to keep prices keen. One slight caveat here is that it makes some sort of sense to attend fairs that are not held in particularly ostentatiously affluent areas, since dealers will automatically mark up prices to reflect the likely affluence of the clientele. The more mundane the surroundings, the greater the likelihood of finding a bargain.

Another issue is condition. A would-be searcher for quality investment-grade material needs to be able to satisfy himself, by inspecting an item, that it is in sufficiently good condition to be of interest.

Fairs are, however, good places to meet and talk to dealers and other serious collectors and investors, and to gauge the strength of the market and the relative price of particular items. There are major fairs held annually, or with greater frequency, for books, coins and banknotes, stamps, art and antiques.

Charity shops

Charity shops, something of a UK phenomenon, acquire items typically from individuals decluttering, perhaps prior to a house move, or disposing of the effects of a deceased relative. In some cases they may acquire antiques, paintings, old books and the like, which have a value to collectors. It is rare, though not entirely unknown, for investment-grade material to crop up in outlets like this, although those running shops like this have an increasingly astute eye (especially in the age of the internet) for the value of the items that pass through their hands.

It is, however, undeniable that they have become a significant factor in the market. Oxfam, for instance, is now the largest UK retailer of second-hand books, much to the chagrin of small professional book dealers. There are occasional bargains to be had, in the form of first editions that have gone unnoticed, or else in older leather-bound volumes priced at less than they would fetch at auction. The same is probably true of other disciplines, but would-be buyers of high-grade material need extreme patience and a keen eye to sift though the dross.

Appendix – Resources

These tables are intended to collect all of the companies referred to in the book, whether alluded to briefly or discussed in detail, into a useful directory.

N.B. "On site" refers to where companies only allow contact via a web email form, or where there are several different email addresses for different departments and these can be found on the site in question.

Art

Entity	Web address	Main location	Email address	Telephone	Category
Art Dealers Association of America (The)	www.artdealers.org	New York	On site	212 488 5550	Organisation
Art in Scotland	www.artinscotland.com	Scotland	aliofabubakar@aol.com	0141 946 5032	Information
Art Loss Register (The)	www.artloss.com	London, Bath	info@artloss.com	020 7841 5780	Miscellaneous
Art Basel	www.artbasel.com	Basel	info@artbasel.com	41 58 200 20 20	Fair
Art Basel Miami Beach	www.artbaselmiamibeach.com	Miami	miamibeach@artbasel.com	41 58 200 20 20	Fair
Art Dubai	www.artdubai.ae	Dubai	On site	971 4 323 3434	Fair
Art Fair Tokyo	www.artfairtokyo.com	Tokyo	info@artfairtokyo.com	83 3 5771 4520	Fair
Art London	www.artlondon.net	London	info@artlondon.net	020 7259 9399	Fair
Armory Show (The)	www.thearmoryshow.com	New York	info@thearmoryshow.com	212 645 6440	Fair
Artnet	www.artnet.com	Berlin	On site	49 30 2091 7850	Information
Art Newspaper (The)	www.theartnewspaper.com	London	On site	020 7735 3331	Publication
Art Review (The)	www.artreview.com	London	info@artreview.com	020 7107 2760	Publication online
Artinfo	www.artinfo.com	New York & London	Various on site	020 7985 9617	Information
Artprice	www.artprice.com	Worldwide	On site	800 2780 0000	Information
Association of International Photography Art Dealers	www.aipad.com	Washington	info@aipad.com	202 367 1158	Association
BADA Antiques and Fine Art Fair	www.bada-antiques-fair.co.uk	London	On site	020 7589 6108	Fair

Art...cont.

Entity	Web address	Main location	Email address	Telephone	Category
Confédération Internationale des Négociants en Oeuvres d'Art	www.cinoa.org.uk	Worldwide	On site	Many on site	Association
Contemporary Art Society	www.contempart.org.uk	London	info@contemporaryartsociety.org	0207 7831 1243	Association
Culture 24	www.culture24.org.uk	Brighton	info@culture24.org.uk	01273 623 266	Information
European Fine Art Fair	www.tefaf.com	Netherlands	info@tefaf.com	31 411 64 50 90	Fair
Frieze	www.frieze.com	London	On site	020 3372 6111	Fair
Galleries	www.galleries.co.uk	London	On site	020 8740 7020	Publication
Glasgow Art Fair	www.glasgowartfair.com	Glasgow	artfair@uzevents.com	0141 552 6027	Fair
Gordons Art	www.gordonsart.com	Arizona	office@gordonsart.com	Various on site	Information
Hong Kong Art Fair	www.hongkongartfair.com	Hong Kong	info@hongkongartfair.com	852 2918 8793	Fair
International Fine Art and Antique Dealers Show	www.haughton.com	New York, London	info@haughton.com	020 7389 6555	Fair
International Fine Print Dealers Association	www.ifpda.org	New York	info@ifpda.org	212 674 6095	Association
Kara Art	www.karaart.com	n/a	On site	n/a	Information
Lapada Art and Antiques Fair	www.lapadalondon.com	London	lapada@lapada.org	020 7823 3511	Fair
London Art Fair	www.lcndonartfair.co.uk	London	On site	020 7288 6482	Fair
London International Fine Arts Fair	www.olympiaartsinternational.com	London	On site	020 7370 8211	Fair
Mei Moses Index	www.artasanasset.com	USA	support@artasanasset.com	n/a	Information
Society of London Art Dealers (The)	www.slad.org.uk	London	office@slad.org	020 7930 6137	Organisation
Venice Biennale	www.labiennale.org	Venice	info@labiennale.org	39 041 521 8711	Fair

Banknotes

Entity	Web address	Main location	Email address	Telephone	Category
Baldwin's	www.baldwin.co.uk	London	On site	020 7930 6879	Dealer
Banknote News	www.banknotenews.com	USA	owen@banknotenews.com	n/a	Information
Banknotes.com	www.banknotes.com	USA	admin@banknotes.com	803 247 5280	Information
Barry Boswell Banknotes	www.collectpapermoney.co.uk	UK	barry.boswell@btinternet.com	01327 261 877	Dealer
Bonhams	www.bonhams.com	London	On site	020 7393 3914	Auction house
Bowers and Merena	www.bowersandmerena.com	California	info@bowersandmerena.com	949 253 0916	Auction house
British Museum	www.britishmuseum.org	London	coins@britishmuseum.org	020 7323 8000	Information
Coincraft	www.coincraft.com	London	info@coincraft.com	020 7636 1188	Dealer
Colin Narbeth	www.colin-narbeth.com	London	colin.narbeth@btinternet.com	0207 379 6975	Dealer
Collect Paper Money	www.collectpapermoney.com	N/A	n/a	n/a	Information
Collector Network	www.collectornetwork.com	N/A	On site	n/a	Information
Dix Noonan Webb	www.dnw.co.uk	London	auctions@dnw.co.uk	020 7016 1700	Auction house
Ian Gradon World Paper Money	www.worldnotes.co.uk	Durham	igradon960@aol.com	0191 371 9700	Dealer
International Bank Note Society	www.theibns.org	USA	On site	n/a	Association
Maastricht Paper Money Show	www.papermoney-maastricht.org	Maastricht	On site	n/a	Fair
Morton and Eden	www.mortonandeden.com	London	info@mortonandeden.com	020 7493 5344	Auction house
Professional Currency Dealers Association	www.pcdaonline.com	USA	On site	n/a	Association
Society of Paper Money Collectors	www.spmc.org	UK	On site	n/a	Association
Spink	www.spink.com	London	enquiry@spink.com	020 7563 4000	Auction house
Stack's	www.stacks.com	New York	On site	212 582 2580	Auction house
Veronafil	www.veronafil.it	Verona	On site	39 0458 00774	Fair
Warwick and Warwick	www.warwickandwarwick.com	Warwick	info@warwickandwarwick.com	01926 499 031	Auction house

Appendix – Resources

Books

Entity	Web address	Main location	Email address	Telephone	Category
Abe Books	www.abebooks.com	Canada	On site	n/a	Online dealer
Alibris	www.alibris.com	USA	On site	n/a	Online dealer
Antiquarian Booksellers Association	www.aba.org.uk	London	admin@aba.org.uk	020 7439 3118	Association
Any Amount of Books	www.anyamountofbooks.com	London	charingx@anyamountofbooks.com	0207 836 3697	Dealer
Biblio	www.biblio.com	North Carolina	On site	n/a	Online marketplace
Biblion	www.biblion.com	London	On site	n/a	Online marketplace
Blackwell Rare Books	www.rarebooks.blackwell.co.uk	UK	rarebooks@blackwell.co.uk	01865 333 555	Dealer
Bloomsbury Auctions	www.bloomsburyauctions.com	London	info@bloomsburyauctions.com	020 7495 9494	Auction house
Bookfinder	www.bookfinder.com	Canada	On site	n/a	Information
Book & Magazine Collector	www.collectors-club-of-great-britain.co.uk	UK	On site	01778 391 180	Publication
Book Guide (The)	www.inprint.co.uk	Stroud	enquiries@inprint.co.uk	01453 759 731	Information
British Library	portico.bl.uk	London	customer-services@bl.uk	020 7412 7676	Information
Bubb Kuyper	www.bubbkuyper.com	Haarlem, Netherlands	info@bubbkuyper.com	31 23 532 3986	Auction house
Burgersdijk and Niemans	www.b-n.nl	Leiden, Netherlands	On site	On site	Auction house
D&M Books	www.dandmbooks.com	Yorkshire	daniel@dandmbooks.com	01924 495 768	Dealer/supplies
Dominic Winter	www.dominicwinter.co.uk	Gloucestershire	info@dominicwinter.co.uk	01285 860 006	Auction house
Francis Edwards	www.francisedwards.co.uk	Hay-on-Wye	sales@francisedwards.co.uk	01497 820 071	Dealer

Books...cont.

Entity	Web address	Main location	Email address	Telephone	Category
Firsts in Print	www.firsts-in-print.co.uk	Somerset	peter@firsts-in-print.co.uk	01823 256 656	Online dealer
Gorringes	www.gorringes.co.uk	Sussex	clientservices@gorringes.co.uk	01273 472 503	Auction house
Horta	www.horta.be	Brussels	info@horta.be	32 741 6060	Auction house
International League of Antiquarian Booksellers	www.ilab.org	Worldwide	info@ilab.org	n/a	Association
Kestenbaum	www.kestenbaum.net	New York	kestenbook@aol.com	212 366 1197	Auction house
Ketterer Kunst	www.kettererkunst.com	Germany	info@kettererkunst.com	49 40 3749 610	Auction house
Lawsons	www.lawsons.com.au	Sydney	On site	02 9566 2377	Auction house
Maggs	www.maggs.com	London	enquiries@maggs.com	020 7493 7160	Dealer
Morgan Library (The)	www.morganlibrary.org	New York	visitorservices@morganlibrary.org	212 685 0008	Information
Pacific Book Auctions	www.pbagalleries.com	San Francisco	On site	415 989 2655	Auction house
Peter Harrington	www.peterharringtonbooks.com	London	mail@peterharringtonbooks.com	020 7591 0220	Dealer
Provincial Booksellers Fairs Association	www.pbfa.org	Hertfordshire	info@pbfa.org	01763 248 400	Association
Quaritch	www.quaritch.com	London	rarebooks@quaritch.com	020 7297 4888	Dealer
Rare Book Review	www.rarebookreview.com	N/A	On site	n/a	Online magazine
Reiss and Sohn	www.reiss-sohn.de	Frankfurt	reiss@reiss-sohn.de	49 61 74 92 720	Auction house
Robert Frew Books	www.robertfrew.com	London	shop@robertfrew.com	0207 590 6650	Dealer
Sotherans	www.sotherans.co.uk	London	books@sotherans.co.uk	020 7439 6151	Dealer
Spink	www.spink.com	London	enquiry@spink.com	020 7563 4000	Auction house
US Library of Congress	catalog.loc.gov	Washington DC	On site	202 707 5000	Information
ViaLibri	www.vialibri.net	USA	On site	n/a	Online Marketplace
Zisska and Schauer	www.zisska.de	Munich	auctions@zisska.de	49 89 263 855	Auction house

Appendix – Resources

Coins

Entity	Web address	Main location	Email address	Telephone	Category
American Numismatic Society	www.numismatics.org	New York	On site	212 571 4470	Association
Ancient Coin Collectors Guild (The)	www.accg.us	USA	director@accg.us	417 679 2142	Association
Ashmolean Museum Oxford	www.ashmolean.org	Oxford	coin-room@ashmus.ox.ac.uk	01865 278 058	Information
Athens Numismatic Museum	www.nma.gr	Athens	On site	210 3612 519	Information
Baldwins	www.baldwin.co.uk	London	On site	020 7930 6879	Dealer
Bonhams (Glendinings)	www.bonhams.com	London	coins@bonhams.com	0207 393 3914	Auction house
Bowers and Merena	www.bowersandmerena.com	California	info@bowersandmerena.com	949 253 0916	Auction house
British Association of Numismatic Societies	www.coinclubs.freeserve.co.uk	Manchester	On site	0161 275 2643	Association
British Museum	www.britishmuseum.org	London	coins@britishmuseum.org	020 7323 8000	Information
British Numismatic Society	www.fitzmuseum.cam.ac.uk	London	fitzmuseum-enquiries@lists.cam.ac.uk	01223 332 900	Association
British Numismatic Trade Association	www.bnta.net	East Sussex	bnta@lineone.net	01797 229 988	Association
Chicago Coin Fair	www.worldcoinnews.net	Ohio	On site	n/a	Fair
Classical Numismatic Group	www.cngcoins.com	London	cng@cngcoins.com	020 7495 1888	Information
Coin Dealers Directory	www.numis.co.uk	Blackpool	contact@numis.co.uk	01253 343 081	Information
Coin News	www.tokenpublishing.com	Devon	info@tokenpublishing.com	01404 46 972	Publication
CoinNews	www.coinnews.net	Texas	On site	n/a	Online publication
Coin Resource	www.coinresource.com	Texas	info@coinresource.com	n/a	Information
Coincraft	www.coincraft.com	London	info@coincraft.com	020 7636 1188	Dealer
Colin Cooke	www.colincooke.com	Altrincham	coins@colincooke.com	0161 927 9524	Dealer
Cornucopia	www.cornucopia.org.uk	London	On site	n/a	Information
Digital Coins Network	www.digitalcoins.org	USA and London	On site	n/a	Information
Dix Noonan Webb	www.dnw.co.uk	London	auctions@dnw.co.uk	020 7016 1700	Auction house
Dr Busso Peus Nachf	www.bussopeus.de	Frankfurt	info@peus-muenzen.de	49 69 959 6620	Dealer
Dorotheum	www.dorotheum.com	Vienna	coins@dorotheum.com	43 1 515 60424	Auction house
Fitzwilliam Museum	www-cm.fitzmuseum.cam.ac.uk/dept/coins	Cambridge	fitzmuseum-coins@lists.cam.ac.uk	01223 332 900	Information

Coins...cont.

Entity	Web address	Main location	Email address	Telephone	Category
Forvm Ancient Coins	www.forumancientcoins.com	North Carolina	On site	252 646 1958	Dealer
Hellenic Numismatic Society (The)	www.coins.gr/hellenum	Athens	hellenum@hotmail.com	30 210 6721 542	Information
Hermitage Museum	www.hermitagemuseum.org	St Petersburg	On site	812 710 9629	Information
Hess-Divo	www.hessdivo.com	Zurich	mailbox@hessdivo.com	41 44 225 4090	Auction house
Hunterian Museum	www.hunterian.gla.ac.uk	Glasgow	hunterian@museum.gla.ac.uk	0141 330 4221	Information
Islamic Coins Group	www.islamiccoinsgroup.50g.com	N/A	jimfarr@nettally.com	n/a	Information
London Coins	www.londoncoins.co.uk	Kent	info@londoncoins.co.uk	01474 871 464	Dealer
Medieval Coins Group	www.medievalcoins.50g.com	N/A	On site	N/A	Information
Monetarium	www.monetarium.com.au	Sydney	info@monetarium.com.au	61 02 9588 7111	Dealer
Morton and Eden	www.mortonandeden.com	London	info@mortonandeden.com	020 7493 5344	Auction house
New York International Numismatic Convention	www.nyinc.info	New York	kfoley2@wi.rr.com	n/a	Fair
Nomos	www.nomosag.com	Zurich	info@nomosag.com	41 44 250 5180	Auction House
Numismata	www.numismata.de	Germany	numismata.modes@t-online.de	49 89 26 83 59	Fair
Numismatica Ars Classica	www.arsclassicacoins.com	London	info@arsclassicacoins.com	020 7839 7270	Auction House
Oriental Numismatic Society	www.onsnumis.org	UK	ons@onsnumis.org	On site	Association
Ponterio	www.bowersandmerena.com	California	info@bowersandmerena.com	949 253 0916	Auction house
Royal Australian Mint	www.ramint.gov.au	Canberra	On site	612 6202 6800	Information
Royal Mint	www.royalmint.com	South Wales	On site	01443 222 111	Information
Royal Numismatic Society, The	www.numismatics.org.uk	London	info@numismatics.org.uk	n/a	Association
Simmons Gallery	www.simmonsgallery.co.uk	London	simmons@simmonsgallery.co.uk	020 8989 8097	Online dealer/auction
Sixbid	www.sixbid.com	Stuttgart	service@sixbid.com	n/a	Online auction platform
Spink	www.spink.com	London	info@spink.com	020 7563 4000	Dealer
Stack's	www.stacks.com	New York	On site	212 582 2580	Auction house
Varesi	www.varesi.it	Italy	On site	39 0382 570 685	Auction house
Warwick and Warwick	www.warwickandwarwick.com	Warwick	info@warwickandwarwick.com	01926 499 031	Auction house

Appendix - Resources

Diamonds

Entity	Web address	Main location	Email address	Telephone	Category
Ajediam	www.ajediam.com	Antwerp	janhuts@ajediam.com	32 479 28 1213	Dealer
Antwerp World Diamond Centre	www.awdc.be	Antwerp	On site	32 032 22 0531	Trade association
De Beers	www.debeers.com	London	clientservices@debeers.com	1 888 376 9230	Dealer
DODAQ	www.dodaq.com	Antwerp	enquiries@dodaq.com	32 3 289 8665	Online market
International Diamond Exchange (The)	www.idexonline.com	New York	On site	1212 3823 528	Online direcory
Israel Precious Stones and Diamond Exchange	www.ipsde-il.com	Israel	ipsde@zahav.net.il	03 575 1177	Directory
Rapaport Diamond Report	www.rapaportdiamondreport.com	USA	info@diamonds.net	1 702 893 9400	Information
Sotheby's	www.sothebysdiamonds.com	London	On site	020 7293 6430	Dealer
Steinmetz	www.steinmetzdiamonds.com	New York	info@rstei.com	1 212 398 1399	Manufacturer
World Federation of Diamond Bourses (The)	www.worldfed.com	Antwerp	info@worldfed.com	32 03 234 9121	Trade federation, information

Forestry

Entity	Web address	Main location	Email address	Telephone	Category
Bidwells	www.bidwells.co.uk	Cambridge	On site	01223 559 210	Agent
CKD Galbraith	www.forestry-scotland.co.uk	Scotland	On site	01463 245 382	Advisor
Confederation of Forest Industries	www.confor.org.uk	Edinburgh	On site	0131 240 1410	Information
Ethical Investments	www.ethicalinvestments.co.uk	Sheffield	dave@ethicalinvestments.co.uk	0114 2368 168	Agent
Forestry Commission	www.forestry.gov.uk	UK	On site	Many on site	Information
Forest Enterprises	www.forestenterprises.co.nz	NZ	pinemail@forestenterprises.co.nz	0800 746 346	Agent
Forest Industry Network	www.forestindustry.com	Canada	On site	1 877 755 2762	Information
Forestry Investment Management	www.fimltd.co.uk	Burford, Oxon	fim@fimltd.co.uk	01451 844 655	Investment Fund
Forestry Journal	www.forestryjournal.co.uk	Dumfries	info@forestryjournal.co.uk	01387 702 272	Information
Forest Research Group	www.forestresearchgroup.com	USA	jlutz@forestresearchgroup.com	978 432 1794	Information
Forest Stewardship Council (The)	www.fsc.org	Germany	fsc.fsc.org	228 367 660	Information
Fountains	www.fountainsforestry.co.uk	UK	On site	Various on site	Agent
FPD Savills	www.savills.co.uk	UK	On site	01356 628 600	Agent
Greenwood	www.greenwood-management.com	Ireland	info@greenwood-management.com	353 1452 0326	Agent
Highfield Forestry Ltd	www.highfieldforestry.com	Scotland	info@highfieldforestry.com	0 1738 442 903	Agent
Institute of Chartered Foresters	www.charteredforesters.org	Edinburgh	On site	0131 240 1425	Association
International Tropical Timber Organization	www.itto.int	Japan	itto@itto.or.jp	45 223 1110	Association
Investment Property Databank (IPD)	www.ipindex.co.uk	London	On site	020 7336 9200	Data

Appendix – Resources

Forestry...cont.

Entity	Web address	Main location	Email address	Telephone	Category
Irish Forestry	www.irish-forestry.ie	Ireland	info@irish-forestry.ie	353 1 284 1777	Advisor
John Clegg	www.johnclegg.co.uk	London	thame@johnclegg.co.uk	01844 215 800	Agent
Malaysian Timber Council	www.mtc.com.my	Malaysia	On site	n/a	Information
New Zealand Forest Owners Association	www.nzfoa.org.nz	NZ	nzfoa@nzfoa.org.nz	64 4 473 4769	Association
New Zealand Ministry of Agriculture and Forestry	www.maf.govt.nz	NZ	info@maf.govt.nz	64 4 894 0100	Information
New Zealand Overseas Investment Offices	www.linz.govt.nz	NZ	info@linz.govt.nz	64 4 460 0110	Advisor
Oxigen Investments	www.oxigen-investments.com	London	enquiries@oxigen-investments.com	0203 405 1480	Investment Fund
Phaunos Timber Fund	www.phaunostimber.com	Guernsey	On site	01481 722260	Investment Fund
Plum Creek Timber	www.plumcreek.com	Seattle	info@plumcreek.com	206 467 3600	REIT
Potlatch	www.potlatchcorp.com	Washington	On site	509 835 1500	REIT
Royal Forestry Society	www.rfs.org.uk	Hertfordshire	rfshq@rfs.org.uk	01422 822 028	Association
Rayonier	www.rayonier.com	Florida	info@rayonier.com	904 357 9100	REIT
Smallwoods	www.smallwoods.org.uk	Telford	On site	01952 432 769	Information
Timber Trades Journal	www.ttjonline.com	Sidcup	On site	020 8269 7844	Publication
Tilhill	www.upm-tilhill.com	Stirling	info@upm-tilhill.com	01786 435 000	Agent
UK Timber Trade Federation	www.ttf.co.uk	London	ttf@ttf.co.uk	020 3205 0067	Association
Food and Agriculture Organization of the United Nations	www.fao.org/forestry	New York	On site	n/a	Information

Gold

Entity	Web address	Main location	Email address	Telephone	Category
Allgold Coins	www.allgoldcoins.co.uk	Surrey	sales@allgoldcoins.co.uk	0844 544 7952	Dealer
ATS Bullion	www.atsbullion.com	London	sales@atsbullion.com	0207 240 4041	Dealer
Baird & Co.	www.goldine.co.uk	London	sales@goldine.co.uk	0207 474 1000	Dealer
Bullion Desk (The)	www.thebulliondesk.com	London	On site	020 7929 2231	Information
Chard	www.24carat.co.uk	Blackpool	enquiries@chards.co.uk	01253 343 081	Dealer
Coinlink	www.coinlinkbullion.com	Florida	On site	n/a	Information
Freemarket Gold and Money Report	www.fgmr.com	USA	contact@fgmr.com	603 323 8182	Information
Gold and Silver Investments	www.goldassets.co.uk	London	info@goldassets.co.uk	020 3086 9200	Dealer
Goldprice	www.goldprice.org	N/A	On site	n/a	Information
London Bullion Market Association	www.lbma.org.uk	London	mail@lbma.org.uk	020 7796 3067	Information
London Coin Company, The	www.thelondoncoincompany.com	London	info@thelondoncoincompany.com	020 8343 2231	Dealer
Perth Mint	www.perthmint.com.au	Perth	bullion@perthmint.com.au	61 8 9421 7428	Dealer
Pobjoy Mint	www.pobjoy.com	Surrey	sales@pobjoy.com	01737 818 181	Dealer
South African Gold Coin Exchange	www.sagoldcoin.com	South Africa	info@sagoldcoin.com	27 11 784 8551	Dealer
Tanaka	gold.tanaka.co.jp/english	Tokyo	On site	n/a	Dealer
Tax Free Gold	www.taxfreegold.co.uk	Blackpool	enquiries@chards.co.uk	01253 343 081	Dealer
United States Mint	www.usmint.gov	USA	On site	202 898 6468	Dealer
World Gold Council	www.gold.org	Worldwide	info@gold.org	n/a	Information

Appendix - Resources

Stamps

Entity	Web address	Main location	Email address	Telephone	Category
American Philatelic Society	www.stamps.org	USA	On site	814 933 3803	Association
American Stamp Dealers Association	www.asdaonline.com	New York	asda@asdaonline.com	516 759 7000	Association
Apex	www.apexstamps.com	Surrey	admin@apexstamps.com	01342 833 413	Dealer/auction house
Arthur Ryan & Co	www.gbstamps.co.uk	Surrey	netenquiry@gbstamps.co.uk	020 8940 7777	Dealer
Association of British Philatelic Societies	www.ukphilately.org.uk	UK	abpssec@ukphilately.org.uk	n/a	Association
Bath Postal Museum	www.bathpostalmuseum.org	Bath	info@bathpostalmuseum.org	01225 460 333	Information
Bonhams	www.bonhams.com	London	info@bonhams.com	020 7393 9789	Auction house
Brandon Galleries	www.brandonstamps.com	Guildford	peter@brandonstamps.com	01483 503 335	Dealer
Bridger and Kay	www.bridgerkay.com	Bristol	sales@bridgerkay.com	01934 863 656	Dealer
British Library Philatelic Collection	www.bl.uk	London	philatelic@bl.uk	020 7412 5120	Information
Cherrystone Philatelic Auctions	www.cherrystoneauctions.com	New York	info@cherrystoneauctions.com	212 977 7734	Auction house
Dorotheum	www.dorotheum.com	Vienna	stamps@dorotheum.at	43 1 515 60298	Auction house
French Stamp Directory	www.philatelie.fr	France	info@philatelie.fr	n/a	Information
Great Britain Philatelic Society	www.gbps.org.uk	UK	gbps@mjpublications.com	n/a	Association
Grosvenor Philatelic Auctions	www.grosvenorauctions.com	London	info@grosvenorauctions.com	020 7379 8789	Auction house
Harmers	www.harmers.com	London	info@harmers.com	020 8747 6100	Auction house
James Bendon	www.jamesbendon.com	Cyprus	info@jamesbendon.com	n/a	Publisher
John Bull Stamp Auctions	www.jbull.com	Hong Kong	info@jbull.com	852 2890 5767	Auction house
Joseph Luft's Philatelic Resources	www.josephluft.com	USA	joeluft@execpc.com	1 262 242 5120	Information
Nalbandian (Jack)	www.nalbandstamp.com	USA	nalbandian@earthlink.net	401 885 5020	Dealer
National Philatelic Society	www.ukphilately.org.uk/nps	UK	nps@ukphilately.org.uk	020 7239 2571	Association
Philaguide	www.philaguide.com	Netherlands	On site	n/a	Information

285

Stamps...cont.

Entity	Web address	Main location	Email address	Telephone	Category
Philatelic Exporter (The)	www.philatelicexporter.com	Hampshire	On site	01425 472 363	Publication
Philatelic Traders' Society	www.philatelic-traders-society.co.uk	Hampshire	On site	01252 628 006	Association
Post Office Archives	www.postalheritage.org.uk	London	info@postalheritage.co.uk	020 7239 2570	Information
Prinz	www.prinz.co.uk	UK	info@prinz.co.uk	01736 751 910	Miscellaneous
Royal Philatelic Collection	www.royal.gov.uk	London	n/a	n/a	Information
Royal Philatelic Society	www.rpsl.org.uk	London	n/a	020 7486 1044	Association
Sandafayre	www.Sandafayre.com	Cheshire	stamps@sandafayre.com	01565 653 214	Dealer
Schlegel	www.auktionshaus-schlegel.de	Berlin	On site	030 8870 9962	Auction house
Scotia Philately	www.scotia-philately.com	Hampton Court	info@scotiaphilately.com	0208 873 2854	Dealer
Sotheby's	www.sothebys.com	London	richard.ashton@sothebys.com	020 7293 5224	Auction house
Spink	www.spink.com	London	info@spink.com	0207 563 4000	Auction house
Stamp Auction Network	www.stampauctionnetwork.com	USA	tldroege@mindspring.com	919 403 9459	Information
Stamp2.com	www.stamp2.com	Singapore	info@stamp2.com	65 629 523 42	Information
Stamp Circuit Club	www.stampcircuit.com	Israel	On site	972 4 837 2831	Information
Stamp Magazine	www.stampmagazine.co.uk	Croydon	On site	020 8726 8243	Publication
Stampshows.com	www.stampshows.com	USA	admin7@stampshows.com	n/a	Information
Stanley Gibbons	www.stanleygibbons.com	London	investments@stanleygibbons.co.uk	0207 836 8444	Dealer
US National Postal Museum	www.postalmuseum.si.edu	Washington	On site	202 633 5555	Information
Wardrop & Co	www.wardrop.co.uk	Colchester	On site	01376 563 764	Miscellaneous
Warwick and Warwick	www.warwickandwarwick.com	Warwick	info@warwickandwarwick.com	01926 499 031	Auction house
Western Auctions	www.westernauctions.co.uk	Cardiff	info@westernauctions.co.uk	029 204 84934	Auction house
Whytes	www.whytes.ie	Dublin	info@whytes.ie	353 01676 2888	Auction house

Wine

Entity	Web address	Main location	Email address	Telephone	Category
Acker, Merrall and Condit	www.ackerwines.com	New York	On site	212 787 1700	Dealer/auction house
Berry Bros. & Rudd	www.bbr.com	London	On site	0800 280 2440	Dealer
Bloomsbury Auctions	www.ny.bloomsburyauctions.com	New York	wine@bloomsburyauctions.com	1 212 719 1000	Auction house
Bonhams	www.bonhams.com	London	wine@bonhams.com	08700 273 622	Auction house
Bordeaux	www.bordeaux.com	Bordeaux	On site	33 5 56 00 2266	Information
Chicago Wine Company, The	www.tcwc.com	Illinois	On site	630 594 2972	Auction house
Christie's	www.christies.com	London	info@christies.com	020 7752 3366	Auction house
Decanter	www.decanter.com	London	On site	020 3148 5000	Publication
Edward Roberts International	www.eriwine.com	Chicago	info@eriwine.com	847 295 8696	Auction house
Fine + Rare	www.frw.co.uk	London	wine@frw.co.uk	020 8960 1995	Dealer
Harpers Wine and Spirit	www.harpers.co.uk	West Sussex	On site	01293 613 400	Publication
James Nicholson	www.jnwine.com	Northern Ireland	shop@jnwine.com	028 4483 0091	Dealer
Jancis Robinson	www.jancisrobinson.com	London	On site	0845 056 4117	Information
Investdrinks	www.investdrinks.org	N/A	jim@investdrinks.org	N/A	Information
Liv-ex	www.liv-ex.com	London	exchange@liv-ex.co.uk	020 7228 2233	Information
London City Bond	www.lcb.co.uk	Tilbury	info@lcb.co.uk	01375 853 700	Cellar
Magnum Fine Wine	www.magnum.co.uk	London	wine@magnum.co.uk	0207 629 5607	Dealer

Wine...cont.

Entity	Web address	Main location	Email address	Telephone	Category
Millesima	www.millesima.co.uk	Bordeaux	On site	0800 917 0352	Dealer
Octavian	www.octavianvaults.co.uk	Wiltshire	care@octavianvaults.co.uk	01225 818 714	Cellar
Premier Cru	www.premiercru.com	London	sales@premiercru.com	020 8905 4495	Dealer
Richard Kihl	www.richardkihl.ltd.uk	Suffolk	sales@richardkihl.ltd.uk	01728 454 455	Dealer
Robert Parker	www.erobertparker.com	USA	info@erobertparker.com	617 938 3984	Information
Sokolin	www.sokolin.com	New York	On site	631 5 37 4434	Dealer
Sotheby's	www.sothebys.com	London	On site	020 7293 5050	Auction house
Vinotheque	www.vinotheque.co.uk	Burton-on-Trent	sales@vinotheque.co.uk	01375 853 777	Cellar
Wineandco	www.wineandco.com	Bordeaux	On site	00800 1000 20	Dealer
Wine and Spirit Education Trust	www.wset.co.uk	London	wset@wset.co.uk	020 7089 3800	Information
Wine Doctor (The)	www.thewinedoctor.com	N/A	chris@thewinedoctor.com	n/a	Information
Wine Gang (The)	www.thewinegang.com	Glasgow	On site	0141 416 4958	Information
Winemega	www.winemega.com	N/A	On site	n/a	Information
Wine Spectator	www.winespectator.com	USA	On site	212 684 4224	Magazine
Wine-Searcher	www.wine-searcher.com	New Zealand	On site	n/a	Information
Wine and Spirit magazine	www.wine-spirit.com	West Sussex	On site	01293 613 400	Magazine
WineBid	www.winebid.com	California	info@winebid.com	888 638 8968	Online auction
Zachys	www.zachys.com	New York	On site	1 866 922 4971	Dealer/auction

Appendix – Resources

Auctions

Entity	Web address	Main location	Email address	Telephone	Category
Artcurial	www.artcurial.com	Paris	On site	33 42 99 20 20	Auction house
Artfact Live!	www.artfact.com	Massachusetts	On site	(617) 219 1090	On line auction database
Bonhams	www.bonhams.com	London	info@bonhams.com	020 7447 7447	Auction house
Bruun Rasmussen	www.bruun-rasmussen.dk	Denmark	info@bruun-rasmussen.dk	45 8818 1111	Auction house
Bukowskis	www.bukowskis.se	Stockholm	On site	46 8 614 08 00	Auction house
Christie's	www.christies.com	Worldwide	info@christies.com	Worldwide	Auction house
Dorotheum	www.dorotheum.com	Vienna	On site	43 1 515 60 0	Auction house
Doyles	www.doylenewyork.com	New York	info@doylenewyork.com	212 427 2730	Auction house
Freemans	www.freemansauction.com	Philadelphia	info@freemansauction.com	215 563 9275	Auction house
International Auctioneers Group	www.internationalauctioneers.com	Geneva	info@internationalauctioneers.com	41 (22) 310 21 80	Auction house alliance
Koller	www.kollerauktionen.ch	Zurich	office@kollerauctions.com	41 44 445 63 63	Auction house
Lempertz	www.lempertz.eu	Cologne	On site	49 221 9257 290	Auction house
Lyon and Turnbull	www.lyonandturnbull.com	Scotland	info@lyonandturnbull.com	0131 557 8844	Auction house
Phillips de Pury	www.phillipsdepury.com	New York	On site	1212 940 1200	Auction house
Pierre Berge	www.pba-auctions.com	Paris	contact@pba-auctions.com	33 01 49 49 90 00	Auction house
Porro	www.porroartconsulting.it	Milan	On site	02 72 094 708	Auction house
Society of Fine Art Auctioneers and Valuers	www.sofaa.org	Surrey	On site	0207 0968 417	Association
Swann Galleries	www.swanngalleries.com	New York	swann@swanngalleries.com	212 254 4710	Auction house
Tajan	www.tajan.com	Paris	On site	Many on site	Auction house
Tennants	www.tennants.co.uk	North Yorkshire	enquiries@tennants-ltd.co.uk	01969 623 780	Auction house
the-saleroom.com	www.the-saleroom.com	Online	On site	n/a	Online link to auctions
Venator and Hanstein	www.venator-hanstein.de	Cologne	info@venator-hanstein.de	49 221 257 54 19	Auction house
Weschler's	www.weschlers.com	Washington	info@weschlers.com	202 628 1281	Auction house
Whytes	www.whytes.ie	Dublin	info@whytes.ie	353 1676 2888	Auction house